BLACK MIRROR

BLACK

MIRROR

THE CULTURAL

CONTRADICTIONS

OF AMERICAN RACISM

Eric Lott

THE BELKNAP PRESS OF HARVARD UNIVERSITY PRESS

Cambridge, Massachusetts ‖ London, England   2017

First printing

Library of Congress Cataloging-in-Publication Data

Names: Lott, Eric, author.
Title: Black mirror : the cultural contradictions of American racism / Eric Lott.
Description: Cambridge, Massachusetts : The Belknap Press of Harvard
  University Press, 2017. | Includes bibliographical references and index.
Identifiers: LCCN 2017013659 | ISBN 9780674967717 (cloth)
Subjects: LCSH: Racism in mass media. | Racism in popular culture—United States. |
  Whites—United States—Attitudes. | Blacks—United States—Public opinion. |
  African Americans in the performing arts—United States. | United States—Race
  relations.
Classification: LCC P94.5.A372 U559 2017 | DDC 305.800973—dc23
  LC record available at https://lccn.loc.gov/2017013659

For Cindi, Coco, and Trixie

and for Cory

CONTENTS

I know I am
The Negro Problem
Being wined and dined,
Answering the usual questions
That come to white mind
Which seeks demurely
To probe in polite way
The why and wherewithal
Of darkness U.S.A.—
Wondering how things got this way
In current democratic night,
Murmuring gently
Over fraises du bois,
"I'm so ashamed of being white."

The lobster is delicious,
The wine divine,
And center of attention
At the damask table, mine.
To be a Problem on
Park Avenue at eight
Is not so bad.
Solutions to the Problem,
Of course, wait.

—Langston Hughes, "Dinner Guest: Me," 1965

I was thinking of a series of dreams
Where nothing comes up to the top
Everything stays down where it's wounded
And comes to a permanent stop
Wasn't thinking of anything specific
Like in a dream when someone wakes up and screams
Nothing too very scientific
Just thinking of a series of dreams

—Bob Dylan, "Series of Dreams," 1989

PREFACE

"I know I am / The Negro Problem / Being wined and dined / Answering the usual questions / That come to white mind," wrote the by-then-celebrated poet Langston Hughes in 1965. Not just a Negro, and as such a "problem," per W. E. B. Du Bois, but The-Negro-Problem-All-Caps, a symbolic construct that the dinner guest, being wined and dined no less, is made to carry or embody. The poem makes all too clear that the problem is a white one and that it consists in part of the very conceptual constructions that have made Hughes's dinner party on "Park Avenue at eight" such a choky good time. That "I" in the very first line is already split, the I who knows observing the I who "am," a state of being unavoidably shot through with the fantasies of white others. Whence the mindful "me" of this poem "Dinner Guest: Me" disappears into race-problem abstraction—and just there Hughes captures the dynamic this book undertakes to study, the dominant-cultural production of and trafficking in symbolic capital generated out of black people and black cultural forms. "Darkness U.S.A.," Hughes terms it: a conceptual apparatus that eclipses the population it names. The poem's speaker is the "center of attention" to the precise extent that such attention displaces the Problem it doesn't solve. This is the realm, obviously, of fantasy and fetish.

I have known for a long time what I am after in the pages that follow, but I couldn't have stated it as plainly before the arc of events I describe in Chapter 1 had come to pass. The 2008 election of Barack Obama may have unfolded within the conceptual outlines of Hughes's poem, the Park Avenue dinner guest now escorted to Pennsylvania Avenue, the full complement of national self-congratulation and racial explaining at fancy banquets following hard thereupon. There was, however, no denying the power of racial fantasy to produce an African American president. The contradictions I have long discerned in such fantasy now had new state consequences. This time around that fantasy went by the name of the "postracial." Here we are, said the crossover dreamwork Obama inspired and in many ways encouraged, in a new age that remaindered old ideas of racial identity and identification. Race no longer "mattered," at least not as much; so long, Cornel West, and thanks for the memories! At one level this was little more than the dream Ralph Ellison invoked in his great 1970 *Time* magazine essay, "What America Would Be Like Without Blacks," the dream of an America free of black people altogether. MSNBC anchor Chris Matthews was heard to remark during a broadcast early in Obama's presidency: "He is postracial by all appearances [savor that line!]." Matthews continued: "You know, I forgot he was black tonight for an hour [savor the syntax! an hour's forgetting or an hour's blackness?]." "Postracial": Good For An Hour's Amnesia. And just why—and what—should one want to forget?

No, the "postracial" wasn't beyond the valley of the shadow of racial mystification, just a different hollow. Another sense in which to take it was not that the racial divide was over or we over it, but that now we could more easily play with and ironize it, stereotype the stereotypes, tease the president about b-ball and his NCAA predictions, poke fun at racial shape-shifting (as in the Steven Spielberg–produced short film that Obama showed at the 2013 White House Correspondents' Dinner—more on which in Chapter 1)—sort of the New Black Aesthetic of the 1980s now street legal, like George C. Wolfe's *Colored Museum* and Percival Everett's *Erasure* had birthed a native son. Sure enough, there was Keegan-Michael Key doing his

Obama Anger Translator *standing next to Obama* at the 2015 WHCD.
Funny as it was to see Obama poking fun at his own habits of com-
posure, it's easy enough to see that this sort of thing resides in just
the sort of subjective splitting, racial ambivalence, disavowal, and
condensation that drive "the stereotype" itself in Homi Bhabha's
once-classic formulation, the postracial burdened with the same varieties of racial fixity as the postcolonial. (There's even a whiff here of
Tambo-and-Bones-style repartee, minstrel-show Interlocutor and
Endman cutting up.) The same goes for the 2016 WHCD skit featuring John Boehner in which the president and the former House
Speaker plot life after Washington responsibility: the two of them
settling into an afternoon screening of the film *Toy Story,* Boehner
quips that Obama will soon be able to "walk right out of the Oval Office singing 'Zip-A-Dee-Doo-Dah'" and "work on your tan." President Obama laughs hard. He's in on the jokes, of course, but they're
still essentially minstrel gags.

Still another resonance of the postracial was its ironic echo
of William Julius Wilson's hotly debated 1978 study *The Declining
Significance of Race,* which argued that class generally and class
differences within black communities particularly outweighed the
importance of structural-racial factors; in this book and in Wilson's
follow-up, *The Truly Disadvantaged* (1987), both of them profoundly
influential, one found the most insistent pathologizing of black
working-class life (which Wilson styled "the underclass") since
Daniel Patrick Moynihan's "The Negro Family: The Case for National Action" (1965). (Henry Louis Gates Jr., who brought Wilson
to Harvard from the University of Chicago, has long peddled this
line, lately, for example, in his February 2016 *New York Times* article
"Black America and the Class Divide," which pins its hopes on the
current generation of college-educated black Talented Tenthers.)
One of Wilson's (and Gates's) most illuminatingly fierce critics for
many years was Adolph Reed Jr., who scored their bourgeois self-
satisfaction and cultural essentialism. Nowadays Reed is one of a
number of thinkers (Barbara Fields being another) who have concluded that the most tough-minded position is to "prove" race's
illusory or ideological or constructed character (as in Fields's *Racecraft*), as though recognizing our cognitive error would make racial inequality go away, and who reach for other, realer social and

political determinants such as, you guessed it, class. Indeed Reed, together with Walter Benn Michaels and Kenneth Warren, form something of a new Chicago School, arguing the importance of class and labor critique and struggle over race-based or other new social movement–oriented criticism and activism; Michaels and Reed go so far as to claim (where Warren just intimates, as in his study *What Was African American Literature?*) that antiracist critique actually sustains and advances class inequality, is one of its engines, a bourgeois ruse. Many of the intellectuals I discussed in my book *The Disappearing Liberal Intellectual* adhere to the notion that racial inequality and antiracist critique are a distraction from or secondary to "common" or "left" or "labor" or "class" concerns—a form of reactionary wish-fulfillment that has its Marxist and socialist adherents as well, alas, both in the academy and on the electoral stump.

"Postracial" wasn't Langston Hughes's dream deferred; it was the wrong dream. Hughes's "Dinner Guest: Me" (1965) captured decades in advance the inextricability of race and fantasy and their dialectical relationship with material inequality and social dominance. This is why you can't simply wish it away, why attending to The Problem—wining and dining it, entertaining solutions—can prolong the "wait," the poem's final thudding word. In many ways—"of course," as Hughes says—The Problem remains today as untouched by this eventuation as it does in "Dinner Guest." I refer to the intensified toll of black death and damage, much of it at the hands of the state, which has like a public X-ray in the last few years opened to view a *longue durée* of racialized state violence. The names of Trayvon Martin, Michael Brown, Eric Garner, Freddie Gray, Walter Scott, Sandra Bland, and many more attest to the character of a regime whose foundational violence extends deeply and broadly beyond the "isolated" incidents that killed them. Their deaths are, as Ta-Nehisi Coates is only the most recent prominent writer to suggest, not tragic exceptions but the shape of the norm.

The seeming paradox of President Obama steering a regime of black death evaporates upon consideration of not just the limits on any single person's power over the state apparatus but also the likely compensatory nature of police power over black populations in the Age of Obama. Racial fantasy may swerve away from The Problem by producing new "centers of attention"; it may even do this by contributing to the election of a black president nominally committed to addressing The Problem. But racial fantasy simultaneously persists in uglier guises, suffusing actual encounters on the ground. For some, a black man in the White House produced new intensities of racial anxiety and paranoia—a new haze of imaginary that mediates every encounter between cop and citizen. Officer Darren Wilson imagined unarmed black teenager Michael Brown to have what he described as Hulk Hogan–like power to harm him, necessitating his death by gun, while more garden-variety pique at black citizenly resistance led Sandra Bland's arresting officer to haul her to jail, where she died allegedly by her own hand. The white supremacist who killed nine worshippers in Charleston's Emanuel A.M.E. Church fantasized more bluntly: "You rape our women and you're taking over our country." To which President Obama responded with an extraordinary counter-fantasy, of shooter Dylann Roof as an instrument of God to demonstrate His grace, concluding his speech with an unprecedented rendering of "Amazing Grace." I argue in Chapter 1 that Obama for years worked adroitly in the domain of racial fantasy to engineer his electoral and other successes. Here too there are nothing but contradictions: from *Saturday Night Live* blackface impressions of him to Washington State NAACP head Rachel Doležal, who turned out to be a white woman passing as black, Obama's rise was crowded by the shadow projections of what Hughes calls "democratic night." Their ne plus ultra came in the form of white Baltimore police officer Bobby "Al Jolson" Berger, who had planned to perform in blackface at a 2015 fundraiser for the six cops charged in the custody killing of Freddie Gray until the event was canceled; Berger claimed for years that his Jolson impersonation, complete with black face paint and a rendition of "Mammy," had nothing to do with race. There is no necessary connection between policing black life and patrolling the black image, perhaps, nor is this an incidental one. The ways of state racial fantasy, I will have no choice but to argue, are volatile and discrepant, never predictable in their outcomes and always productive in the sense of having consequences as opposed to being spare parts on the real motors of history. *Black Mirror* seeks to plumb the contradictions and some of the consequences of U.S. racism's theaters of fantasy—classic American literature, Hollywood film, pop musical artistry, and venturesome social commentary among them—across the long twentieth century, culminating in a moment of black moral power in the grip of institutionalized black death.

A series of dreams, you might say, where nothing comes up to the top and everything stays down where it's wounded, as Bob Dylan once sang: dreams my book *Love and Theft: Blackface Minstrelsy and the American Working Class* set out to explore in a different but hardly unrelated moment and format. I sought in that book to do a number of things at once. I wanted to offer close analysis of a various and still-influential U.S. entertainment form, to speculate on the vagaries of popular antebellum racial feeling arising from and visible in it, and to provide an account of plebeian racial politics in the decades before the Civil War. At the heart of the book was a theory of white appropriations of African American cultural materials for sport and profit, appropriations that sometimes produced unintended cultural and historical results. In September 2001, on 9/11 in fact, Dylan released an album that appropriated the title of my book, a tribute of sorts to its themes, just as I had riffed on the title of Leslie Fiedler's *Love and Death in the American Novel* for mine. Dylan's *"Love and Theft"*—the only one of his many albums whose title is in quotation marks—contributes its share to thinking about racialized cross-cultural borrowing, as I describe in Chapter 8. *Black Mirror* extends and expands the story of white America's way with black symbolic and cultural capital, its uses as inspiration and as raw material (though it is anything but) and most importantly as a modality of self-recognition, in music and performative force, narrative depiction and visual representation, social occasion and subject position. U.S. dominant cultural makers have taken up African America in various forms of interracial embrace with variable and uncertain results, often as a way to reproduce themselves and their own hegemony, occasionally with liberating consequences, all of it a blue tangle of impacted self-regard: a kind of black mirror. Fantasies of white plenitude dance with misrecognition in the looking-glass culture industries, which have based themselves substantially on the skin trade.

Having pursued the affective life of whiteness in nineteenth-century America by looking at one of its principal cultural forms, I turn here to some of the cultural institutions that subsequently erected the screens and templates of black mirroring, the mechanics, dispositions, and effects of the dominant culture's looking at itself always through a fantasized black Other. If Du Bois's "double consciousness" captured the way African Americans are made to see themselves through the eyes of white dominance, black mirroring is its dialectically related but asymmetrical inverse, the very medium of white luxury and privilege. Hence Fiedler's stirring (if imperfect) analyses long ago of the aching white desire for cross-racial love to coexist with the caste system, or Hughes's biting nod to the frisson of dinner table white shame (" 'I'm so ashamed of being white' "). "Mirror mirror on the wall / Can you see my face at all?" sings Merrill Garbus in tUnE-yArDs's "Powa," a screaming demand for female recognition that extends to black power in the white-Narcissus wellspring I am studying (and in which tUnE-yArDs self-consciously know they swim). One intellectual achievement of the last two decades has been to displace—somewhat—the sterile middlebrow moralism and handwringing that used to rule the study of race and culture (though here and there a David Brooks will rear his goofy head: I speak among other things of his *New York Times* epistolary column in response to Ta-Nehisi Coates's epistolary *Between the World and Me,* Brooks addressing Coates as Coates in his book addresses his son, Brooks's column an exemplary instance of willful mirroring—mimicking Coates's work in order to refuse its summons). Nowadays the unequal terms of racial power in the United States have become so starkly visible that a bracing anger has raised the stakes. This circumstance, salutary as it is, doesn't encourage a full attention to the rather wayward dimensions of the hysterical and sometimes downright bizarre cultural forms white America has produced to explain itself to itself over the last century. Over the course of twentieth-century liberalism, cultural shapes arose in which Caucasoid self-definition depended ever more fiercely—and weirdly—on its dialectical other. The race-liberal cross-dressing of Mark Twain (*Huckleberry Finn*) and John Howard Griffin (*Black Like Me*), race-curious Hollywood noir and Elvis impersonation, white-ethnic blackface badinage (Frank Sinatra) and corrosive irony (Steely Dan), and rock 'n' roll bootlegging and pimp gaming (Dylan, Joni Mitchell) are spaces of fantasy that require a whole new kind of "reflection theory" to account for the speculations they enact

through racialized mirror-gazing. Mirrors don't reflect; they reverse and distort for starters, and what you offer up to them is precisely what swerves away (per John Ashbery's *Self-Portrait in a Convex Mirror*). *Black Mirror* takes up a slightly idiosyncratic but highly influential vein of cultural production and iconography in order to explore the condensations and displacements, disavowals and ruthless demands of white affect in the throes of racial capitalism—very, very far from the fairest one of all.

I HAVE BEEN WAITING a long time to celebrate the institutional and collective formations that have been crucial to this study's itinerary. The UC-Berkeley 1997 Making and Unmaking of Whiteness conference lies in its formative deep background; the two camps of work on whiteness that emerged there (one "abolitionist," the other "pro–white trash"), the united front it encouraged despite the prevailing disagreements (having Walter Benn Michaels around tends to unite everyone else), and certain of its moments that I continue to cherish have all shaped the book you hold in your hands. Walter and I still amuse ourselves remembering the scene when a white-supremacist agitator ("I go by my indigenous name of Thor!"—I am not making this up) erupted during Mab Segrest's presentation and the both of us, cowering in the back of the room, thought we might be doomed. (They could have played Alanis Morissette's latest hit "Ironic" at our funerals.) Meanwhile there was smoking weed and listening to Pavement with Fred Pfeil and others late one conference night and wondering aloud if doing just that said something about whiteness studies in the 1990s. Thanks are due the organizers of the Berkeley events, Matt Wray, Birgit Brander Rasmussen, Eric Klinenberg, and Annalee Newitz. My world-altering experiences during Anna Deavere Smith's 1998 Harvard University Institute for the Arts and Civic Dialogue annealed, as I like to think of it, some of this book's themes and emotional force. I thank Anna herself, Carrie Mae Weems, Michael Ray Charles, Rip Lhamon, Donald Byrd, Roger Guenveur Smith, Oliver Lake, Patricia Williams, and all

Fig. 1. Michael Ray Charles, *REWOP ETIHW*, 1994, courtesy of the artist

the other participants for their ideas, revelations, and sheer commitment to honest feeling that week and after. (Never stop asking why, why, why, why, why, Why, WHY, right y'all?) I am proud to have been a part of the University of Virginia Afterlives of Identity Politics workshop in 1999, sponsored by Ralph Cohen and *New Literary History* but spearheaded by a stellar collective of graduate students who have all gone on to even better contributions (as you will know from the names Bryan Wagner, Heather Love, Michael Millner, Ben Lee, Alice Rutkowski, Bill Albertini, and Ken Parille). The NYU Africana Studies event that Manthia Diawara and Patricia Blanchet organized upon the release of Spike Lee's *Bamboozled* has resonated for me well beyond the confines of that long-ass and exhilarating evening; my co-panelists Stanley Crouch, Margo Jefferson, Clyde Taylor, and Michele Wallace ratcheted up the stakes, as they will, and I, at least, left the room better equipped than when I entered it (and not one fistfight!). My time at Princeton on a Council for the Humanities Fellowship in the spring of 2001 was buoyed by Michael Wood, Diana Fuss, Bill Gleason, Sean Wilentz, and Eduardo Cadava. I have little in the way of pages to show for my 2001 time in Cuba with a deliciously raucous crew of scholars and writers hosted by the journal *Callaloo* and its editor and my friend Charles Rowell, but I still believe the friendships deepened or inaugurated there suffuse everything I do. A commemorative shout-out to Brent Edwards, Fred Moten, Laura Harris, David Kazanjian, Josie Saldaña, Kevin Young, Carla Peterson, Harryette Mullen, Toi Derricotte, Mae Henderson, Cathy Cohen, Farah Griffin, Salim Washington, and Barbara Browning. The Experience Music Project Pop Conferences in Seattle and other locales have for over a decade now become for me a home away from home, for which thanks and praise are due above all to Eric Weisbard and Ann Powers but to many other friends as well. The 2006 Dartmouth Bob Dylan conference convened by Lou Renza got to the bottom of many mysteries once and for all, I swear, and Michael Denning and Christopher Ricks had a lot to do with that. I hope my pals at the Society for the Humanities at Cornell know how much that pivotal year on Sound (2011–2012) meant to me; its fruits will I hope issue in a different book, but its spirit entered into this one: thank you to Tim Murray and my fellow fellows (especially Trevor Pinch, Jenny Stoever, Damien Keane, Marcus

Boon, Tom McInerney, Sarah Ensor, and Michael Jonik), and here's
to the once and future A.D. White House Band. The City University of New York Graduate Center's *"The Black Atlantic at Twenty"*
symposium gave me the opportunity, as that institution so often
has of late, to collaborate with some of my favorite people, among
them Duncan Faherty, Kandice Chuh, Robert Reid-Pharr, Louise
Lennihan, Ken Wissoker, Cathy Davidson, and Herman Bennett, to
say nothing of Paul Gilroy, Ruth Wilson Gilmore, and Tina Campt.
Finally, it is quite impossible to say just how much the Dartmouth
Futures of American Studies Institute, for me a sustaining annual
pilgrimage since 2000, has nurtured, nourished, and challenged
my work. Certainly there is no thanking my comrade Donald Pease,
whom I have been exhilarated and honored to work with all these
years, and as for the rest of our beloved circle—Elizabeth Maddock
Dillon, Robyn Wiegman, Hamilton Carroll, Wini Fluck, Donatella
Izzo, Tony Bogues, John Carlos Rowe, Colleen Boggs, Alan Nadel,
Michael Chaney, Marty Favor, Soyica Diggs Colbert, Ivy Schweitzer,
Hortense Spillers, Lisa Lowe, Liam Kennedy, Jed Dobson, Alex
Corey, and others besides—these puny words of gratitude will have
to suffice.

I am more delighted than ever to acknowledge the funding of
some of this work by a fellowship from the National Endowment
for the Humanities. Former CUNY Graduate Center president Bill
Kelly, whose name rings like unto bullion, deserves special thanks
for centrally transforming my life and work. Thanks are due as
well to the venues and editors that occasioned early versions of
some of these pages, and for permission to reprint them here: for
Twain, Forrest Robinson and *The Cambridge Companion to Mark
Twain;* for Sinatra, Jill Lane and *hemisferíca;* for film noir, Gordon
Hutner and *American Literary History;* for John Howard Griffin,
Don Pease, Amy Kaplan, and *Cultures of U.S. Imperialism;* for
Elvis, Harry Stecopoulos, Mike Uebel, and *Race and the Subject of
Masculinities;* for Dylan, Kevin Dettmar and *The Cambridge Companion to Bob Dylan.*

My thinking about Barack Obama and the workings of racial
fantasy, especially as the latter circulates in the film *Candyman,*
was aided to no end by Donald Pease, Meg Wesling, Carlo Rotella,
Sean McCann, Kate Nickerson, Avery Gordon, Sianne Ngai, Mitch

Duneier, Harry Stecopoulos, Mark Maslan, Laura Goldblatt, Maria Damon, Jani Scandura, William Savage, Samuele Pardini, George Justice, Devoney Looser, Jack Hamilton, Gwendolyn DuBois Shaw, and audiences at the University of California–Santa Barbara, UC-Irvine, the University of Minnesota, Michigan State, Northwestern, the University of Illinois, the Andy Warhol Museum, Wayne State, the University of Richmond, Southern Illinois University, the CUNY Graduate Center, Dartmouth, the Smithsonian National Portrait Gallery, UCLA, UVA, Elon University, Arizona State, Montana State, and the University of Nevada–Reno. My thanks to Forrest Robinson for commissioning my writing on Mark Twain, to Shelley Fisher Fishkin for convening an American Studies Association panel in Boston that helped deepen my ideas, to Hal Holbrook (Twain impersonator extraordinaire) for cracking wise about them on that same panel, and to Lillian Robinson, Henry Louis Gates Jr., David Bradley, Ann Ryan, and Jonathan Arac for their various responses. Sitting around with Michael Rogin and Marshall Berman after delivering an early version of the ideas in Chapter 3 is one of my fondest memories; thanks also to David Yaffe, Herman Beavers, Eric Weisbard, Rob Wilson, Tom Ferraro, John Gennari, Samuele Pardini, Susan Gubar, Robert Christgau, and Stanley Crouch for various kinds of instructive response. Many thanks to Nancy Loevinger for putting together the panel on film noir at the Virginia Film Festival (all those years ago!) that generated the first version of my work on the genre; Philomena Mariani offered extremely generous and indispensable help (including bootleg VHS tapes of many films back when that was, well, extremely generous and indispensable) in getting my ideas off the ground, and audiences at Texas A&M, SUNY–Stony Brook, and Wesleyan engaged and challenged those ideas, as did Susan Fraiman, Richard Herskowitz, Larry Reynolds, E. Ann Kaplan, Sara Blair, Carlo Rotella, Sean McCann, Michael Denning, Harry Stecopoulos, and Paul Buhle (who tipped me to crucial leads). Long ago, when I began to take an annoyed interest in the ubiquity of *Black Like Me* in the African American Studies sections of Barnes & Noble and Waldenbooks stores nationwide, my writing on John Howard Griffin benefited from the attention of Amy Kaplan (who took productive issue with it), Chris Looby (a virtual collaborator), Jeff Melnick, Walter Michaels, Tania Modleski, Don

Pease (who brilliantly edited the first version), David Roediger, Kirk Savage, Bart Bull, Werner Sollors, and Gayatri Spivak, as well as audiences at the Dartmouth Cultures of U.S. Imperialism Conference, the College of William and Mary, and the American Studies Association in Costa Mesa, California. David Yaffe and his work on Joni Mitchell provoked and sharpened my ideas about her strange and brilliant career; Lindsay Andrews, Alex Corey, Tony Bogues, Jonathan Flatley, Bob Ivry, Kandia Crazy Horse, Miles Grier, Rodrigo Lazo, Michael Szalay, and Richard Godden shrewdly clarified some of the things I was trying to address; Duane Corpis and Damien Keane immeasurably broadened and deepened my engagement with the material; and audiences at the Dartmouth American Studies Institute, Syracuse University, UC-Irvine, and a Columbia graduate history workshop led by Karl Jacoby were informed, immensely helpful, and gracious. Some early notes toward Chapter 7 on Elvis impersonators were published in *The Nation* and are incorporated here; many thanks to Ruth DeJauregui of American Graphic Systems, Inc. for various tips and inside information on Elvis impersonators; to the impersonators and fans themselves for sharing their thoughts and ideas so generously; to friends and audiences at Rutgers, Wesleyan, Michigan, Southern Maine, and Chicago; to Steve Arata, Karen Bock, Lisa Brawley, Lucinda Cole, Rita Felski, Rick Livingston, Greil Marcus, Sean McCann, Jahan Ramazani, and Caroline Rody for critical suggestions on early drafts and for useful information of various kinds; and to my brother, Brian, for helping me learn from Las Vegas. One day in the summer of 2001, Greil Marcus called to tell me he'd heard that Bob Dylan's forthcoming record "had an interesting title"; David Yaffe brainstormed with me about the record's implications, Lou Renza finally provoked me to write about it, and Kevin Dettmar helped me articulate what I was trying to say; and I found patient listeners to what I came up with in wonderful audiences at a UVA Music Department Colloquium (thank you, Michael Puri and Bonnie Gordon), Hunter College (thank you, Paul Fess and Richard Goldstein), and Dickinson College (thank you, Cotten Seiler and Barry Shank—my mates, along with Charlie McGovern, in the short-lived but blazing band The Structure of Feeling, upon hearing which Eric Weisbard uttered the immortal verdict: "That was surprisingly not that bad"). Michael

Denning's responses to a number of these chapters affirmed a long-standing intellectual comradeship.

I HAVE BEEN WAITING just about twenty-five years to do a book with Lindsay Waters, across which time we have had many conversations telephonic and not, swaps of writing and musical tips, rhapsodic exchanges and testy ones, and I am proud not only to count him a friend but to have this book done for him at last. I am very grateful to the Harvard University Press production team for making it all happen so smoothly: Amanda Peery, Joy Deng, and Stephanie Vyce, you are the best. Greil Marcus, Donald Pease, and Elizabeth Maddock Dillon gave the manuscript the once-over it deserved and kept it from being twice-told. Adam Cohen's research assistance helped enormously with enormous changes at the last minute. Marissa Brostoff's amazing line editing and proofreading saved me from any number of stupidities. I have been blessed across many years with gifted students whose work has engaged me and enriched mine: Harry Stecopoulos, Bluford Adams, Doris Witt, Dorri Beam, Mike Bennett, Will Kazmier, David Scott, Anthony Rizzuto, Rebecca Hyman, Derek Nystrom, Allen Durgin, Joon Lee, Chris Krentz, Mason Stokes, Ian McGuire, Karlyn Crowley, John Charles, Finnie Coleman, Tom Jehn, Evelyn Chien, Rod Waterman, Matt Brown, Dan Rosensweig, Walton Muyumba, Mike Millner, Bryan Wagner, Ben Lee, Bill Albertini, Tom Kane, Justin Gifford, Mike Lundblad, Jolie Sheffer, Rei Magosaki, Sarah Hagelin, Jim Cocola, Ben Fagan, Brenna Munro, Brian Roberts, Ray Malewitz, Erich Nunn, Scott Selisker, Nathan Ragain, Wes King, Sam Turner, Phil Maciak, Tiffany Gilbert, Kendra Hamilton, Sarah Ingle, Sonya Donaldson, Maria Windell, Shaun Cullen, Morten Hansen, Laura Goldblatt, Lindsay O'Connor, and Jean Franzino. It has been a true joy to watch them flourish and to call them friends. Laura Goldblatt helped and pestered me in such equal measure that it made me wonder fondly whether she was the new Harry Stecopoulos. I have enjoyed and learned a ton from close collaborations in recent years with Hilarie Ashton, Danica Savonick, Sean Gerrity, Jenny LeRoy, Paul Fess, Nicole Zeftel, Wendy Tronrud, Simone White, Chris Eng, Kristin Moriah, Kristina Huang, Marissa Brostoff, Nick Gamso, Melissa Phruksachart, and Timothy Griffiths:

long may you run. I could always count on Carlo Rotella, Franny Nudelman, Sandhya Shukla, John Gennari, Robyn Wiegman, Michael Denning, Chip Tucker, Craig Barton, Tavia Nyong'o, Lara Cohen, Gordon Hutner, David Roediger, Kandice Chuh, Liam Kennedy, Robert Reid-Pharr, Duncan Faherty, José Muñoz, Bryan Wagner, Jack Hamilton, Chris Looby, Alexandra Vazquez, Daphne Brooks, Matt Jacobson, Harry Stecopoulos, Laura Goldblatt, and Scott Saul to wake me from merely professional slumbers and also to make me laugh. The love and encouragement and critique and cajolery coming at me from two Massachusetts weirdos, Benj DeMott and Jonathan Flatley, have been keeping me going for a long time now; to capture the importance of their example and influence on my life and work would take another book, but for now, hey fellas, thanks, you know I love you. Much love to Arthur Katz, Susan Katz, Phyllis Katz, and Marshall Feigin, with whom I have enjoyed talking about the ideas in this book, as I have with MGM—Maggie Magee, Gary Katz, and Maeve Magee Katz—who rarely overslept and gave me yokes too deadly to mention. I think my loving parents, Judy and Dick, became skeptical this book would ever get done, and who can blame them, but like my brother, Brian, they held fast, and I thank them for that. Brian could have written this book but wisely was otherwise engaged. Being in the company of Cory Fraiman-Lott is one of the great joys of my life. Whether speaking to each other entirely in lines from *The Big Lebowski* or off on some mad caper, we continue to take it to the next level. Cory's wit, blazing intelligence, and love mean everything to me. As for Cindi Robin Katz, one person in three names (at least; see this book's dedication)—quite possibly three persons (or more) in one name—her zany brilliance keeps me aloft even when times get rough, especially when times get rough, and I never feel far from my joy in living with her smile, her songs, her patience, and her insight. There is no thanking her.

CHAPTER 1

BLACK MIRROR

States of Fantasy and Symbolic Surplus Value

*Since the beginning of the nation, white Americans have suffered from
a deep inner uncertainty as to who they really are. One of the ways
that has been used to simplify the answer has been to seize upon the
presence of black Americans and use them as a marker, a symbol of
limits, a metaphor for the "outsider." . . . Despite his racial difference
and social status, something indisputably American about Negroes not
only raised doubts about the white man's value system but aroused the
troubling suspicion that whatever else the true American is, he is also
somehow black.*

—Ralph Ellison, "What America
Would Be Like Without Blacks," 1970

THE ELECTION OF THE FIRST African American president of the
United States occasioned the legitimate return of blackface comedy.
All across Barack Obama's first term the burnt cork snuck back, most
notably in comedian Fred Armisen's many Obama impressions on
Saturday Night Live. Heads were scratched: was this kosher? Armisen had already ventured his version of pop star Prince; his blackface (and "blindface") New York governor David Paterson was a big

hit. Before you knew it, *Mad Men* principal Jon Hamm was cooning opposite a protesting Tracy Morgan in a spoof of *Amos 'n' Andy* on TV's *30 Rock* (Jane Krakowski did some "mock" blacking up too), *Fox NFL Sunday*'s Frank Caliendo blacked up *for a broadcast* as basketball star Charles Barkley, Billy Crystal resurrected his blackface Sammy Davis Jr. for the opening segment of the 2012 Academy Awards telecast, and the gang on *It's Always Sunny in Philadelphia* pursued more than one greasepaint remake of *Lethal Weapon.* Even Robert Downey Jr. got into the act, however ironically, using blackface to lampoon a white Method actor playing a hard-bitten black G.I. in the Ben Stiller lark *Tropic Thunder* (2008), recalling his father, Robert Downey Sr.'s, dubbing of lead actor Arnold Johnson's voice in Downey's radical satire *Putney Swope* (1969). The kitchen heating up, *SNL* replaced Armisen's Obama during election season with that of African American Jay Pharoah, whose artificially lightened skin on top of the inevitable comparisons to his comedic predecessor only redoubled the minstrel quotient. A state fantasy of what C. Wright Mills once called the new men of power played out serially on American screens. Earlier in the decade, Dennis Haysbert had laid important representational track for Obama's advancement in his portrayal of black president David Palmer on Fox's *24,* solemnizing somewhat comedian Chris Rock's conceit in the 2003 film *Head of State.* With Obama's actual triumph came the conscious restoration of what they used to call "negro minstrelsy."[1]

Should the specter of a blackface Obama surprise us? After all, commercial blackface stage performance first appeared at the turn of the 1830s in tandem with William Lloyd Garrison's abolitionist movement (and its paper *The Liberator*); isn't this always the dialectic of racial representation in America? It's never clear in any case what the relation is between off-color comedy and advances of color. Counterweights or complementarities? Could Obama in cork have been a backward testament to Americans' investment in a black president? Or are we in the realm of what Jacques Derrida in *Specters of Marx* referred to as "hauntologie," ontology haunted by a pun on haunting, in which the noncontemporaneity of time, the always out-of-joint unsettledness of temporality, is prey to repetition and ghosted past acts that consort uneasily with present purposes? What Ian Baucom in *Specters of the Atlantic* calls time's heterochronic "accumulation"?[2] This book takes the measure of such contradictions—the cultural contradictions of American racism, as I think of it, with Daniel Bell's *Cultural Contradictions of Capitalism* in mind. Where in Bell's work the desires and pleasures unleashed by capitalist consumption threaten to undermine the very system that gave rise to them, my project explores some of the ways dominant U.S. cultural institutions have relied insistently and repeatedly on a kind of racial symbolic capital, including and above all black-face, in the process threatening to betray—at the very least to reveal, sometimes to destabilize—the racial hegemony that generated such forms and that they exist in order to maintain.[3] In the case of Zip Coon Obama, a mostly affectionate recreational fantasy worked to expose the material and psychic operations of racial symbolic capital itself—operations that team Obama cunningly deployed to engineer its own success in 2008 and 2012. Here in this first chapter I spin a somewhat circuitous tale of those operations, catching up the subjects I address across subsequent chapters and making plain the stakes involved in each of them.

A crowning instance of what I am talking about came in a mock movie trailer produced for President Obama's April 2013 appearance at the yearly White House Correspondents' Dinner. Presidential second terms very often being chiefly symbolic, Obama's was no less so, starting with the densely allusive second inauguration that happened to fall on Martin Luther King Day in January of 2013, inevitably recalling the 1963 March on Washington fifty years earlier. The symbolism radiated across this moment's array of inevitably allusive popular fictions of state, all of them with some kind of White House resonance—Steven Spielberg's *Lincoln,* Quentin Tarantino's *Django Unchained,* Robert Zemeckis's *Flight,* Ben Affleck's *Argo* (awarded the Oscar for Best Picture by Michelle Obama herself live from the White House in late February), Kathryn Bigelow's *Zero Dark Thirty,* Roland Emmerich's *White House Down,* Lee Daniels's *The Butler,* Steve McQueen's *12 Years a Slave,* Ava DuVernay's *Selma,* and more besides; in the realm of pop symbolic capital, this is a period that stretches from Beyoncé Knowles's halftime performance at the 2013 Super Bowl in New Orleans to D'Angelo's long-awaited *Black Messiah* (2014) to Kendrick Lamar's *To Pimp a Butterfly* (2015) (with its cover featuring the White House lawn crowded with uproarious OGs) and beyond; and the actual factual realm of force and violence punctuated by the notable instances of police harassment and murder in Staten Island, suburban St. Louis, Baltimore, and many more found Obama in an even more distantly symbolic role—until that extraordinarily immediate (if no less symbolic) June 2015 moment he sang "Amazing Grace" in the Charleston church where nine parishioners had been murdered by a young white supremacist. In any case this two-minute confection (see it on YouTube) cast light on all these accumulating dimensions of what Donald Pease calls state fantasy and the state power it mediates and facilitates.[4] It opens with a deadpan Steven Spielberg recalling how it hit him to follow up his award-winning biopic of Lincoln with—Steven Spielberg's *Obama*. But who on earth to play him? "As it turns out," the director says, "the answer was right in front of me all along: Daniel Day-Lewis!" The actor so brilliant as Hawkeye in *Last of the Mohicans,* as Bill the Butcher in *Gangs of New York,* and most recently as Spielberg's Abraham Lincoln, a quick montage of clips certifies, "becomes his characters." "And you know what?" crows Spielberg, "He *nailed* it." Cut to Barack Obama being interviewed with the large caption, "DANIEL DAY-LEWIS, Method Actor." The joke has arrived. "Was it hard playing Obama? I'll be honest, yeah it was," says Obama as Day-Lewis as Obama. Shots of Obama in the mirror practicing "his accent": "Hello Ohio! Hello Ohio! I love you back!" For one thing, the actor avers, "the cosmetics were challenging"—and almost 200 years of blacking up roll into the picture. After a quick, almost obligatory bit with Tracy Morgan talking about his performance as (who else?) Joe Biden, we're back to "Day-Lewis." "The hardest part? Trying to understand his motivations. . . . What makes him tick? Why doesn't he get mad? If I were him [sic] I'd be mad *all the time.* But I'm not him. I'm Daniel Day-Lewis." Fade to black on "Obama" doing his hair and checking his hand gestures in the mirror.[5]

  In the face of such an astonishing artifact, it's hard to decide: amazing they thought of it or obviously overdue? Obama as Day-Lewis as Obama not only doesn't dissolve Obama's blackface nimbus, it perfectly realizes it. There's a white man inside him (white viewers' spectatorial surrogate) looking in the mirror and seeing the black face of power. That face fronts a persona always reflecting on how

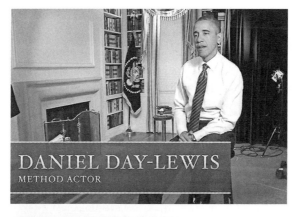

Fig. 2a and Fig. 2b. Barack Obama playing Daniel Day-Lewis playing Barack Obama: *Steven Spielberg's* Obama, 2013

to get the performance just right according to the dictates of white desire ("I love you back!"). The performance is always just that, an approximation or copy, never true or originary: the cosmetics are challenging. Obama was always already blackface Obama, presumptive imposter in many senses (not really black, not really left, not really American, not really patriotic, etc.). No less than Cornel West has called Obama a "Rockefeller Republican in blackface." (Why is blackface germane to the charge of crypto-conservatism? Black Republicans do exist. Or is the imputation of fake blackness the real assertion here?)[6] It is consoling both that a white man is inside pulling the strings and that he is able to summon the seductive contours of "blackness." For great swaths of the republic, "Steven Spielberg's Obama" *was* Obama, racial ambivalence and state playacting intact and defining. To follow the thread of West's remark, we loved (or despised) him for knowing just how to play us (in both senses). This is just one in a series of what in this book I call the black mirror: black mask for my white face, all the beautiful (or demonic) attractions of "blackness," generated out of a thousand media sources and ideological state apparatuses, the apparently fundamental precondition for the reproduction of national white selfhood if not dominance. Whites need that mirror to see ourselves healed, allied in innocence (or angrily disgusted) with the symbolic figure our reliance on whom reveals the violence and guilt we attempt by this means to overcome. For black citizens, certainly, other fantasies are in operation; wielding precisely these, scenarios of struggle duly rewarded, Obama carried the mirror as the very fulfillment of self-sustaining misrecognition—ourselves made delusively whole.[7]

Only this fragile dynamic sometimes undermines its own interests. From the early-nineteenth-century era of blackface minstrelsy (at least) to the present day, the generation of black images and self-interested Others has crucially buttressed white social and cultural dominance; but even in antebellum days this could be a risky proposition, and all across the long twentieth century such operations have occasionally played havoc with the dominance that brings them about, as I hope to show in the chapters that follow. I begin with Obama's interesting mirrors because they indicate how much we are heir to an ongoing racial imaginary structured in dominance, how much that imaginary can occasionally surprise us (not least by producing a black president), and how much its own operations can leave it vulnerable to self-exposure at the very moments it seems most intractable. All of this certainly puts the lie to the notion that our moment is "postracial," as the pundits say (or disclaim, with vehemence). Not even in your dreams—*least* of all in your dreams. Conversely, though, those writers who have made the obvious but necessary cases against the postracial fantasy have themselves understated the predicament.[8] White racial hegemony fueled by white racial desire stubbornly refuses to die; it is the latter's unpredictability as well as persistence that interests me here. It clearly interests President Obama as well, more about which below, and the funny thing is how aware of it he was both before and after being elected to high office—electorally, he made this awareness pay off twice; in media gambit and legislative maneuver, many times over. This never, to my mind, and contra Cornel West, involved him somehow cooning or corking up (let alone "niggerizing" the presidency, as West outrageously claimed on TV's CNN in June of 2015).[9] It is not that Obama metaphorically donned blackface in his more conservative gestures, as though blackness were essentially leftist and "good," or essentially anything at all. The blackface comes in with the contours of white desire, white fantasy about the president, and it is this we ought to know more about. Barack Obama is an apt starting place for this study because the fantasies to which he has given rise indicate that the black mirror, while very often involving the appropriation or approximation of blackness by whites—through blackface, through control of black images, through other kinds of cultural claim—actually depends less on appropriation or impersonation than on the theatricalization of race itself, the production of a kind of fantasy zone amenable to racial phantasmagoria. Not unlike drag, black mirroring seeks less to reproduce blackness with any accuracy than to activate it for white purposes, in the first instance those of social dominance and self-regard. What artist Kara Walker calls the Emancipation Approximation is that asymptotic vector of misrecognition and fetishism, a pure playing in the dark (as Toni Morrison has it), whereby classic American literature, Hollywood film, pop musical artistry, and concerned social commentary (to name my objects of study here) summon blackness in order to redeem the Republic and instead reveal their supremacist redundancy.[10]

Exhibit: John Howard Griffin, white author of *Black Like Me* (1961), the subject of my Chapter 5, blacked up for the purposes of undercover investigative journalism, beholding the mirror:

> Turning off all the lights, I went into the bathroom and closed the door. I stood in the darkness before the mirror, my hand on the light switch. I forced myself to flick it on.
>
> In the flood of light against white tile, the face and shoulders of a stranger—a fierce, bald, very dark Negro— glared at me from the glass. He in no way resembled me.

The transformation was total and shocking. I had expected to see myself disguised, but this was something else. I was imprisoned in the flesh of an utter stranger, an unsympathetic one with whom I felt no kinship. All traces of the John Griffin I had been were wiped from existence. Even the senses underwent a change so profound it filled me with distress. I looked into the mirror and saw reflected nothing of the white John Griffin's past. No, the reflections led back to Africa, back to the shanty and ghetto, back to the fruitless struggles against the mark of blackness. . . . I had gone too far. . . . The black man is wholly a Negro, regardless of what he once may have been. . . . The Griffin that was had become invisible.[11]

The writer who in the late 1950s famously made a tour of the South to discover "what it was really like" to be black finds utter self-estrangement in blackface. It is an exemplary instance of the black mirror. Racial crossover means that the "Griffin I had been" ceases to exist, though he looks on from his black prison. Which is to say, first, that even this liberal white journalist imagines whiteness and blackness as insuperably distinct, "wholly" different, devoid of kinship despite the obvious counterevidence of history. His foray into otherness amounts not to Keats's negative capability but sheer negation—blackness for Griffin is Shakespeare's "undiscovered country," not Africa, that is, but death. Note that he nonetheless manages to produce a (for him) wholly convincing impersonation of black American manhood. All this strikes me as superbly (if somewhat hideously) revealing of a well-meaning U.S. white man's racial imaginary at the turn of the 1960s, in the very year Barack Obama was born. For isn't it also the case that Griffin fully grasps his whiteness just here, at the moment it is apparently obliterated? Who but a white "I" is "imprisoned in the flesh of an utter stranger" and feels his whiteness wiped away, "invisible" (à la Ralph Ellison)? Though everything begins to transform, right down to his senses, there lurks a presumptively universal, normatively white self capable of imagining a new past—Africa (not America too?), shanty and ghetto, fruitless resistance against the mark of blackness. The black mirror stages white access to, even dependence on, a black-ness imagined to be both other and intimate, and while that black-ness engenders a certain pedagogy for whites, it also threatens white annihilation. It is all at once crucial to white dominance, funda-mental to cross-racial understanding, and a potential disruption of white hegemony. It is the key to a world of symptoms. Perhaps this is why artist Glenn Ligon chose Griffin's charged words for one of his signature works, *Black Like Me #2* (1992), an earlier study for which graces the cover of this book, which consists entirely of the repeated lines of type "ALL TRACES OF THE GRIFFIN I HAD BEEN WERE WIPED FROM EXISTENCE," over and over and over, blurring as they proceed into almost completely smudged areas of illegible black ink. Perhaps, too, this is why the Obamas chose Li-gon's work for their private living space at the White House.[12]

What all this suggests is that the specular logic of resemblance— the "like-me-ness" of Griffin over against, and as, his imagined other; of Ligon refracting Griffin's plight; of the Obamas recognizing Ligon's art—is fundamental to the idea of racial identity or self-identification. It gives rise to the very impulse of self-reflection, the self-conscious affirmation that "I am white" (or not). We have absorbed the idea of gendered identities as iterative and performative—as masquerade— more quickly than we have racial ones.[13] Here, too, seemingly essen-tial or inherent racial predispositions are not the cause or ground of "racial" practices, culture, and behavior but rather their misrec-ognized results. That race and racial difference are structured in (if not like) language has become more or less axiomatic in studies of literature (and is part of the winking point, I think, of much of Glenn Ligon's work). The encounter between poststructuralist theory and race studies has ensured that we think of race not as an essence but as an inscription, a signifier of instituted difference; race partakes of the symbolic realm of cultural construction, not that of what Jacques Lacan terms the real; and it thrives on the swirl of pronoun functions producing and undermining self and other. To my mind it follows that that other thing we think to be struc-tured like a language, the unconscious, plays a crucial part in what we think of when we think of race. Race and racial difference, that is to say, are structured by fantasy: structures of fantasy, if you will, to play on Raymond Williams's well-known and useful formulation about affect and feeling.[14] The space this structure opens—the lack that drives it, in which fantasy lives—requires the mirror, that speculum, per Lacan, where imaginary or "orthopaedic" fullness emerges, revealing as it does so "a certain dehiscence at the heart of the organism, a primordial Discord."[15] In this study, the mirrors of and in performance, film, literature, and music, reflections both imaging back and producing moments of U.S. self-(un)knowing, are essentially my subject.

Just about the last thing it means for race to be structured in fantasy is that it has no real-world consequences. However fictional, race simply is one of the modalities in and by which we experience human life and human difference—which also means categories of social difference such as class and sexuality. A variety of thinkers in recent years have concluded that the most productive stance is to demonstrate race's incoherence, as though showing our mistake would make racism disappear; or reach for firmer social and political determinants such as class; or suggest race's declining or properly historical significance, now past. The most popular gambit for writers all across the ideological spectrum has been to insist on the importance of class over race.[16] My view is and always has been that we should explore the dimensions and especially the consequences of the fantasy race is—consequences that suffuse the consciousness of class, sexuality, gender, and other lines of force. Live there a while, in thought as in life. That is what this book tries to do.

THE AFOREMENTIONED Sammy Davis Jr.'s first autobiography was titled *Yes I Can* (and published in 1965—the year of the Selma marches, the second of which Davis attended). By the time of the 2008 presidential election, Barack Obama had taken a close approximation of the phrase for his campaign slogan, "Yes We Can" (through the crucial intervening filter of Cesar Chavez and Dolores Huerta's "Sí se puede"). Sammy Davis's very first movie, it turns out, was *Rufus Jones for President* (1933), in which a seven-year-old Davis ascends to high office. A Warner Brothers Vitaphone song-and-dance short from early in the history of sound motion pictures, and according to Davis shot in Brooklyn, *Rufus Jones* is a Jim Crow fever dream.[17] Bullied by some kids in the street, Rufus runs for solace to Ethel Waters, who tells him he can be anything he wants to be, even president of the United States; when Rufus drifts off to sleep in her lap, his dream realizes the fantasy. Despite some fine performances by Waters (and Davis!), the film is essentially a vehicle for *Birth of a Nation*–style burlesques of African Americans wielding the sort of political power Barack Obama would assume exactly seventy-five years later. How interesting, then, that an effigy Sammy Davis would feature in a *Saturday Night Live* opening skit with Billy Crystal and Obama's signal predecessor, Jesse Jackson, during the latter's 1984 presidential run (20 October 1984). (Think here of Bill Clinton's comparison of Obama to Jackson, in South Carolina no less, during the 2008 primaries in a desperate attempt to discredit him; think too of Jackson crying in Chicago's Grant Park the night of Obama's first victory.) Coming later in the year of Jackson's pitiful "Hymietown" references to New York City, the bit cheerfully legitimates Crystal's blackface Sammy Davis even as Crystal invokes and indeed authenticates Davis's famous conversion to Judaism. The skit features a couple of bad jokes about the Republicans; a Davis-administered Yiddish lesson; a little duet with "Davis" and Jackson singing a Vegas version of Paul Simon's 1966 song "Red Rubber Ball"; and—"Live from New York!" in Yiddish. The charm of the piece, I suppose, inheres not only in Crystal's funny Davis impersonation but also in Jackson's self-consciously second-fiddle status—he's the inadequate student of showbiz and of the cultural markers of his fantasized "Hymietown." Jackson is humbled and forced to pay his respects to the culture he's traduced. The lyrics of "Red Rubber Ball" even suggest absolution for Jackson as a result of this very performance: "And I think it's gonna be all right / Yeah, the worst is over now / The mornin' sun is shinin' like a red rubber ball." Announcing the show's opening not as he would have done it, in the tones of the Baptist reverend he is, but in mimicry of Billy Crystal's Yiddish, Jackson comes to New York on Jewish terms.

But not unlike the dream of a black president in the hands of the brothers Warner, and fully in step with Michael Rogin's well-known analysis of Hollywood racial representation in *Blackface, White Noise,* this is a charade of amity. Crystal and Jackson mime interracial brotherhood though Crystal is blacked up. They confirm

Jackson's political penitence for his anti-Semitic remarks but do so at the parodic expense of Davis, Davis's earnest Jewishness, and indeed interracialism itself. For sure Sammy made himself a Rat Pack mascot. But here any reaffirmation of Jackson's political credibility can apparently come only at the expense of black representation— Crystal's blackface, the imputation of Davis's Jewface—pretty much the equivocal political dynamic I have outlined thus far.[18] Most insidiously, in the end, the political and representational crisis at hand is displaced onto the terrain of black *intraracial* politics, the conflict between blacks and Jews restaged as one between Jackson the insurgent Democrat and Davis the Kennedy-turned-Nixon man ("no hugs," Jackson warns Davis at the end of the skit, probably referencing the latter's notorious public embrace of Richard Nixon on live television during the 1972 Republican convention).[19] Neither man is kosher, but the matter is left to them to fight out. (Precisely what Tarantino accomplishes in his scripted clashes between Jamie Foxx's badass Django and Samuel L. Jackson's house-Negro Stephen at the end of *Django Unchained*.)[20]

Just here it would be nice to have a little sense of how President Obama, so often the target of this sort of thing, thinks about such matters. As it happens, we do. Obama's *Dreams from My Father* (1995) suggests the president's dialectical cast of mind when it comes to the burdens of racial representation. On one occasion while a Columbia undergraduate, Obama receives a visit from his mother and sister. Paging through the *Village Voice,* Mom spots an ad and enthusiastically enjoins everyone to see the famous 1959 French-Brazilian film directed by Marcel Camus, *Black Orpheus,* at a downtown art house. Obama writes: "The story line was simple: the myth of the ill-fated lovers Orpheus and Eurydice set in the favelas of Rio during Carnival. In Technicolor splendor, set against scenic green hills, the black and brown Brazilians sang and danced and strummed guitars like carefree birds in colorful plumage." The son is not pleased, quite dismayed rather by the romantic racialism onscreen. Ready to split about halfway through, he turns to his mother: "But her face, lit by the blue glow of the screen, was set in a wistful gaze. At that moment, I felt as if I were being given a window into her heart, the unreflective heart of her youth. I suddenly realized that the depiction of childlike blacks I was now seeing on the screen, the reverse image of

Conrad's dark savages, was what my mother had carried with her to Hawaii all those years before, a reflection of the simple fantasies that had been forbidden to a white middle-class girl from Kansas, the promise of another life: warm, sensual, exotic, different."[21] The eternal racial gulf, he despairs, even among kin. "The emotions between the races could never be pure; even love was tarnished by the desire to find in the other some element that was missing in ourselves," Obama writes. "Whether we sought out our demons or salvation, the other race would always remain just that: menacing, alien, and apart" (124). For a few days after this, he avoids situations where he might have to talk to his mother—a remarkable confession. One day, though, she asks if he's planning on visiting his dad, about whom she begins to recollect at length; and hearing his mother speak of his father, a deeper feeling settles over him. His mom is still "that girl with the movie of beautiful black people in her head," full of "misconceptions," but Obama realizes that her love for his father was guileless and unself-conscious like any other love, transformed if we're lucky into something firmer. "What I heard from my mother that day, speaking about my father, was something that I suspect most Americans will never hear from the lips of those of another race, and so cannot be expected to believe might exist between black and white: the love of someone who knows your life in the round, a love that will survive disappointment" (127). Even as that exoticizing "girl" she finds her way to real love. *Despite* the blandishments of *Black Orpheus,* that notable instance of the black Atlantic imaginary? *By way of it* somehow? By transcending it altogether, as though that were possible? Obama doesn't venture to say. In any case that text doesn't foreclose, and as Obama renders it may even help afford, the commitment across racial lines. The point is that contradictions in racial representation, even rather dicey ones, can provide the conditions for social movement—in this case the quite literal generation of our former president. The president in turn mobilized a vast constituency out of these, or similar, contradictions.

Indeed in a powerful essay Donald Pease has gone so far as to see in this *Black Orpheus* episode the origins of Obama's understanding of how to construct a social movement—a collective imaginary resulting in the presidency—across racial lines. Obama, Pease argues, found a way to inhabit the "breach" between romanticized embrace ("childlike blacks") and demonizing recoil ("dark savages"), red state and blue, sovereign and (as Giorgio Agamben would have it) *homo sacer*. "Neither the one nor the other," Pease writes, "Obama's oscillation between the positions of the sovereign and the *homo sacer* enabled him to deploy both of the positions within the structuring racist antinomy—the venerated racial prophet / the demonized terrorist—to his political advantage," reworking this seemingly endless oscillation "into the energies animating the momentum of his political movement." Converting what Pease calls this "Orphic machinery" into the precondition for his emergence, Obama "impersonat[ed] a new iteration of Black Orpheus."[22] Black Orpheus's descent into the underworld—curiously echoed by the use of Gounod's *Faust* in Spielberg's *Lincoln* and the source story of Broomhilda's name in Tarantino's *Django* (if not indeed the whole southern-descent theme of the entire film), both of them subtending an Obaman imaginary—fundamentally reworked what Pease has for years been calling the "Bush settlement" even as it assumes Orpheus's mythic power to liberate the machinery of state from political impasse.[23]

I would contend, however, that Pease's argument is a state fantasy in its own right and finesses the force of its own point: the descent into underworld governmentality depicted, for one, by Max Weber in his famous essay "Politics as a Vocation" (1919). "The early Christians knew full well the world is governed by demons and that he who lets himself in for politics, that is, for power and force as means, contracts with diabolical powers and for his action it is *not* true that good can follow only from good and evil only from evil, but that often the opposite is true."[24] In short, writes Weber, "Whoever wants to engage in politics at all, and especially in politics as a vocation . . . must know that he is responsible for what may become of himself under the impact of [commanding a monopoly on the legitimate use of force and violence over a given territory]. . . . I repeat, he lets himself in for the diabolic forces lurking in all violence" (125–26). Those who enter politics enter a deal with the devil, and not only are positive ends not guaranteed to follow from good intentions, the means of politics—force—often make wholesome ends impossible: a desperate state contradiction resulting precisely from the Orphic bargain. To put it in the bluntest possible terms, on one side Obama could proselytize about elementary school shootings and gun control and even mean it while on the other authorizing the unchecked and unbalanced use of drones—estimated by one review of classified CIA documents for a fourteen-month period beginning in September of 2010 to have killed 613 people (in 114 strikes), many of them children, some of them only best guesses ("signature" as opposed to "personality" strikes) as to the identity of their targets.[25] Grasped in pop terms, this is something like the political unconscious of Spielberg's *Lincoln* underwriting the tactics of Tarantino's *Django*, the gun power behind state power made all too real. Preemptive and not popularly mandated drone strikes, their results more than once exactly the same as that of the Newtown, Connecticut, school shootings, are not a casually necessary part of the national defense but a component of ongoing state-sponsored primitive accumulation. One hates to drag George W. Bush press secretary Ari Fleischer back from wherever he was, but his comments on the Obama administration are worth noting: "Drone strikes. Wiretaps. Gitmo. Renditions. Military commissions. Obama is carrying out Bush's fourth term, yet he attacked Bush for violating the Constitution."[26] The state monopoly on legitimate violence that Obama won through his Orphic maneuvering redounds to state fantasy deployed to the state's diabolical ends—demonism's return.

As Sammy Davis—himself a mix, in Gerald Early's fine phrase, of Ragged Dick and Faust—once sang: "Who can take tomorrow, dip it in a dream / Separate the sorrow and collect up all the cream . . . / Who can take a sunrise, sprinkle it with dew / Cover it with chocolate and a miracle or two / The Candy Man, the Candy Man can."[27] Obama's state fantasy couldn't possibly have come through on all its promises. That's the logic inherent in state fantasy—to say nothing of the state itself. I agree with Pease when he writes in *The New American Exceptionalism* that in 2008 Obama became "the placeholder for all who could not be constitutively included within the social order . . . the originative lack out of which our individual desires arise," the "odd man in," the "embodiment of the void introduced by desire into objective reality" (210). But lacks and voids are wayward states, the very homes of racial cross-purposes and contradiction, fetishism and *meconnaissance*. If Obama's mother's affective antinomies—so strikingly given expression in ambivalent forms like blackface—supplied his template for the creation of a national, dominantly white investment in black Atlantic value, from Kansas to Kenya, an investment that put Obama in the White House, his habitation there generated its own state contradictions. The "audacity of hope"—cousin-german to Ernst Bloch's utopian *Principle of Hope,* if you need Frankfurt School filigree for Obama's slightly hucksterish coinage (Bloch's original title, interestingly enough, was the Obamaesque *Dreams of a Better Life)*—and *dreams,* dreams from his father and others erected into a sort of state dreamwork, always both condensing and displacing per Freud's analysis, provided both the energy and the snare of Obama's administration.[28] For Freud, as Jacqueline Rose observes, fantasy makes group identification possible and impossible at one and the same time; it is social reality's psychic glue or ambivalent precondition.[29] At least where Obama is concerned, state fantasy was a site of both knowing and not knowing, embrace and disavowal, a scene of subjective splitting; there are left and right versions of this, differently double for his believers (Obama both savior and failure) and his haters (Obama both ill-equipped and overweening un-American socialist terrorist dictator); and this splitting is reproduced as and in terms of fetishism and misrecognition at the level of racial representation—that is, fantasy's incarnation as film, mediated image, mimicry, and more besides. Race fantasy and state fantasy in the age of Obama worked similarly in different registers but with no immediate or instrumental relations between them—lags and imperfect alignments of all kinds, prima facie meanings liable to turn into their opposites, unpredictable political results strangely arising from predictable forms of depiction.

Displacing and condensing, Obama in his Second Inaugural Address invoked "Seneca Falls and Selma and Stonewall." Thrilling, to be sure, in the mouth of a U.S. president, especially with all that is condensed there, these instances of history-making masses in motion. But Obama's trope may have played too much on a reading of progress unimpeded by the state's diabolism. Two of the above three name moments of horrific if routine state violence: the state's reliance on what Bryan Wagner has called the police power.[30] The Selma marchers were first beaten and tear-gassed, in their next attempt pushed back across the Edmund Pettus Bridge, before on their third try they made it all the way to Montgomery; and the Greenwich

Village cops were wielding nightsticks and guns along with homophobic slurs the night Village people fought back with garbage cans and uprooted parking meters. Invoking these instances of obstructions overcome, Obama displaced the legitimate state violence he wielded onto his movement's enemies, othering it in a triumphal narrative of civil-rights progress—wearing his shackles, you might say, on his sleeve. Obama is very much a son of Selma, that movement pushing precisely for black voting rights in 1965 without which he would not have become president. If it is too much to suggest he betrayed that legacy, it would be foolish not to note the contradiction that found him with a monopoly on the legitimate use of force and violence, from Guantánamo to drones, and about which he was less forthright than about the ghosts of enemies past. The chains belonged to him.

Unclarity on this front was exhibited quite visibly in the summer of 2009 when Harvard's Du Bois Institute director Henry Louis Gates Jr. was arrested trying to enter his own home. President Obama first correctly remarked that the police "acted stupidly" in the affair but then retracted his remarks in the face of political pressure. Whereupon the famous "beer summit" was announced. An egregious malfeasance of police power was met with—*mediation,* a friendly sit-down with the cops. One "teachable moment" wasted. In a certain way, though, the conduct of this whole episode was consonant with the displacements and condensations of Gates's own PBS DNA specials, which downplay masses in motion against injustice in favor of individualist glory stories. Those shows, *African American Lives* and *African American Lives 2,* and more lately *Finding Your Roots,* engage what the *New York Times* termed "the poetry of history, the magic of science and the allure of the family trees of Morgan Freeman, Chris Rock, Tina Turner, Don Cheadle, Tom Joyner and Maya Angelou."[31] (Poetry, magic, and celebrity allure: sounds like fantasy to me.) Conducting DNA analyses once the genealogical paper trail runs out—and it runs out pretty quickly, given that the enslaved were recorded in census lists as chattel personal rather than people with names—Gates enters the dizzying sphere of mitochondrial and Y-chromosome tests, genetic admixture tests, sample populations, the Cambridge reference sequence, haplotypes, single nucleotide polymorphisms (SNPs), ancestral components, and the like, to say nothing of the perplexities and uncertainties of rendering the resulting "racial" mixes of a given family or person. (The money moment in these searches comes when Gates reveals, *Voila!,* the racial percentages, European, Native American, African, of one's makeup—the obverse of, but no less phantasmatic than, blackface itself.) Gates's companion volume *Finding Oprah's Roots* brims with confidence about the capacity of genealogical research "to heal the rupture and the wounds of the Middle Passage" and "to stake our claim, ever more deeply, on the American tradition."[32] Finding Oprah's roots, it turns out, demonstrates the following: "Education and property ownership: These are the two most important aspects of Oprah's family history" (167). Making it, that is—not, say, collective political struggle—turns you into a "hero," Gates's term for Oprah Winfrey's Reconstruction-era great-great-grandfather Constantine, who managed to acquire eighty acres of land (138). A remarkable achievement, no doubt about it, and objectively speaking a revolutionary one, since just a decade earlier Constantine had himself been property. But the political lesson for Gates lies elsewhere: "owning land was the conduit to middle-class status, because it implied economic stability and promised mobility, the mobility of subsequent generations" (73). (Never mind Oprah's notoriously hardscrabble youth.) Gates is frank about his interest in the making of the black middle class—particularly its celebrity exponents. What Gates rather astonishingly refers to as "roots in a test tube" is one more instance of symbolic surplus value, material interest generated out of racial fantasy.[33]

It's a wonder Gates hasn't gotten to pop stars Beyoncé and Jay-Z, during the Obama administration something of a surrogate First Couple. True to form, they availed themselves of U.S. state protection in order to travel to Cuba, and when they got flak for it Jay-Z produced "Open Letter," a rap that urged Obama to "chill with me on the beach": something of a right relation between state contradiction and the perils of racial fantasy in which the first couple of R&B found themselves caught.[34] More generally they tend to represent the better dreams and bigger responses of the R&B diaspora's fractured, insubordinate creations, the kind Obama saluted at a 2012 White House celebration of the blues (the president sang a verse of "Sweet Home Chicago"), or the Al Green songs he enjoyed singing on the stump. Diaspora "arts of darkness," as Paul Gilroy calls them, as if they issued from the underworld; and if Gilroy stresses the centrality of music to the black Atlantic's self-reflection and political agency, it is not merely because of the close guard whites placed on literacy but also because "words, even words stretched by melisma and supplemented or mutated by the screams which still index the conspicuous power of the slave sublime," are not enough to communicate the unsayable claims of black utopian political desire (perhaps why you found Obama singing all the time). Love songs, Gilroy rightly argues, songs crazy in love, traversed by plaint and challenge, reconciliation and reclamation, offer displaced meditations on exile and dispersal, social desire and different dreams, in a "syncopated temporality" that recalls the Orphic descent that was the Middle Passage.[35] In New Orleans in February of 2013, Beyoncé Knowles made the Super Bowl her own. (What was it Brecht said? "We pin our hopes to the sporting public," so much more discerning than that for the theater.)[36] Not only this, she staged a post-Katrina retaking of the Superdome for the age of Obama, a resonant symbolic act if it is true, as Pease has argued, that "Obama inaugurated [his] movement at [this] very site where Bush's [state] fantasy was washed away," only to ground it, Pease writes, in a "much more pervasive fantasy of dispossession."[37] Demanding a little sugar in *her* super bowl, as Bessie Smith would have said, Beyoncé brought to the Big Easy a very different, down home Houston (H-town!) ethos than that of our former First Clan, the Bush family. Answering water with fire, Bey arrived at halftime amid infernal towers of flame. With melisma and martial steps, ring shout and girl-game defiance, off the chain for sure, she found a "Halo"—the song she went out on—for what Lincoln in his First Inaugural called the "better angels of our nature." Midset, Beyoncé reunited with the two other members of her former group Destiny's Child, who shot up from beneath the stage as though from the underworld itself. A light Charlie's Angels thematic not only supplanted white versions of this ass-kicking pop crime-fighting unit but raised the question: in whose service was this troupe operating? (It didn't appear to be Mr. Charlie's, if you follow me.) In stark contrast with January's White House festivities, there was no state-sponsored lip-synching here; Beyoncé may not have come out and said it, but her troops effectively offered a countermemory to

Obama's parlous state apparatus. With Obama totem Jay-Z nowhere in sight, Beyoncé's sisterly army—every single person in her onstage collective was female—offered up a state fantasy to think with, righteous force in place of colorful plumage. One had to wonder whether Spielberg's Obama, our man in the mirror, was ready, in the words of the song, for *that* jelly.[38]

I SUPPOSE IT WOULD BE akin to occupying the tain of the mirror—the mirror's tin backing that allows it to reflect at all—for Obama or any president to square the circle of state contradiction. The modern state apparatus puts beyond the mirror's field of reflection any action uncompromised by force and social dominance; Obama could at most gesture to the kind of social justice the state can approximate but that lies properly beyond its purview. Even before that, the mechanics of representation—of representative government, of discursive framing and access, laws of genre, revolutions per minute—open themselves to no outside. As Jacques Derrida once wrote of theoretical discourse, that very medium of self-reflexivity, any "breakthrough toward radical otherness" must take place within philosophy itself, according to the "specular nature of philosophical reflection."[39] What is most important for my present purposes is that the self-and-other mirroring of racial symbolic capital gives rise to circuits of imaginative speculation and representation, cross-racial fantasy rendered into significant form, crossover dreamwork revealing as it conceals its ultimate investments. The black mirror is simultaneously shot through with another register of speculation, that of cultural and economic value, the capitalizing on which, whenever racial imaging comes into play, is the bedrock of white cultural dominance. Michael Rogin is responsible for the coinage "surplus symbolic value" that I am appropriating with slight modification to describe the cultural dynamics I study in the chapters ahead; and the happy fact is that his terminology, appropriately redolent of Marx, was produced to name "the power to make African Americans represent something beside themselves" that he rightly suggested was my subject in *Love and Theft*.[40] The material process of cultural extraction grounded in the expropriation of black sexuality and labor has its commercial

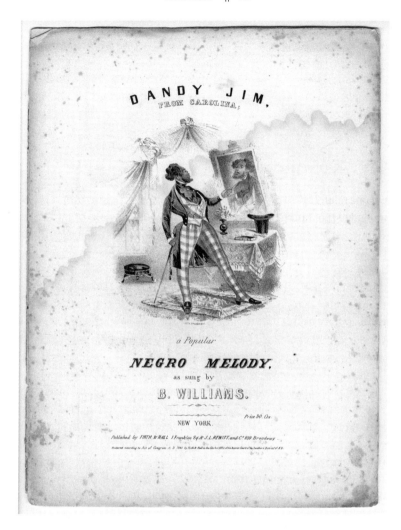

Fig. 3. "Dandy Jim from Carolina," sheet music cover, 1843, American Antiquarian Society

roots in the blackface minstrel show, and in *Black Mirror* I extend the analysis of its operations to arts and artists ranging from Mark Twain to film noir to Elvis impersonators. Like many of the most vital products of U.S. cultural life, they depend on—enact in their innermost workings—modes of production of racialized cultural value.

I take it to be relatively clear that when white men got on stage in antebellum America advertising themselves as fit representatives of African American dance, music, speech, song, and wit, in hues and sartorial styles claiming to be "Ethiopian," they were engaged in violent acts of value-creation. White and near-white (Irish and Irish American) performers and brokers capitalized on black cultural forms and dominant ideas about black cultural life, profiting financially as their audiences did culturally and psychologically. But well beyond the entertainment cash nexus, the actual scene in which "African American" arts were put up for exchange on the market, a template was created for a long-term traffic in "blackness." Black arts now had value beyond their "use value" for black Americans themselves; activated as exchange by whites for other whites, black cultural practices were subjugated by an invisible hand, where anyone could play and the people who had collectively produced them had no special claim. (To some extent, as Bryan Wagner has shown, even the use value of black cultural practices would from now on be interrupted by their exchange value—as when late-nineteenth-century vernacular forms incorporated as part of their purpose a response to white cultural and social expropriation.) When black commercial entertainers finally entered the picture after the Civil War, they did so as entrepreneurs entering an already established and externally governed system of exchange, one to which they had to adapt (not least through blackface) rather than the other way around and whose cross-racial mirrorings, featuring white performers as well as black, for increasingly racially mixed audiences across multiple media formats leading up to the present day, have made for such a dizzyingly complex and indeed alienated scene of cultural circulation and value production.[41]

I regard symbolic surplus value in black cultural forms as the appropriated capital, both cultural and actual, that accrues to white cultural producers and institutions whenever they traffic in "blackness"—a political economy of the sign, as Jean Baudrillard once framed it.[42] As in Marx's analysis of the workings of capital, it all proceeds according to routine, no moment of theft is visible, the object is sociocultural reproduction after all, and yet at the end of the day the customary exchange of black cultural labor has managed to earn dominant cultural workers a world of bling, an expression I use advisedly to underscore the effortless transfer of African American symbolic forms (here, slang terms of art) into mainstream usage. The best face to put on this process is Ralph Ellison's celebration of the "deceptive metamorphoses and blending of identities, values, and life-styles" that have made U.S. whites "culturally part Negro American without even realizing it," and this position does indeed have immense democratic salience.[43] But such "blending" was from its beginnings underwritten by the material relations of chattel slavery. Not only did the latter incubate the black melting-pot cultural labor so ripe for dominant-cultural expropriation, slavery also, as Michael O'Malley has argued, seemed to ground antebellum America's volatile markets, and especially its dizzyingly various forms of paper currency, in something like a gold standard of commodified black bodies. "More than simply labor power," O'Malley writes, "slaves formed a stock of actual capital that supported the issue of paper credit. . . . The idea of African Americans as a stock, a commodity of natural value, allowed them to 'regulate' other forms of meaning, other systems of value, in the North as well as the South."[44] "Blackness" both anchored value and, because of this, floated as one of its signifiers; it gave the lie to counterfeits, the suspicion of which always clung to paper money, and became itself a kind of currency, as I have elsewhere described the play of authenticity and mimicry in early minstrelsy.[45] The subsequent circulation of signs of "blackness" in the U.S. culture industries echoes its economic coloration even as it continues to generate surplus out of its extractions and exchanges. For every heartstring tugged by fare such as *The Help* (2011), a lot of people get paid, most of them white, all of them for maintaining a system of symbolic value-creation that transcends any single agent and that therefore awaits further activation for good or ill.[46]

The idea of symbolic surplus suggests that even beyond the antebellum moment of cultural services forcibly taken, some mysterious process of appropriation occurs, a siphoning off of value, in black cultural circulation, no matter how much black cultural producers themselves happen to be remunerated. As with so many things, Marx described this process best—and especially useful for our purposes is that his analysis dovetails with the psychoanalytic accounts of fetishism and disavowal so indispensable to the study of racial fantasy. In *Capital* Marx demonstrates that surplus value is generated out of the excess labor time demanded by an employer in an ordinary working day; all the value generated beyond that required to meet a worker's daily needs (a fraction of the working day) is quietly pocketed by the owner of the means of production. Something analogous to this happens when African American cultural practices (whoever performs or mimics or transforms them) circulate for money in entertainment industries beyond the scene and moment of their creation and actualization in local contexts of use. But there is more. Speaking of the "mysterious character" of the commodity form, Marx insists that it stems from making relations among humans seem like objective characteristics of the products that arise from those relations, a reification or congealing of the social forms of labor into the artifactual or "socio-natural" properties of the things labor produces. By extension this also "reflects the social relation of the producers to the sum total of labour as a social relation between objects, a relation which exists apart from and outside the producers," as though, in the context of racial cultures and their products, the latter had an independent and "natural" existence apart from the social institution and maintenance of racial difference. This substitution produces commodities, Marx says, "sensuous things which are at the same time supra-sensible or social. In the same way, the impression made by a thing on the optic nerve is perceived not as a subjective excitation of that nerve but as the objective form of a thing outside the eye. . . . It is nothing but the definite social relation between men themselves which assumes here, for them, the fantastic form of a relation between things. In order, therefore, to find an analogy we must take flight into the misty realm of religion." Or indeed race: this is the "fetishism of the world of commodities," an object-world that one cannot not misrecognize—its truth is quite literally invisible—and to my mind it extends to all social relations, including the misty realm of racial construction, in which the outcomes of human interaction, negotiation, and dominance are misconstrued as having a genesis and natural life of their own.[47]

    This circumstance is at the heart of a film I have long admired, the 1992 slasher picture *Candyman,* directed by Bernard Rose. To be sure, in its portrayal of a white female graduate student researching

urban legends in a black public housing project, the film gets itself into places it cannot finally get out of; but this is just another
way of saying it has the courage as well as the intelligence to pose
indelicate questions about specters of race whose surplus value
governs the postindustrial landscape the movie depicts as much as
it does the apparently debased cinematic form of its depiction. In
many ways *Candyman* allegorizes the states of fantasy and expro-
priations of value that are the subject of this book.[48] It has the virtue
to boot of taking place in Chicago—Barack Obama's Chicago, if you
will, since the year the film was released Obama (fresh out of Harvard Law) returned there, one node in the happenstance geography,
near enough to the Mississippi Valley, that features in several of my
chapters. The film also resonates with certain of their urgencies:
the hair-raising interracial involvements of Mark Twain and others,
the imaginary interlocutors and detective paradigms of film noir, the
mirror stages of John Howard Griffin and Melvin Van Peebles, Joni
Mitchell's fascination with black manhood, Elvis as crossover figure,
even the racialized melancholia of late Bob Dylan.

The black mirror is *Candyman*'s motivating device but also its
major theme, the vehicle of its political intervention but also its final
enigma. (It also literally underwrites the existence of the film, which
transports and transposes to Chicago the plot and characters of a
Clive Barker short story, "The Forbidden," set in an English Council
Estate—and in doing so outdoes its already very fine double.)[49] The
rumor of Candyman comes to the attention of Helen Lyle (Virginia
Madsen), a white University of Illinois–Chicago anthropology
graduate student writing a dissertation on urban legends. The story
goes that if you say the word "Candyman" five times in the mirror, he
will appear: the ghost of a black man maimed (his hand cut off, now
replaced by a hook) and then killed (by swarms of bees, to avenge
his having impregnated the daughter of a rich white man) in the Reconstruction period on the site of what became Chicago's notorious
Cabrini-Green public housing project. In a prologue we see the
specter summoned in a suburban bathroom mirror by a young white
couple about to have (premarital) sex; momentarily Candyman arrives to punish (per slasher genre convention) the young woman for
her transgression. This is the sort of timeless tale told to our protagonist Helen by white UIC undergraduate informants, but a couple

of black female Cabrini-Green residents, UIC housekeeping staff who overhear Helen's research interviews, suggest more pointedly that Candyman is to blame for the recent Cabrini murder of their neighbor Ruthie Jean. This sends Helen to the other side of the (El) tracks to investigate, yet however much Candyman's existence seems independently verified by these and other Cabrini tenants, the film goes out of its way to explore the situational demands of white fantasy that provide the medium for Candyman's returns, from his various mirror conjurings to the pressures of scholarly cupidity. Helen's interest in scooping her snarky and sexually unfaithful anthro professor husband, Trevor, and his ultracondescending colleague Purcell (neither of whom gives such folk myths any credence) leads her, along with her black grad-student friend Bernadette, to stake out Cabrini-Green for fresh material. At first a nonbeliever, Helen begins to take seriously the possible existence of Candyman, but her very interestedness—the dimensions of her desire—works at the same time to cast doubt on her discoveries. Indeed, Helen is eventually institutionalized after Bernadette is found stabbed to death next to an unconscious Helen holding a knife in her hand. We "know" Candyman to have been present when the murder occurred—we see him terrorizing Helen as Bernadette arrives upon the scene—but facts appear to be facts.[50]

Nonetheless, the movie perhaps purposely never resolves the question of whether Candyman (Tony Todd) is merely the spectral emanation of Helen's white ethnographic fantasy or a spirit of the ghetto generated out of Chicago urban transformations the film visually and otherwise insists on calling to our attention. Plenty of Cabrini's black residents believe he exists, but we see him appear only upon Helen's various mirror solicitations, and it is anyone's guess if he is responsible for all the villainous activity ascribed to him: more than one garden-variety Cabrini gangster evidently operates in his name. This means Candyman the specter walks the line between white fetish and the afterlife of social death—the racist violence that originally killed him and its new variation as constituted by carceral postwar "urban renewal" complexes such as Cabrini. The film's refusal to distinguish between these options elegantly makes Marx's point about the commodity's "mysterious character." Candyman the mysterious character is reputed (we learn) to have been the son of a quite literal American commodity, a slave who upon emancipation made good in the mass manufacture of shoes and was thus able to send Candyman to all the best academies, where he became a brilliant painter and thereafter a portraitist of the Chicago rich (one of whose daughters—Helen's precursor—fell in love with him). The loving detail with which the film renders Chicago urban space and spatial histories turns the city into a (mysterious) character in its own right and vastly enriches the depiction of all these "specters of Marx" (to invoke Derrida again). Restlessly roaming the built environment, the camera discerns the sovereignty Henri Lefebvre understood to be lodged there and suggests the "unrequited desires, bizarre ideologies, and hidden productivities" Patricia Yaeger argues are therein encrypted, requiring a "poetics of geography" capable of recovering "what is repressed or forgotten in space"—what she strikingly terms a "geographic equivalent of the ghost story."[51] The stunning opening aerial shot (one of many in the film) takes us from the downtown Loop out west to UIC along the Eisenhower Expressway (I-290), hovering above stretches of freeway full of commuting suburbanites with such mesmeric cinematography and musical repetition (in the score by Philip Glass) that we are enjoined to ponder the meaning of those convolutedly layered blocks, trestled freeway exit by sunken cloverleaf inlay, commuter campus by municipal post office. The congregated voices of Glass's music suggest at once a collective subject and a free-floating evanescence, gesturing perhaps to an entranced or phantasmatic witness to urban horror, or a summons to attend to it.[52] This effect is literalized a few seconds later in a shot that dissolves the Chicago skyline into the face of a entranced Helen, holding it there as she listens to a student recounting one of the urban horror stories she believes might make sense of her mental cityscape. Not long after, Helen and Bernadette in another aerial shot drive into the Cabrini area (again subtended by Glass's score), charting the project's willed seclusion from a surrounding city so obviously proximate that it forces one to reflect on such a momentous boundary's historical construction and enforcement. Above all there is the movie's supremely clever decision to have Candyman materialize chiefly in locations that attest to Chicago urban transition and built succession: a postindustrial parking garage (where Helen first meets him), Cabrini itself, Helen's apartment at the film's start (more on which below), and Helen's apartment again at the end as it undergoes "renewal" by ex-husband Trevor and his new (adoring undergraduate) girlfriend. Hauntological specimens like Candyman are key to unleashing and adducing oppressions that are, in the words of Joseph Roach, "forgotten but not gone," present but unseen; ghosts attest to injury but also suggest the unfulfilled possibility of redress.[53]

In short, *Candyman* seems bent on narrating the formation (or at least consequences) of Chicago's "second ghetto" as well as implicating white fantasy in aiding and abetting that formation.[54] Centering its gaze on Chicago as canonical site of urban study but knowingly diverting its focus from the "Chicago School's" classic 1920s formulations (by Robert E. Park and others at the University of Chicago) to post–World War II developments like Cabrini-Green (which came to maturity under Chicago mayor Richard J. Daley at the turn of the 1960s) and the University of Illinois–Chicago (whose current campus opened in 1965)—rotating, that is, from the Chicago School's Near North Side–South Side axis in the direction of the suburban Near West—*Candyman* operates as seriously in the register of urban investigation as it does in that of the phantasmagorical, and makes each crucial to the other. The restless academic and the remorseless specter equally traverse contested territory and operate with the similar cinematic goals of making visible the proximate but determinedly cordoned-off zones of developed downtown, underdeveloped public housing, and residential / suburban peripheries—making them visible, that is, as a coordinated, *manufactured* dialectical unity produced in history. The full story of this enormous transformation is better told elsewhere, but the postwar enterprise of urban redevelopment was rooted in racially unequal practices of public works construction, real estate development, home ownership loaning, legal intervention, waste management, and taxation, which contributed fundamentally to the logic of a postindustrial landscape that authors Douglas Massey and Nancy Denton term "American apartheid." A massive state-capital collaboration featuring among other things the firmly segregationist practices of the Federal Housing Authority; a federally mandated program of "urban renewal" in the interests of downtown private redevelopment; the resulting evisceration and displacement of black communities and near-literal containment of black residents in massive though inadequate high-rise public housing developments like Cabrini-Green; the concomitant economic and social push-pull of whites to the suburbs; and the enormous postwar investment in a federal highway system (not least *Candyman*'s Eisenhower Expressway) that would transport these white-collar workers to and from the developed urban core's large banks, insurance companies, and other service industries: all of it produced the Chicago that haunts *Candyman*—and that Candyman haunts.[55]

Even in this sociological vein the black mirror abides. Helen learns that the layout of her apartment (in "Lincoln Village" no less) is the mirror image of those in the Cabrini-Green complex owing to the fact that her building was constructed originally as part of that complex but later deemed "too close to the Gold Coast" (Chicago's Loop) for comfort and so converted to condominiums. She shows her friend Bernadette the "proof": her mirrored bathroom medicine chest backs directly onto the one in the adjoining apartment and pulls out easily, affording a killer access, say, to Cabrini victim Ruthie Jean. This also affords Helen the intimate knowledge of the Cabrini units' layout that she calls on in her explorations there, in particular the passage to neighboring apartments offered up by the removal of the bathroom medicine chest. (These mirrors irresistibly solicit the Candyman summons; he always, eventually, arrives.) This fanciful but clever device yields a mimic scene in which the two explore Ruthie Jean's (now empty) apartment. Helen pulls out the medicine chest and crawls (like a predator) through the resulting hole, leaving Bernadette behind her—alone in Ruthie Jean's apartment and just as vulnerable—establishing quite clearly the way Helen's ethnographic gain capitalizes on black endangerment. Going all the way through the looking-glass, Helen climbs into the adjoining apartment, what turns out to be a graffiti-covered gang lair; a shocking reverse shot reveals her emerging from the terrified screaming mouth of a huge, agonized black male face painted around the hole in the wall. Jeopardizing Bernadette, she unstops a black man's scream, or occasions it, or both. This silent scream is one of a number of representational instances and modes that take the form of fantasy mirror-screens: the Cabrini graffiti and wall paintings—one of them of Helen's nineteenth-century avatar, which looks very much like her; Helen's own photographs, which seem to yield eerie evidence of the specter; the slides of those photos she screens on her apartment wall; and the four televisions in hospital psychiatrist Dr. Burke's office that replay surveillance footage of her highly agitated discourse with a Candyman who is of course not visible onscreen (though we saw him hover above Helen in the event, and when Helen speaks his name five times in an office mirror, he shortly arrives to gut Dr. Burke and free Helen). These and more suggest the intricate knotting together of white and black life in both imagined and very real ways, an intimacy built into the architecture that the geography of urban formation must proscribe.

For above all Helen confronts in Candyman the spectral emanation of a repressed, ongoing history of sexualized racial violence by white men against black men and women, sited as if in the cornerstone of such segregated structures as Cabrini. *Candyman* plays off Chicago militant Ida B. Wells-Barnett's 1890s antilynching pamphlets in offering us the ghost of a nineteenth-century lynching victim who returns as the vengeful product of white men's attempts to police the province of the white woman's body. Candyman's psychic hold arises not least from a history of racial exploitation rooted in a hysterical fear of sexual congress between black men and white women. In a far-reaching analysis, Heidi Nast has suggested the ways a white-supremacist oedipal family "unconscious" both drove and derived from the colonized terrain of Chicago's South Side.[56] Nast argues that the Chicago School itself helped rationalize a "spatial castration" in Hyde Park that kept good daughters separate from native sons. *Candyman* returns agency to the white woman in whose name the whole edifice was erected, giving her the power to intervene in the lynching-for-rape scenario, at some level championing Helen's attempts to defeat white male power in her pursuit of Candyman and investigations of Cabrini-Green. At one point exploring a Cabrini public men's room where her native informant, a boy named Jake, tells her a resident was once murdered and castrated, Helen meets up with a thug who bludgeons her with a hook. Now herself symbolically castrated, she permits the film to unfold the ways white women and black men are mirror threats to the white male Imaginary. Refusing the role of rape-ready cover story for white male terror/ism,

Helen in her sleuthing removes the gag on the counterknowledge that circulates in tales and graffiti of Candyman—even as she appropriates those materials for her own purposes of research. When she first meets Candyman in the parking garage, Helen's memories of the Cabrini artwork she's photographed come back to her like bolts to the brain, and she begins to internalize the history by which such specters have been produced. The stories Candyman charges Helen with disbelieving become figures for a redressed social and spatial amnesia, and even if they are pure fantasy on Helen's part, they mirror something historical and real.[57]

To be sure, Candyman wants to recommit his original "crime," as it were, to take Helen again as his lover. But he asks her consent so that stories of their love will live forever—that narrative surplus value on black expropriation and lynching which results in the very film we are watching. Candyman's constantly avowed interest in keeping this story and others circulating becomes a bit clearer when we understand the political geography his legend incarnates. The ghetto ghost enunciates a spectral metaphysics of eternal life; he can't understand why Helen won't "join his congregation" by agreeing to "be [his] victim," guaranteeing them both immortality through the stories, the activated subterranean knowledges, to which the film's profs condescend. Candyman lives only through the vast network of spectral, indeed Orphic, communication the film shows us, the urban legends, the graffiti, the rumors, and the rest, what Candyman himself calls "the writing on the wall, the whisper in the classroom." This all works until a final twist, a final mirroring, a suddenly emancipatory outcome of white fantasy, when Helen eludes Candyman by becoming a version of him. Candyman and Helen both perish in a Cabrini community bonfire out of which Helen is attempting to rescue an abducted baby (as usual with this movie: Candyman or Helen or neither may be responsible; who's to say?). She returns after death to haunt the film's true villain, her faithless and cynical former professor-husband Trevor. Weeping alone in the bathroom while his new wife makes dinner, Trevor chances to moan Helen's name five times into the mirror. Helen the avenging angel returns to slice Trevor from crotch to crown, castrator castrated as it were. The family romance that would exile Candyman to the margins is here affirmed the white heteropatriarchal enemy. This does leave Trevor's new partner on the hook—she finds her dead husband butcher knife in hand—but at least the target is choice.

LIKE THE MATERIAL I study in this book, *Candyman* poses the question of our racialized relationship to time. It will not do to "dissipate the phantom," Derrida contends, so much rides on it: Obama in blackface alone suggests the phantom lives well enough still. Such specters make the present waver, unsettle any too solid sense of temporality, embroil us constantly in fantasy's contradictions, repetitions, and returns. As Derrida says, we must "learn to live *with* ghosts."[58] This transgenerational haunting adduces a spectral nationality whose eternal recurrences define racial life in the United States. I agree with Jacqueline Rose's contention that "there is no way of understanding political identities and destinies without letting fantasy into the frame"; and fantasy, moreover, is always "a journey through the past" (4–5), time piling up and overdetermining any instance of significant form: Mark Twain's black characters and dialect, depicting difficulties of democracy they meanwhile enact; white-ethnic entertainers' cross-racial solidarity double-crossed by self-regard; film noir's dark tropes of national critique that end up affirming white Hollywood; John Howard Griffin's clumsy attempt at cross-racial understanding that depends on and reconfirms the racial divide; Joni Mitchell's perverse pimp game that actually exposes a complacent Laurel Canyon scene; Elvis impersonators' garish yet acute negotiations of class as well as color; Bob Dylan's knowing stealing. Dylan himself makes the Orphic descent in the *"Love and Theft"* song "Mississippi," a shadow tour of everything from Huck and Jim to Elvis's men to Joni's fantastic voyage. In 2012, Barack Obama brought all of this back home when he awarded Dylan the Medal of Freedom. The ceremony was a little surreal. Dylan, in shades, appeared uncomfortable; Obama, standing behind him, seemed delighted and amused; and when the president clasped the medal's ribbon around Dylan's neck, it looked for all the world like a noose.

CHAPTER 2

OUR BLACKFACE AMERICA

Mr. Clemens and Jim Crow

SOON AFTER LEAVING HANNIBAL for New York in 1853, Sam Clemens wrote home to his mother: "I reckon I had better black my face, for in these Eastern States niggers are considerably better than white people."[1] As the youth who would be Mark Twain wrote these words, Christy's Minstrels were at the peak of their extraordinary eight-year run (1846–54) at New York City's Mechanics' Hall, and many other blackface troupes battled them for public attention. Meanwhile, the new phenomenon of the "Tom show"—dramatic blackface productions of Harriet Beecher Stowe's *Uncle Tom's Cabin*, published the year before—was emerging to (briefly) displace and re-orient the minstrel tradition; by 1854 there were several such shows running in New York alone. Probably the prominence of blackface in New York only clinched Clemens's love of minstrelsy, which extended back to his Hannibal childhood.

Blackface minstrelsy—"the genuine nigger show, the extravagant nigger show," Twain calls it in the autobiography he dictated in his last years—had burst upon the unwitting town in the early 1840s as a "glad and stunning surprise."[2] Small bands of white men everywhere armed with banjos, fiddles, tambourines, and bone castanets and arrayed in blackface makeup and ludicrous dress had taken both city and countryside, and Twain fell immediately for their pop appeal. Songs, breakdowns, gags, puns, novelty acts, bone-headed "stump speeches" and "lectures," and burlesque skits comprised a demotic new form in the register of raucous. In his *Autobiography* Twain averred: "If I could have the nigger show back again, in its pristine purity and perfection, I should have but little further use for opera" (294), which tells you something about the minstrel show's class aura. This quite unguarded attraction to "blacking up" perhaps made it inevitable that in a letter to his mother, Twain would reach for the blackface mask to finesse his response to racial difference and rural defensiveness in the northern city. For the rest of his life, Twain's imaginative encounters with race would be unavoidably bound up with blackface minstrelsy, joined at the hip like Twain's tales of extraordinary twins.[3]

We now take for granted minstrelsy's centrality to white racial fantasy and Mark Twain's centrality to U.S. literary self-regard. It should hardly surprise us that these come together in the racialized mirror structures that have helped make Twain America's most "hypercanonized" author, especially given the degree to which he was immersed in the cultures of everyday life that gave rise to works like *Tom Sawyer, Adventures of Huckleberry Finn,* and *Pudd'nhead Wilson.*[4] Critical commitment to "classic" American literary form has for some time now made clear the indebtedness of such work to pop life and pulp lit in the United States.[5] Yet a corollary commitment has often been to redeem the classics from the muck that spawned them or to demonstrate the ways they transcended and subverted American common wisdom. With Twain (as with most of the others) this is impossible, not even desirable. The symbolic surplus Twain derived from minstrelsy and everyday American racism proved more productively scabrous than can be tamed—which is why we're still arguing about him, his gift to us. If young Sam Clemens's class- and race-conscious recoil from free blacks sounds a lot like Huck Finn's Pap—"And to see the cool way of that nigger—why, he wouldn't a give me the road if I hadn't shoved him out o' the way"[6]— it also reminds us that such consciousness, as in minstrelsy, often acknowledged the lure to *be* black ("I reckon I had better black my face"), to use the mirror for self-protection or self-enlargement. Pap himself, in Twain's sly depiction of his rage against the black professor, is actually as black as the hated "mulatter," since he is, as Huck says, "just all mud" after a drunken night lying in the gutter (26). These subterranean links between black and lower-class white men called forth in the minstrel show, as in Mark Twain's work, interracial recognitions and identifications no less than the imperative to disavow them. This is the contradictory structure of fantasy that drives Twain's best work, and part of that work's value is to lay this structure open to view.

There is no question that nineteenth-century blackface acts cast doubt on the idea that blacks and whites shared a common humanity. Their racist gibes and pastoral gambols asserted that slavery was amusing, right, and natural; their racial portrayals turned black people into simps, dupes, and docile tunesmiths.[7] A whole new performance industry sprang up to entertain tradesmen, teamsters, and shopkeepers (and, in the 1850s and after, their female counterparts) in a broad range of northern and western frontier venues both hip and hick, the cultural flank of a generalized working-class hostility to African Americans. Yet the minstrel show very often twinned black and white, equating as much as differentiating them. The sources of this equation lay in exactly the same social conditions that gave rise to racist violence. One glimpses in the violence a severe white insecurity about the status of whiteness. To be lower class and white in the early nineteenth century, as the industrial revolution began to grind into high gear, was to be subject to remorseless assaults on one's independence and livelihood. The terms and conditions of work were steadily and alarmingly deteriorating; the status and character of white manhood struck masculinist workingmen as increasingly like that of women and blacks, like "wage slavery." Blackface minstrelsy was founded on this social antinomy.[8] The interracial mirroring on which minstrelsy often called was visible in the artisan abolitionism that competed with artisan racism for the hearts and minds of workingmen; working-class antislavery feeling was intermittently strong in the antebellum years and may have aided blackface minstrelsy's turn toward a liberating sentimentalism in the late 1840s.[9] Stephen Foster's "Old Folks at Home" (1851) and "My Old Kentucky Home, Good-Night!" (1853), sung from behind the blackface mask, unquestionably evoked sympathy for separated slave families and generally implied the feeling humanity of slaves, though in doing so it relied on the old racial stereotypes. As Ralph Ellison once remarked, even when the intentions of minstrel performers were least palatable, still "these fellows had to go and listen, they had to open their ears to [black] speech even if their purpose was to make it comic."[10] The complex and active exchanges of white self and black Other in black-face performance, however derisive, opened the color line to efface-ment in the very moment of its construction.

Twain's own response to blackface minstrelsy illustrates the ambivalence of lower-class white racial feeling, which suffuses his greatest novelistic treatments of race and slavery. Twain said of the minstrel show:

> The minstrels appeared with coal-black hands and faces, and their clothing was a loud and extravagant burlesque of the clothing worn by the plantation slave of the time; not that the rags of the poor slave were burlesqued, for that would not have been possible; burlesque could have added nothing in the way of extravagance to the sorrowful accumulation of rags and patches which constituted his costume; it was the form and color of his dress that was burlesqued. (AU 294)

Twain proceeds here with some caution and not a little sympathy for the slave; he senses, perhaps uncomfortably, that the pleasures of stage burlesque have been wrought out of the quotidian violence of slavery. He even observes that blackface minstrels had "buttons as big as a blacking-box," collapsing blackface masquerade, the means of its artifice, and an echo of one of its literal models—Negro boot-blacks—in a single self-conscious figure. But Twain easily abandons such self-consciousness, as his reference to the slave's "costume," a clearly aestheticizing gesture, might lead us to expect:

> The minstrel used a very broad negro dialect; he used it competently, and with easy facility, and *it* was funny—delightfully and satisfyingly funny. . . . [Minstrels'] lips were thickened and lengthened with bright red paint to such a de-gree that their mouths resembled slices cut in a ripe water-melon. . . . The minstrel troupes had good voices, and both their solos and their choruses were a delight to me as long as the negro show continued in existence. (AU 294–96)

Twain is undeniably attracted to and celebratory of black culture. Yet just what that culture *is* to him is not altogether easy to make out, distorted and filtered as it is by white fantasy, desire, and delight. When views like Twain's do not simply fall into ridicule, they are certainly the patronizing flip side of it, suggesting Twain's ability to lose sight of the sorry circumstances that underlie his mirth and his continued and unexamined interest in racial exoticism. Ralph Ellison once observed that *Huckleberry Finn*'s Jim rarely emerges from behind the minstrel mask; reading Twain's remarks on the minstrel show lends a great deal of force to that observation.[11]

Already in *Tom Sawyer* (1876), Twain had called on the pleasures of minstrelsy in his portrayal of an earlier version of Jim; in chapter 2 a boy Jim comes "skipping out at the gate" singing "Buffalo Gals"—a blackface tune previously known as "Lubly Fan" (1844):

> Den lubly Fan will you cum out to night,
> > will you cum out to night,
> > will you cum out to night,
> Den lubly Fan will you cum out to night,
> An dance by de lite ob de moon.

> I stopt her an I had some talk,
> > Had some talk,
> > Had some talk,
> But her foot covered up de whole side-walk
> An left no room for me.

> Her lips are like de oyster plant,
> > De oyster plant,
> > De oyster plant,
> I try to kiss dem but I cant,
> Dey am so berry large.[12]

It may well be that black people picked up even outrageously untoward songs from the blackface theater and adapted them to their own uses, as the long history of black "signifying" on such white productions, and the rowdy misogyny of much black oral culture, suggest.[13] Conversely, Twain's own intent might have been irony rather than realism: a black Jim sings this blackface ditty as Tom whitewashes his aunt's fence in punishment for his truancy, the heightening of racial markers working up a certain self-consciousness here. There may even be an implied equation between Tom and Jim, since Tom's frequent disappearances mimic the escapes of fugitive slaves (which Jim would soon become in *Huckleberry Finn*) and require a constant whitening or chastening in order to distinguish Tom from such a status. Or perhaps Aunt Polly is merely the "lubly" object of a veiled blackface joke on Twain's part (if so, this puts Twain himself in blackface). Just as surely as all of these conjectures, however, Twain saw the character of Jim through lenses the minstrel show had afforded—he let a racist song go out of Jim's heart. The minstrel show's influence on Twain oddly redoubled over the next eight years, the years of *Huckleberry Finn*'s composition.

Blackface minstrelsy indeed underwrote one of the nineteenth century's most powerful antiracist novels—a tribute to the political fractures of minstrelsy and *Huckleberry Finn* both. This is no simple matter of minstrel show "trappings" or "residues" in Twain's novel (as we often hurry to say), an issue of unfortunate, merely historical formal qualities in the portrayal of Jim disrupting Twain's liberal thematic intentions. The text is shot through with blackface thinking. Written as well as situated in the minstrel show's boom years, *Adventures of Huckleberry Finn* (1884), as Anthony J. Berret has argued, relies on comic dialogues between Huck and Jim (much of the humor at Jim's expense), many and various novelty acts (the king and the duke's scams, the circus, etc.), and riotous burlesques of social and cultural matters (Emmeline Grangerford's sentimental poetry, the final setting-free of an already free Jim). The whole book may thus conform to a tripartite minstrel show structure of comic dialogues, olio, and southern burlesque.[14] And circumstances surrounding *Huckleberry Finn*'s writing only clarify its indebtedness to the minstrel tradition.

In 1882 Twain got the idea for a lecture tour (which he termed a circus or menagerie) to include himself, William Dean Howells, Thomas Bailey Aldrich, George Washington Cable, and Joel Chandler Harris. This authorial circus seems hardly more than the variety acts of a minstrel show, and the reading tour that came out of the idea, featuring Cable's straight man and Twain's clown, was in a sense precisely one, since both authors read the roles of black characters onstage, Cable even singing black songs.[15] This was the tour during which Twain first read parts of *Huckleberry Finn,* significantly the "King Sollermun" and "How come a Frenchman doan' talk like a man?" passages, whose blackface resonances are very clear. These passages may even have been written to be so performed after *Adventures of Huckleberry Finn* was already completed.[16] The political complexity of this affair is compounded by Cable's having published, midtour, "The Freedman's Case in Equity," a forthright attack on southern racism that appeared in the same issue of *Century Magazine* that ran an excerpt from *Huckleberry Finn.* Somehow the authors' views did not arrest the blackface tones of their readings, or Twain's naming of one of his selections "Can't Learn a Nigger to Argue," a title he changed only when Cable requested it.[17] These events no doubt put a highly ambiguous spin on *Huckleberry Finn,* but they indicate as well that the contradiction between the book's overt politics and its indebtedness to the minstrel show was less cumbrous in the nineteenth century. Even the most enlightened nineteenth-century political thinkers, for example, adhered to "romantic racialism," as historian George Fredrickson has termed it, which celebrated the supposedly greater emotional depth and spiritual resources of black people even as it postulated innate differences between the races, just as the minstrel show seemed to do.[18] *Huckleberry Finn*'s limitations can surely be laid at the minstrel show's doorstep, but its strengths are oddly imbricated with strains of thought and feeling that inspired blackface performance.

We are thus led to a rather scandalous conclusion. The liberatory coupling of Huck and Jim *and* the gruesome blackface sources of Jim's character are the unseparate and equal results of minstrelsy's influence on the work of Mark Twain. Writers who have rightly denounced the minstrel show aura of *Huckleberry Finn* miss the extent to which even the best moments have a blackface cast.[19] True enough, Twain's lapses are easy to spot, and we ought to remark on a few of these. There is, for instance, the slave down on the Phelps farm who at the end of *Huckleberry Finn* tends to Jim in his reenslavement. Named Nat in what one can only assume is jocular homage to Nat Turner, this character is so reminiscent of Jim's portrayal at the novel's beginning that he undermines the steady commitment Jim exhibits in the final chapters; the blackface aspersions against him taint Jim as well. Possessed of what Huck/Twain calls a "good-natured, chuckle-headed face," obsessed with fending off the witches he says have been haunting him, Nat is a sort of hysterical paranoiac (186). (The reference to Nat Turner's obsessive, visionary Christianity works to discredit both men.) Nat observes that Jim sings out when he first sees Huck and Tom, and says so; but the boys flatly deny having heard it, pushing Nat to resort to mystical explanations. "'Oh, it's de dad-blame' witches, sah, en I wisht I was dead, I do. Dey's awluz at it, sah, en dey do mos' kill me, dey sk'yers me so'" (187). Even if we remark that Nat is forced to this conclusion by the boys' denial, his squirms are rendered with infantilizing exactitude. Shortly after, amid one of Tom's stratagems in the digressive freeing of Jim, some hounds rush into the hut and Nat is again afrighted: "'You'll say I's a fool, but if I didn't b'lieve I see most a million dogs, er devils, er some'n, I wisht I may die right heah in dese tracks. I did, mos' sholy'" (196). Tom offers to make Nat a witch pie to ward them off, to which Nat responds: "'Will you do it, honey?—will you? I'll wusshup de groun' und' yo' foot, I will!'" (197). Twain may have intended us to pick up on Tom's callousness in fanning the flames of Nat's fear: we note, for instance, that Nat has never heard of the now-implanted idea of a witch pie and indeed that Nat promises not to disregard Tom's request that he let alone the witch preparations, "'not f'r ten hund'd thous'n' billion dollars'" (197)—a sum that would probably free Nat from his fetters. But the very uncertainty of Twain's intentions, together with his seemingly happy blackface depiction of Nat's self-abasement, undercuts all but racist meanings from the scene.

At the same time, moments very like this one may reveal more sympathetic dimensions. At the beginning of *Huckleberry Finn,* Tom Sawyer can't help playing a trick on Jim while he sleeps; he puts his hat on a branch above his head. Jim believes he's been bewitched and put in a trance and ridden by witches. Huck says Jim tells demonstrably self-serving tales of his adventures:

> Jim was monstrous proud about it, and he got so he wouldn't hardly notice the other niggers. Niggers would come miles to hear Jim tell about it, and he was more

looked up to than any nigger in that country. Strange niggers would stand with their mouths open and look him all
over, same as if he was a wonder. . . . Jim was most ruined,
for a servant, because he got so stuck up on account of
having seen the devil and been rode by witches. (11)

In one sense this is standard "darky" fare. Huck even supplies the
proper white exasperation with such charlatanism. Yet as several
scholars have shown, this moment of apparent blackface foolishness
is an occasion in which Jim seizes rhetorical and perhaps actual power.
Despite Huck's rather harsh judgment of Jim's self-investment, the
fact is that Jim becomes a "wonder" within the black community and
is "most ruined" for a servant—unsuited for slavery—in the wake of
his tales. The superstition to which we are encouraged by Huck to
condescend has real and potentially subverting results in the world
of the novel. One notes that Jim's actual words are not rendered
here, which in the orthographic hierarchy of white dialect writing
might have had the effect of reducing their impact. This is a moment
when Jim, as he does in other ways throughout *Huckleberry Finn,*
uses tricks and deceits to his advantage.[20] We may call this a kind of
blackface antiracism, of whose political duplicity and indeed vari-
ability Twain was not always the complete master.

This may even be a moment, as Shelley Fisher Fishkin has argued, that reveals Twain's intimacy with black life. For beliefs and
stories such as Jim's were present and alive within black culture,
which coded terrifying "night rides" by patrolling whites or Ku Klux
Klan brigades as those of ghouls and spirits.[21] Tales of such night
rides, says Gladys-Marie Fry, duly suffered and survived by resilient
blacks, allowed the heroic exploits of a subject people free expression.[22] Yet Twain leaves his white readers to divine for themselves the
pressing uses of such tales as Jim tells, and in doing so steps again into
the uncharmed circle of blackface—for it is, after all, Twain who is de-
ploying black lore for his own ambiguous uses. Ambiguity arises also
in scenes where racialist assumptions seem to be under the novelist's
scrutinizing gaze. Soon after Huck and Tom arrive on the Phelps farm,
with Jim still to be located, Tom suddenly realizes that the dinners
the boys see regularly transported to a certain hut seem suspicious:

"Looky here, Huck, what fools we are, to not think of it before! I bet I know where Jim is."

"No! Where?"

"In that hut down by the ash-hopper. Why, looky here. When we was at dinner, didn't you see a nigger man go in there with some vittles?"

"Yes."

"What did you think the vittles was for?"

"For a dog."

"So'd I. Well, it wasn't for a dog."

"Why?"

"Because part of it was watermelon."

"So it was—I noticed it. Well, it does beat all that I never thought about a dog not eating watermelon. It shows how a body can see and don't see at the same time." (183)

Working on the assumption that, as Tom puts it, "watermelon shows man," Huck and Tom detect Jim's whereabouts. This is a craftily constructed scene, one that makes some of Twain's largest political points. Huck's recognition that one can see and not see simultaneously is perhaps the aptest self-description in his whole twisted history of antislavery antiabolitionism. The scene pointedly distinguishes man from dog. And yet the means of this distinction is the cliché watermelon reference, as though that stereotypical food in particular were the one to best locate Jim. It is true that Tom's words suggest only that dogs do not eat watermelon, not that black people do; and even if the latter is implied, it is Tom and Huck, not Twain, speaking. But Twain is joking around here even in the midst of one of his most earnest moral observations. I think we are justified in concluding that the closer Twain got to black cultural practices and to racially subversive meanings, the more, paradoxically, his blackface debts multiplied. Blackface was something like the device or code or signifying system through which Twain worked out his least self-conscious and most sophisticated impulses regarding race in the United States. Jim's triumphs and Twain's ironies have to be as elaborately deciphered as Huck's future through Jim's hair ball, so self-evident are their minstrel roots.

What is more, scenes we always take as Twain's most enlightened strokes suggest a surprising complicity with the minstrel show. Jim's emotionalism and the fugitives' several joyous reunions on the raft call on the romantic racialism that underwrote minstrelsy's sentimental strain—its broken-family nostalgia and long-suffered separations. Stephen Foster's "Old Folks at Home" (1851), for instance, depends for its effect on the pathos culled from black families forced to split up:

> Way down upon de Swanee ribber,
> Far, far away,
> Dere's wha my heart is turning ebber,
> Dere's wha de old folks stay.
>
> All up and down de whole creation,
> Sadly I roam,
> Still longing for de old plantation,
> And for de old folks at home.

Foster's "Oh! Susanna" (1848) exploits the poignance of black attempts to reunite:

> I came from Alabama wid
> my banjo on my knee,
> I'm g'wan to Lousiana
> My true love for to see,
> It rain'd all night the day I left,
> The weather it was dry,
> The sun so hot I frose to death;
> Susanna, dont you cry.
>
> Oh! Susanna,
> Oh! dont you cry for me,
> I've come from Alabama,
> wid my banjo on my knee.[23]

Twain's novel relies on similar familial predicaments whose resonance derives from the slave's stereotyped emotionality, his deeper well of feeling. Jim does not ache for the old plantation but he does miss his children, from whom he has been separated: "He was often moaning and mourning that way, nights, when he judged I was asleep, and saying, 'Po' little 'Lizabeth! po' little Johnny! its mighty hard; I spec' I ain't ever gwyne to see you no mo', no mo'!' He was a mighty good nigger, Jim was" (125). This moment demonstrates to Huck that Jim "cared just as much for his people as white folks does for their'n" (125), one of Twain's heavier-handed interventions, but in calling on the black types evident in minstrelsy, the scene qualifies the very point it wants to make. Investing black people with human feeling, in the minstrel show or in *Huckleberry Finn,* was no doubt an advance over other less charitable views. Yet doing it by way of the postulated inequality of romantic racialism troubled the commitment to American freedom.

In their flight down the river, Jim and Huck are themselves occasionally separated, whereupon the two are placed in the longing position of the lovers in "Oh! Susanna" (as Leslie Fiedler somewhat anxiously suspicioned long ago).[24] The most famous of their reunions, after Huck and Jim lose each other in a fog, is an aesthetic and political triumph. Adrift in a canoe on the foggy river with no idea as to Jim's and the raft's whereabouts, Huck falls into uneasy sleep. When he wakes up, it takes him a moment to recall his dilemma. The fog is gone, and in no time Huck has made it to the raft. Jim is asleep, the raft littered with evidence of its difficult passage in the fog. Huck decides to play a trick on Jim—shades of Tom Sawyer—by telling him that he dreamed the whole thing. Jim rouses: " 'Goodness gracious, is dat you, Huck? En you ain' dead—you ain' drowned—you's back agin? It's too good for true, honey, it's too good for true. Lemme look at you, chile, lemme feel o' you. No, you ain' dead! you's back agin,' live en soun', jis de same old Huck—de same ole Huck, thanks to goodness!' " (70). Huck mutes Jim's gladness as he gets him to adopt the theory that the fog was all a dream. Once convinced, Jim sets out to interpret the dream, to Huck's considerable derision. Huck lets on that it was a joke after all, and Jim's response to Huck's prank apportions most of the humanity on the raft to himself:

> "When I got all wore out wid work, en wid de callin' for you, en went to sleep, my heart wuz mos' broke bekase you wuz los', en I didn' k'yer no mo' what become er me en de raf'. En when I wake up en fine you back agin', all safe en soun',

de tears come en I could a got down on my knees en kiss'
yo' foot I's so thankful. En all you wuz thinkin' 'bout wuz
how you could make a fool uv ole Jim wid a lie. Dat truck
dah is *trash;* en trash is what people is dat puts dirt on de
head er dey fren's en makes 'em ashamed." (72)

Jim gets to call Huck white trash. Jim's concern for Huck
transcends mere worry over his own safety as a fugitive; it is a concern that is not visibly reciprocated by Huck. Indeed Huck, whose
experience of the fog curiously resembles that of Jim—he is lost and
lonely, falls asleep and feels like he is dreaming, then is glad to see
Jim—denies his vulnerability by projecting it onto the slave. Unable to deal with his own experience, treat Jim like a human being,
or express his feelings, Huck concocts a trick that makes Jim do all
the work—first of articulating Huck's joy at reuniting, then of expe-
riencing Huck's puzzlement and frustration. The "solid white fog"
(68), that apt metaphor for white supremacy, which separated Huck
and Jim even from the sight of each other, now dissolves only to find
Huck reerecting racial barriers. It takes Jim's speech to make Huck
"humble myself to a nigger" (72). We might remark, however, that
Twain himself is leaning heavily on Jim in this scene to do his work
for him. Even as he exposes Huck's racist failings, he needs the pathos
that minstrel shows in the 1840s and 1850s had begun to pin to
the slaves to make his case. Not only does Jim's joy reiterate the
steadfast urge to reunion of "Oh! Susanna," his delivery of Huck's
comeuppance is swelled by its air of brokenhearted disappointment.
Twain knew well the aggregated sources of racial guilt, racial desire,
and racial longing that make just the kind of emotional strategy Jim
uses irresistibly effective to whites, whether Huck, Twain himself,
or his white reader; and his working of the white audience through
his manipulations of Jim's character is not the least of *Huckleberry
Finn*'s convergences with the minstrel tradition. That Twain may
have come to know the appeal of racial emotionalism from the minstrel show itself only shows how variable the political work of minstrelsy could be. If, in other words, some of *Huckleberry Finn*'s best
scenes come close to blackface minstrelsy, this hardly cancels their
impact (though it does show how little literature transcends its
cultural moment). The duplicity of these scenes simply evidences

how implicated we remain in the contradictions of North American racial life.

Perhaps Twain was remarking on the absurd consequences of this fundamental cultural fact when he put Jim in what can only be called Arabface. In order to free the fugitive slave from being tied up all day while the king, the duke, and Huck go ashore, the duke disguises Jim as an insane Arab to keep the curious at bay. Attired in a King Lear outfit and horse-hair wig and whiskers, and his face and hands theater-painted a "dead dull solid blue" (26), Jim's appearance surely recalls the art of blackface at the same time that it explodes the very idea of racial performance. Twain no doubt means to lampoon the racial thinking behind forms such as blackface when he has the duke tell Jim that should anyone draw near the raft, Jim must "hop out of the wigwam, and carry on a little, and fetch a howl or two like a wild beast" (126). Savage injuns and niggers and A-rabs too are invoked here as figments of the white supremacist imagination. The effect of Jim's costuming, we note, is to make him look, as Huck puts it, "like a man that's been drownded nine days" and "like he was dead" (126–27)—racist caricature is itself a kind of death.

Despite Twain's self-consciousness, though, the evidence suggests we take Huck's admiring remark about Jim in chapter 40—that he "knowed" Jim was "white inside"—as the crowning statement on the centrality of blackface's contradictions to Twain's imagination. The remark is a perfect specimen of the imperial psychological orientation Homi Bhabha calls "ambivalence."[25] Convinced of the humanity and identity of American blacks, Twain seems nonetheless to have been haunted by their difference. Hence he returned over and over to the actual practice and literary trope of blackface, which hedges by imagining the Other as black only in exterior, still white inside. A delicate black-mirror balance must be maintained here. To think of blacks as altogether the same—as all white—threatens white supremacist identity; to think of them as altogether different—as all black—raises the specter of white annihilation and superfluity. As in many societies with subject populations at home or abroad, the Other must be rendered not quite black and yet not white. "They" must be versions of "us," caught in a cycle of mimicry (usually construed as "civilizing" or benevolent rule), and yet perennially unable to make the grade. Racist ideologies, even the relatively gentle ones Twain deploys, insert the boundaries that ever threaten to evaporate between the kinds of human beings stuck in such a hierarchical relationship. Why should it surprise us that, even in a dissenter like Twain, the colonial mentality, so routinely unsettled by an anxiety of otherness, produced a need to preserve the differentness of black people through blackface gestures even as it nervously asserted that "they" were like "us" after all?

Exploring as well as enacting this logic, Twain anticipated Antonio Gramsci's remarks on "national-popular" literature—that it emerges out of extant popular materials rather than artificially refined or imposed ideas.[26] Twain took up the American dilemma not by avoiding popular racial representations but by inhabiting them so forcefully that he produced an immanent criticism of them. It is not just that Huck more or less fulfills Twain's intention of making nonsense of America's racial strictures (including those of Twain's readers) by living up to them the best anyone can; Twain himself pushed his blackface devices so far that they turned back on themselves, revealing the contradictory character of white racial feeling.[27] It is this simultaneous inhabitance and critique that makes *Huckleberry Finn* so thorny, unassimilable, and perhaps unteachable to our own time. I don't think Twain chose to work within the popular racial codes of his day out of calculation, as a way of exploiting racist entertainment for antiracist uses, though that often turns out to be *Huckleberry Finn*'s effect. He did it with an odd relish, out of a sense of inwardness and intimacy with the mass audience who shared his love of minstrelsy—the "mighty mass of the uncultivated" he said he wanted to reach with his novel (sold door to door by canvassing agents) and with whom he felt the greatest kinship.[28] It is worth noting here Twain's own willingness in effect to put on the blackface mask. After dinner one night at an 1874 Twain dinner party in Hartford, Twain dropped into his version of several slave spirituals, which had begun to be disseminated by black university singing groups in the early 1870s. Later, an overimbibed Twain mimicked a black man at a hoedown, dancing black dances for his guests in his drawing room.[29] Out of this sensibility came writing based on Twain's immersion in lower- or working-class racial feeling: writing that still resists attempts to tamp down or clean up its engagements with race and class in America and that is as partial, flawed, and disturbing as it is penetrating, emblematic, and current.

It is such contradictions that allow *Huckleberry Finn* and many other Twain writings yet to grate on our nerves. These same contradictions, however, make Twain's work valuable, if hard to take. Ecstatic in blackface, Twain touched on a form that conveyed exactly the brutality, insecurity, omnipotence, envy, condescension, jealousy, and fascination that characterize popular white racial responses to black people. Arguments either pro or con Mark Twain and race flatten out this complexity. Much of Twain's work enacts (Twain's own) white lower- or working-class affective racial alliances, which have always been more ambiguous and variable than bourgeois culture and its educational apparatuses can safely admit. Working-class whites negotiate the color line demonstratively, intimately, with a sort of wisecracking wonder; this structure of feeling eludes middlebrow aesthetics (see any film version of *Huckleberry Finn*) no less than it exceeds the proper boundaries of "respectable" political discourse. In this sense Twain scandalizes liberal racial moralizers of our day as he scandalized the complacent racists of his own. *Huckleberry Finn*'s narrator and even more its author suggest the capacities for antiracist transformation that lie far more promisingly in the popular classes than in their enemies, for whom manners only hide the privilege of blaming racial "insensitivity" on those they dominate.

The contradictions of lower-class racial feeling inform the notorious quip Twain made in a letter to William Dean Howells in 1872 after reading Howells's review of Twain's *Roughing It*. "I am as uplifted and reassured as a mother who has given birth to a white baby when she was awfully afraid it was going to be a mulatto."[30] This is an unfortunate remark from the author of "The United States of Lyncherdom" (1901). Yet we ought to reflect on its complex provenance. For the remark puts Twain in the position of a white woman unsure about the consequences of what in the nineteenth century would have been called her "past." No doubt this anxiety speaks to Twain's own past, as two years after marrying Olivia Langdon, a coal magnate's daughter, he battled still to establish himself in the ways of eastern respectability. In his joke to Howells, Twain imagines his own rural, artisan-class upbringing, however obliquely, coming back in his brainchild *Roughing It* to haunt him as a curiously racial specter—and he imagines his work itself to be the offspring of a mixed-race culture. This mapping of class matters by way of race metaphors indicates the degree of commonality that could be imagined between blacks and lower-class whites even as Twain feared the effects of that commonality in respectable society. Twain's occasional "black" self-representations, for instance the 1882 black-dialect note he wrote to his publisher, James Osgood, may bear out this duality.[31] Certainly the sympathy necessary for a piece such as Twain's "A True Story" (1874), told almost entirely in the voice of a black mother who has lived through slavery, could only have come from some deep source of interracial identification such as lower-class life might have afforded.

And yet if we follow out the speculative logic of Twain's quip, we find his genteel wife, Olivia, put in the place of a white woman suffering Twain's own "black" intrusions into the respectable East. From this angle Twain is the black man whose unholy past traduces the unsullied and unmixed literary whiteness he wants to inherit. This tendency—no less a part of Twain's racial contradictions—points up the unself-conscious and frightening index of white racial emotional life suffusing Twain's writing. The radical egalitarianism of that work is compromised by the unwarranted reliance on blackface gags and black gulls. Even the impressive evidence in Twain's life of transgressions against the color line runs up against the pale gaze through which Twain absorbed black cultural practices and the inevitably partial character of all such crossover dreamwork.[32] Staying true to the complexities of Mark Twain also means recognizing the whiteness of his tales, a quality illuminated by another of Twain's encounters with the minstrel show. In the *Autobiography* Twain tells us he once took his mother and one Aunt Betsey Smith to see Christy's Minstrels in St. Louis. Twain's anxiety about being sullied by race, as with the "mulatto" *Roughing It,* takes him again into the area of sexuality and gender; this anxiety surfaces in the oedipal hostility he vents toward his mother in what is, after all, a relatively minor episode. The comic situation Twain constructs centers upon getting his mother to attend a minstrel show, since she is a religious woman who takes her dissipation, Twain notes, only when it can be proved not to be irreligious. One almost senses Twain rubbing his hands together as he prepares to sink his mother into some real dissipation—a desacralizing impulse on the part of the son inspired by the unease minstrelsy has provoked in the writer.

Twain tells his mother and Aunt Betsey Smith that they are attending an exhibition of African music by some lately returned missionaries:

> When the grotesque negroes [Twain here gets carried away with his own conceit] came filing out on the stage in their extravagant costumes, the old ladies were almost speechless with astonishment. I explained to them that the missionaries always dressed like that in Africa.
>
> But Aunt Betsey said, reproachfully, "But they're niggers!" (297)

Very soon the newcomers begin to enjoy themselves, "their consciences . . . quiet now—quiet enough to be dead," Twain writes. They gaze on "that long curved line of artistic mountebanks with devouring eyes" (297), and in the end revivify the show by laughing at a stale pun from the endmen. Twain jokes in this account not only at the expense of blacks but at that of his mother. The linking of race and motherhood as objects of Twain's aggression is registered in the syntactical ambiguity as to who possesses the devouring eyes, a double threat Twain assuages through degradation of both. This retreat to the haven of whiteness is triggered by Twain's response to his mother, which somehow, here and elsewhere, so raises the frightening bar of race as to become confused with it. Blackness and motherhood stand as suffocating obstacles to Twain's most intimate and unconscious feeling of white manhood, and they occasionally call forth from him vivid disavowals. Maternity, race, and blackface revealingly unsettle Twain's novel *Pudd'nhead Wilson* (1894).

The premise of *Pudd'nhead Wilson* is the switching at birth of a slave boy, Valet de Chambre (called Chambers), and a scion of a distinguished white family, Thomas à Becket Driscoll (called Tom). The boys are switched by Roxy, the slave mother of Chambers, who has sole care over the two and who, like her son, is virtually white in appearance. As Twain trenchantly puts it: "To all intents and purposes Roxy was as white as anybody, but the one-sixteenth of her which was black out-voted the other fifteen parts and made her a 'negro.'"[33] This kick at the one-drop "fiction of law and custom" (9) persists throughout the novel; indeed, Twain's hackneyed plot device is there to explore questions of blood and breeding, racial genetics and social conditioning. But Twain's inquiry into American racial customs is confused by the ambiguities incident to the category of race itself, by other plot devices (such as a pair of visiting Italian twins—originally Siamese twins whose story Twain wrenched from the novel and published as *Those Extraordinary Twins*), by generic swerves (a detective story that involves failed lawyer Pudd'nhead Wilson's interest in fingerprinting), and by the maternal role of Roxy.[34]

Roxy's relationship with her son after she enters him into the world of whiteness is the first ambiguous intrusion on Twain's investigation of the color line. Having renamed her son Tom (and conducted a similar reversal on the real Tom), she no longer feels so heavily the weight of slavery. Her master dies, setting her free, and both the rechristened Tom and Chambers go to live with an uncle while Roxy leaves the Missouri town of Dawson's Landing to work aboard Mississippi steamboats. Tom turns out a gambler forever in debt, a wretched, purposeless, and mean specimen who treats his mother with all the viciousness of the white master he has become; Chambers, the former heir, grows up a courageous, strong, but perforce submissive youth who functions as both whipping boy and bodyguard for Tom. Roxy's return has all the earmarks of the maternal power Twain attacks in his minstrel show episode and in *Tom Sawyer's* whitewashing scene. Rankled by Tom's way with her and attempting to reform at least this part of his behavior, Roxy essentially blackmails her son with the knowledge that he is black: "'You is a *nigger!*—*bawn* a nigger en a *slave!* . . . en if I opens my mouf, ole Marse Driscoll'll sell you down de river befo' you is two days older den what you is now! . . . you's my *son*—'" (41). If earlier Tom lorded over his mother in a fantasy of filial domination, he now suffers subjugation by her; this oedipal distress is triggered once again by the eruption of race, as though the categories of "son" and "nigger" inevitably overlapped and together best named the abjection of a white male child's relation to his mother.[35] The exceedingly odd thing about this turn is that Roxy threatens Tom with the very evidence of blood that Twain at first and intermittently questions—and that Roxy herself has subverted in switching the babies in the first place.

Tom's one drop is made visible, as it were, by Roxy's presence (one thinks of Twain on the verge of blacking up in the letter to his mother), a conjoining of maternity and race that confounds the former emphasis on nurture. Roxy returns to cancel with blood the racial masquerade she set in motion. If this perhaps seems inevitable given Twain's fear of female power—the family romance that mixes up this work on racial categorizing—it is nonetheless strange when one recognizes how alive Twain is in *Pudd'nhead Wilson* to precisely the racial masquerade produced by law and custom and theatricalized by blackface minstrelsy. Indeed, this novel is Twain's most sustained blackface production—one that is inspired but ultimately destroyed by the racial contradictions on which blackface rests.

Blackface perfectly mediates the implicit argument in *Pudd'nhead Wilson* between social and genetic explanations for "racial" behavior. Emphasizing race as theater, blackface speaks to the performative and manufactured character of identity; emanating from racist ideologies of blood, it continually threatens to collapse race into biology. This is by and large what happens to Twain's novel, and its interest in blackface, an apt expression of the dilemmas it wants to expose, finally traps Twain in retrograde racialist thinking. Much of *Pudd'nhead Wilson* attends to the fictionality or theatricalizing of race. When Tom returns from his stint at Yale, for example, the town boys have a "negro bellringer . . . tricked out in a flamboyant curtain-calico exaggeration of his finery, and imitating his fancy eastern graces" (24). This act is a sort of minstrel gag in reverse; the black man burlesques Tom's acquired graces, and does so at the behest of an audience of village white boys. While the absurdity of the act assumes an insuperable barrier between black and white, it also suggests that Tom's whiteness is itself an act, a suggestion that is truer than either the bell ringer or Tom can know since Tom's identity is precisely a black man's whiteface performance. Racial theater is here and throughout Tom's plot a way for Twain to rebut or interrogate the claims of blood—the assigning of attributes and traits according to racial lineage. It is true enough that social conditioning goes so deep that its effects are more than mere theater, in some sense difficult to distinguish from biology. But Twain plays on its humanly constructed character even when he may seem to be giving in to blood. After Roxy tells Tom he is black, and Tom wakes up a Negro like Godfrey Cambridge in Melvin Van Peebles's film *Watermelon Man* (1970), all of his old habits begin to wither and he begins to act the part. "It was the 'nigger' in him asserting its humility," writes Twain, just as Tom finds "the 'nigger' in him involuntarily giving the road, on the sidewalk, to the white rowdy and loafer" (44–45). Twain's seemingly geneticized insistence is qualified by the scare quotes he wraps around the racial indicator, and indeed an adjacent passage Twain inexplicably cut from the published novel so crosses blood with circumstance that biologism is in effect rejected.[36] At the very least the status of Tom's new attitude—blood legacy? psychological metaphor? racial fiction?—remains in doubt.

At the same time, Twain rightly acknowledges the way racial fictions such as blackface assume the status of truth. Soon after Roxy switches the black and white babies, she comes to think of her own son, "by the fiction created by herself" (19), as legitimately her master. Practicing the forms of submission becomes habit, then nature; "the little counterfeit rift of separation between imitation-slave and imitation-master widened and widened, and became an abyss, and a very real one—and on one side of it stood Roxy, the dupe of her own deceptions, and on the other stood her child, no longer a usurper to her, but her accepted and recognized master" (19). Roxy has indeed become an imitation slave—a minstrel performer. But as Twain's narrator hints, this is no easy act: it is a world. When Roxy returns after eight years on steamboats, broke after a bank failure and in need of some form of income, she hopes to appeal to Tom: "She would go and fawn upon him, slave-like—for this would have to be her attitude, of course—and maybe she would find that time had modified him, and that he would be glad to see his long forgotten old nurse and treat her gently" (34). There is, to be sure, some distance between Roxy and her slave-like act. The very need for blackface formality, however, indicates the foregone conclusion. Race is theater but race is real, and no amount of blackface accoutrements wins Tom's pleasure:

> "Look at me good; does you 'member ole Roxy?—does you know yo' ole nigger mammy, honey? Well, now, I kin lay down en die in peace, caze I's seed—"
> "Cut it short, damn it, cut it short! What is it you want?"

"You heah dat? Jes' de same old Marse Tom, allays so
gay and funnin' wid de ole mammy. I 'uz jes' as shore—"
"Cut it short, I tell you, and get along! What do you
want?" (37)

Roxy's self-minstrelizing has become the rule, and only her threat of
exposing Tom changes his view of her. The great irony of Roxy's later
blackface cross-dressed masquerade (89), put on to deflect her capture after Tom (per Roxy's selfless request) sells her to pay his debts,
is that blackface both disguises and reveals her. Too light-skinned
to be noticed in black makeup, Roxy in blackface comes out, though
paradoxically in secret, as a black woman and a slave.

This is the sense in which Chambers is right to refuse Roxy's
description of him as an "imitation nigger." Amid a minstrel show
dialogue that does Twain little credit, Roxy labels Chambers, born
to a first family of Virginia, a "'misable imitation nigger dat I bore in
sorrow en tribbilation'" (35). She means blackface, quite literally, but
Chambers, who can know nothing of this meaning, responds with
sense: "'If I's imitation, what is you? Bofe of us is imitation *white*—
dat's what we is—en pow'full good imitation, too—Yah-yah-yah! [this
incidentally a standard ejaculation from the minstrel show]—We
don't 'mount to noth'n as imitation *niggers*'" (35). The last remark
is apt commentary on the way racial fictions like blackface and the
law amount to reality for black people, whatever their genetic provenance. (Twain ironically bears this out in observing the interaction between these two black characters through the blackface
glass, darkly.) Not only do "imitation niggers" not amount to much,
Chambers and Roxy imitate pointlessly because by "fictional" decree
they already occupy the despised category in question. Indeed the
suggestion here is that blood actually confounds the color line up-
held by racial fictions, since African Americans can on occasion look
"pow'full" white. This is the double bind of American racial demarcation: for Roxy and Chambers to be imitation black is to *be* black and
gird racial boundaries; for them to be imitation white is to be mere
mimics, once removed, "mulatto."

The chief tribute to the forceful sway of such instituted fictions is Roxy's and possibly Twain's resort to explanations of blood in
glossing Tom's behavior. Racial acts so easily seem acts of racial pre-

disposition that even those aware of this fact succumb to myths of racial biology. Pudd'nhead Wilson is the most notable believer in a genetics of race; as he says to himself when Roxy refuses to have her fingerprints taken, "The drop of black blood in her is superstitious" (23). Wilson's ultimate triumph, his discovery through his eccentric interest in fingerprinting that Tom has murdered his uncle—a conclusion that "corrects" the racial identities of Tom and Chambers, redrawing the color line, and results in Tom being sold down the river—allies his belief in blood with white supremacy even as it causes one to doubt Twain's clarity and allegiances on matters of racial definition. Roxy herself plumps for blood. As she says to Tom of his rascal nature, countering Twain's earlier wariness: "'It's de nigger in you, dat's what it is. Thirty-one parts o' you is white, en on'y one part nigger, en dat po' little one part is yo' soul'" (70). My reader may well object that Roxy's racial genealogy includes not only Tom's white father, Colonel Cecil Burleigh Essex, and other white men ("ole Cap'n John Smith") but also Pocahontas and "a nigger king outen Africa." And Roxy later mutters, "'Ain't nigger enough in him to show in his finger-nails . . . yit dey's enough to paint his soul'" (70), perhaps a succinct bit of irony about the "painted" and put-on nature even of racial "blood." But when profligate, swindling Tom enters the house of the man everyone thinks is his uncle and murders him *in a blackface disguise,* it is difficult to escape the conclusion that Twain has himself painted not only Tom's soul but his face the color ordained by his one drop of black blood.

The murder of Judge Driscoll is the last in a long line of actions that prove Tom's ill character, the shiftless, fruitless existence that leads him to kill for money and the casual viciousness he sows generally. Tom seems to be acting on his one-thirty-second of black blood, acting racially rather than racially acting—motivated, that is to say, by heredity. Twain suggests early on that Tom's upbringing among the planter class accounts for his failings (18–19), but no one of that gentry comes close to Tom's sorry history. Tom is a "bad baby" (17) from the cradle, before much conditioning at all has taken hold; later, he stabs Chambers with a pocketknife in a scene straight out of the coon show, blackface minstrelsy's 1890s legacy on the black stage (21). Twain underscores Tom's difference by alluding to his youthful plan to have his father sell Chambers down the river, at which point

Judge Driscoll steps in to buy him—"for public sentiment did not approve of that way of treating family servants for light cause or for no cause" (22). Tom even sells his own mother, once at her behest, admittedly, but that sale delivers Roxy (contrary to their agreement) down the river, and when she escapes with a bounty on her head Tom comes very close to turning her in. It is worth noting that in Twain's working conception of the novel Tom began as a scoundrel and was given a mulatto mother only after the fact, as though to explain his devilry.[37] The textual gaps and lapses owing to the notoriously chaotic composition of *Pudd'nhead Wilson* surely account for some of its inconsistencies of racial definition, but not even these explain the curiously inherent nature of Tom's flaws amid a self-conscious context of racial masquerade and play.

Tom's murder of his supposed uncle caps his unwholesome career. Telling historical resonances crowd this scene. Tom in blackface, killing Judge Driscoll as Driscoll counts his money, is the avenger of Tom's race against the planter class, who, as Twain writes earlier in the novel, "daily robbed [the slave] of an inestimable treasure—his liberty" (12). Tom's escape in female dress adds to the killing an element of black female revenge for the master's rape of slave women, one of whose issue is Tom himself. Tom's murder with the knife owned by one of the Italian twins, a knife previously used, we are told, in the twins' self-defense (52–53), reinforces the sense of justifiable homicide. However, such resonances make sense only if heredity, not history, is the cause of Tom's crime. He is, after all, so alienated from blackness that he finds oppressive even occasional intimacies with Roxy (Roxy's love makes him "wince, secretly—for she was a 'nigger'" [80]). He has spent far more of his life white than black, and his blackness is still a secret. In this sense he kills his uncle not out of a sense of oppression but to prevent his mixed heritage from being revealed. Tom's hatred of his uncle does increase after Roxy's disclosure that he is black, and in killing the judge he strikes at the legal representative whose juridical fictions would consign Tom to the black side of the color line. Yet the blackface disguise achieves a kind of transparency when Pudd'nhead Wilson secures Tom's "true" racial identity. Not Tom's fingernails but his fingerprints betray his blackness. This "sure identifier," as Wilson calls it, this "mysterious and marvelous natal autograph," reinstitutes the racist fictions of law and custom. The bearer of its physiological truth cannot mask it, "nor can he disguise it or hide it away, nor can it become illegible by the wear and the mutations of time" (108–9). Racial crossing and masquerade, performance and play founder on Wilson's restored hierarchy of racial biology, a restoration in which Twain seems to acquiesce.

Twain's decision to put Tom in blackface during his uncle's murder let minstrelsy's legacy of blood cloud minstrelsy's racial theatrics. As in most of his experiments along the color line, Twain in *Pudd'nhead Wilson* was so attuned to the racial complexities of his time as to be incapable of critical distance from them. Twain's devotion to the minstrel show, recorded autobiographically a decade after the publication of *Pudd'nhead Wilson,* was in no small part responsible for his racial ambivalence and the confusions thereof. "It seems to me that to the elevated mind and the sensitive spirit, the hand-organ and the nigger show are a standard and a summit to whose rarefied altitude the other forms of musical art may not hope to reach" (AU 294). Blackface furnished Twain's very language of race, a language riddled with ambiguities Twain did not so much illuminate as reiterate.

Coda: Jim Too

Wesley Brown's early 1990s novel *Darktown Strutters* came as such a glad and stunning surprise, as Twain might have said, because it took up but drilled deep into the ambivalences Twain's own work had left critics debating right up into that decade.[38] An often profound meditation on performance, masking, identity, and equality in the American skin game, written in the surreal spirit of minstrelsy itself, peppered with wit and lancing dialogue, full of implications for black-mirror brooding, *Darktown Strutters* is a novel of ideas devoted to exploring the complex fate of black and white Americans caught, as ever, in a racial history they can neither surmount nor escape. A hundred years on, and quite self-consciously, it goes *Adventures of Huckleberry Finn* one better.

The novel spans forty or more years, from the advent of blackface performance in the 1830s through the up-tempo revolutionary drama of the Civil War and the improvised quality of postwar life to the centennial celebration of 1876 (fittingly enough, the span of time from *Huckleberry Finn*'s setting to the moment of its initial composition). Brown is learned in the national and performance history that forms the backdrop of his tale, but he freely riffs on the known facts, which gives his story the aura of an alternate or parallel racial history, this time with (as it were) the bones laid bare. The novel opens with minstrelsy's primal scene: the appropriation of black dance, song, and style from an enslaved man named Jim Crow by white performer Thomas Rice. Rice is soon making a name for himself in blackface, where before long he hears of the remarkable dancing of the son Brown bestows upon Jim Crow, Jim Too. Rice makes a deal with Jim's owner, a Mr. Churchill, who agrees to hire out Jim to dance with Rice's traveling minstrel show in a distant echo of antebellum America's only black minstrel star, Juba (William Henry Lane). Jim is thereby launched on a performance career that features, among many other events, dance contests against whites such as Jack Diamond (who was indeed Juba's terpsichorean sparring partner), run-ins with white mobs upset by the excellence of Jim's dancing and his refusal to wear blackface makeup, secret meetings with slaves to discuss abolitionist ideas and with Juba himself, a harrowing encounter with the 1863 New York Draft Riots, and, after manumission, a long stint with a women-led mixed-race minstrel troupe known as the Featherstone Traveling Theatre. All of this emerges from taut scenes that raise the largest questions of U.S. racial-cultural formation in the intimate occasions of everyday life. Part of the point of *Darktown Strutters* is to suggest the local, personal consequences of and motives for major historical processes. Thus Brown acutely and energetically gauges the psychodynamics of white cultural appropriation (and black reappropriation), the emotional (not to mention political) economy of slavery and its aftermath, the interiority and racial affect of lower-class whites befuddled by imminent black emancipation, the connection of black arts to personal and political liberation (not to mention the potential conflict between personal and political liberation)—in short, the *feel* of living through what Karl Marx referred to as America's mid-nineteenth-century "revolutionary turn."[39]

"Turn" implies performance as well as change, and Brown concerns himself not only with both of these but with both at once. In

contrast to the conventional view of blackface minstrelsy as the nail
in the coffin of antebellum racial stasis, Brown sees it, rightly I think,
as an arena in which ripping social transformation was registered and
even activated. Putting on the Negro in more than one sense, white
minstrels crossed in fantasy the racial lines they had been raised to
respect; momentarily commanding white stages, the occasional black
minstrel forced acknowledgment and even respect for arts and artists who had made minstrelsy possible. Brown lucidly imagines his
way into this quite unstable situation. Rice is so taken with Jim Crow's
dancing that he first mimics it and then ponders wearing blackface
offstage as well as on—which, as Jack Diamond remarks, " 'puts him
several cuts above most men I've known who do a lotta damage tryin
too hard to be white' " (81). Meanwhile, the black men exploited for
such white self-enlargement may profit too; as Diamond shrewdly
says to Rice: " 'Well, when he showed you that dance, he was more
than just some broken-down nigger slave. And once you allow somebody to be more than one thing at a time, ain't nothin nailed down no
more, includin you!' " (27). Generating interest often means getting
respect, and maybe more than that. These scenes and others capture
the shape-shifting social momentum, the creeping fissures in the racial status quo, that seemed to drive blackface performance amid its
desperate attempts to contain the changes to come. In the process
they decisively recast our understanding of the minstrel show's cultural thefts, undeniably founded on a slave economy yet resulting in
a certain degree of white self-othering and black agency. They point,
that is, to the crucial shaping part black performers played in and
around an unfortunate and peculiar entertainment institution that
was nonetheless a central avenue of American cultural creolization.

Such ironies lie near the heart of Brown's tale. True to its epi-
graph from Ralph Ellison about the ambiguities that attend the
mask in a land of masking jokers, *Darktown Strutters* explores the
ruses of black masking and performance in a culture saturated and
confounded by the masks and performances of a racial caste system.
Reckoning Rice correct when he quips that at least in minstrelsy, unlike slavery, " 'there's somethin in it for you' " (62), Jim makes good
on his obviously constricted opportunity. He realizes a sense of personal and collective liberation through his dancing, at one point
inciting a black uprising during a plantation dance contest, more

generally rallying underground resistance and acquiring literacy through the travel minstrel-show touring affords. So strong is the connection of minstrel dancing and freedom that, in a surprising move (for Jim and for novelist Brown), he refuses the idea of escape. A form of unfreedom, minstrelsy is at the same time a venue of possibility; Brown repeatedly compares Jim's role in minstrelsy to that of black liberation orators and agitators (Jim even gets to meet Frederick Douglass), and minstrelsy here is less the especial villain of much cultural historiography than one more American obstacle black people have had to thread their way through. This strikes me as an unusually sober and acute line of historical reflection, which Brown presents with some dialectical subtlety. Jim's friend Jubilee, for example, is one hell of a masking joker who specializes in taming his murderous resentment and rebutting white supremacy in riotous, anarchic laughter; rejecting the evident hostility encased in white amusement at minstrel antics, Jubilee spits it back in grins and watermelon rinds—until at last he explodes in righteous violence. Indeed because even prewar minstrelsy so resonated with the black cultural urgency behind its popularity, it carries with it in *Darktown Strutters* a whiff of danger that, to my understanding, did trail nineteenth-century minstrel shows. In the late 1850s, we know, Richmond and certain other cities outlawed minstrelsy for its hint of insurrection, perhaps an unthinkable prospect to us now; Brown has Rice assassinated, pointedly, by a Confederate loyalist, and he everywhere portrays minstrel shows delivering humanist home truths refracted through the distorting stage form appropriate to a society upended by racial confusion.

To wit, *Darktown Strutters'* central exhibit, a minstrel skit called "Who's Who In Paducah?," prods America's predicament of skin: "Are we who we are when we open our eyes?/Is my face myself or just a disguise?/Do we know who's who when our eyes are shut?/When the lids go down, do we know what's what?" (90). This too is reminiscent of certain nineteenth-century blackface confections, which occasionally had a surprising capacity for self-consciousness. (As do the white characters in Brown's novel, which eschews the luxuries of demonizing to portray whites caught up in major change and moved to entertain its ramifications; Rice feels a certain guilt about "'dancin the darky business'" [26] while Diamond, the better democrat, relishes his intimacy with otherness.) "Who's Who?" moreover articulates the novel's ultimate concern with the performative nature of racial identities—the baffles and bafflements of the visible in a world where we're all alike in the dark. Masking, Brown intimates, is the way of the stage because it's the way of the world, which has in turn taken the stage to heart and redoubled the confusion. Offstage antics in the novel increasingly take on the aspect of stage performances, and underscore the quotidian masking enjoined upon all by the racialist buffoonery of caste categories and codes. Collapsing, in the manner of Melville's *The Confidence Man,* two senses of the verb "to act," Brown shows the regulatory force of the mask for black people who must live up to white scripts even as they work them to other purposes. As one of Jim's fellow performers says: "'I know blackin up is US DOIN WHITE FOLKS DOIN US! But minstrelsy ain't the only place where that goes on. Like most of our people, I know I gotta stretch the truth in order to live. But long as WE know what we doin, it don't matter what white folks think!'" (138).

It is an inquiry into the ultimate stakes of the black mask's burden that propels *Darktown Strutters.* Having been affixed a priori, the mask defines an African American condition, but it may also be subversive equipment for living. In many ways the central drama is Jim's persistent refusal to wear blackface. As long as he can keep the cork off, he surmises, he's untouched by the "nigger act" that is his meal ticket. Finally, in a very moving scene, Jim is forced by his co-performer / lover Starletta to acknowledge his implication in the tar with which they, and black people generally, have been brushed.

> "It don't matter that you never blacked up. You made a
> name for yourself from it, same as those of us who used it."
> "That ain't the same thing!"
> "No it ain't. But that don't mean it didn't leave a smell
> on you."
> "Ain't no smell on me!"
> "If there wasn't, baby, you wouldn't be alive; and I
> wouldn't be bothered with you! . . . Jim. We all hurt
> when somebody tries to turn us into something that ain't
> human." (184)

There are no hiding places down here. Brown's acknowledgment of this dilemma rebukes claims to an authentic blackness above the fray in the name of accurately recognizing the terms of struggle, without which, Brown hints, there's no possibility of effective rejoinder. Pop life in these United States is a mixed-up, commercially saturated venture at its root, blackface all the way down. There are no names apart, no selves outside the regimes of representation that box in black folk. Up against that, only guerrilla mimicry, performative marronage, blistering reappropriations of racist myths, types, and masks remain. These don't amount to transcendence, but they do change the joke.

Indeed, *Darktown Strutters* suggests that black selves are not hostage to the labels and masks they are nonetheless forced to labor under. A performative negotiation of them, whether on the stage or in everyday life, has the effect in Brown's text of undermining and reorienting them. " 'When I black-up,' " says Jubilee, " 'I ain't gotta follow in behind what no white man did who put it on before me' " (93). Certainly the mask doesn't entirely colonize black identity. As Brown depicts it, blackface is merely the stage uniform of its cultural moment, one's ticket to public notice, where the struggle begins rather than ends. The terrific final scene of the novel—in which Jim in 1876 comes across a P. T. Barnum re-creation of the "Southland as it really is" (220) complete with black actors playing the parts of The Contented Slave, The Wretched Freedman, The Comic Negro, and so on—seems familiar enough to raise the question of our current uniforms of racial representation while suggesting again the performative devices that reroute them. Captured for no reason by some nearby police, Jim is hauled to a photographer's tent to have his picture taken for a national police "Rogue's Gallery" with a tag around his neck reading THE CONNIVING UNCLE TOM. As the photographer snaps, an idea for a new dance step flashes into Jim's mind; when the photo is developed, the conniving Uncle Tom both has and has not lived up to his name: Jim's movements have ruined the picture. This splendid evasion is an apt figure for all the frame-ups foiled in *Darktown Strutters*—and for those subtly conniving moments Twain allowed *Huckleberry Finn*'s Jim before he sold him out again.

CHAPTER 3

THE MIRROR HAS TWO FACES

White Ethnic Semi-Mojo

[Dreams] show a particular preference for combining contraries into a unity or for representing them as one and the same thing.
—Sigmund Freud, 1910

BY THE TIME MARK TWAIN died in April 1910, his brand of racial satire and evasion had been taken over by the vaudeville stage, an equally national-popular institution with a new-immigrant stamp. The vernacular stage, and after it Hollywood film and certain forms of musical offspring, picked up more or less where Twain left off and elaborated new domains and dispositions of cross-racial fantasy. I take my title from the 1996 Barbra Streisand film *The Mirror Has Two Faces,* which in the present context works to indicate the ways white-ethnic cultural production across the twentieth century trafficked in blackness as a foil for its own situational rigors—a series of dreams, as Freud said, tending to represent two contrary predicaments as one thing, a link between marginalized groups that often ended up exploiting the cultures on which it depended. Consider the following.

Oscar night 1994, when *Schindler's List* won seven awards and *Jurassic Park* took three others: a makeup artist had applied some

dark aerosol to cover Steven Spielberg's bald spot, and by the time
of the post-Oscar party, the evening's star had absently patted his
head a few times and then stroked his face. His wife rushed over and
said, "You look like Al Jolson!" As Spielberg joked to *Time* magazine,
"I was mortified. I was also relieved that I hadn't rubbed my head
during the ceremony and, in front of God and a billion people, given
my thanks in blackface."[1] Journalist and author Joe Klein, seeking to
avoid the same fate, published his best-selling 1996 political roman à
clef *Primary Colors* under the nom de plume "Anonymous" (though
Klein was later forced to admit authorship); its first-person narrator
is black campaign staffer Henry Burton. Burton opens the novel with
the words, "I am small and not so dark," that is, not your stereotypical
black man. This little ventriloquial bit is clever; "small" in German is
klein, making the above line translate as "I am Klein and not actually
black."[2] Some years before, singer Neil Diamond embraced just this
turn in his version of Jolson's most famous movie, *The Jazz Singer*
(1980). Early in the film, Diamond's black buddy (Franklin Ajaye)
convinces him to substitute for a sick member of their soul foursome. Only one problem: it's a black club, and its manager wants
a black group. No sweat: Neil just blacks up. All goes surreally well
until a black audience member (Ernie Hudson) notices Diamond's
white hands; some black men approach the stage—but Diamond
throws the first punch. No wonder the 1973 blaxploitation feature *Black Caesar,* directed by Larry Cohen, climaxes with Harlem
kingpin Fred Williamson fatally beating his longtime nemesis, an
Irish cop, with a shoe-shine box after blacking him up and making
him scream Jolson classic "Mammy!" Or that Melvin Van Peebles's
Watermelon Man (1970) has white suburbanite Jeff Gerber (Godfrey Cambridge in whiteface) cry out, upon realizing in the bathroom
mirror that he has been transformed into a black man (too much time
under the sunlamp): "Maybe [my kids] will recognize me if I get on
my knee and I sing 'Mammy'!" You can keep going earlier and earlier,
all the way back to 1927 and the Warner Brothers' original Jolson vehicle *The Jazz Singer,* as Michael Rogin did in *Blackface, White Noise*
(1996), and still not get to the bottom of this white-ethnic/African
American "fix": it extends at least as far back as black-Irish minstrel-
show politics in the middle decades of the nineteenth century.[3] In
fully demystifying the institutional racial unconscious of Jewish im-

migrants in the "Hollywood melting pot" (as he calls it), Rogin brilliantly brought up for review the long, internalized, not altogether intentional deployment of black cultural practices by white artists and apparatuses as well as by those bent on achieving their racial status. To judge from the outrage *Blackface, White Noise* generated in some quarters, Rogin offended by pushing the notion of a blackface liberalism that could work against the grain of even antiracist artists, as I hope to have shown occurred in the case of Mark Twain. The cover image of Rogin's book featured Eddie Cantor blacking up in a makeup mirror, Jew disappearing into dark Other—which is to say the prerogative of whiteness: routine showbiz protocol suddenly catching the stage pro in a state of surprised, two-faced transition.

Whether it is Spielberg's bald spot, Klein's smallness, or Diamond's suspiciously performative sucker punch, blackface may be a way to resolve gender trouble with a racial mask—the maintenance of virility through the imaginary embrace of African American manhood. *Watermelon Man* knows this and more when it has a now-black Godfrey Cambridge look down his pants hopefully only to find that "that's an old wives' tale"; and *Black Caesar*'s Williamson, the film suggests, is beating to death not only a terrorist cop but also an image of himself saddled with the white meanings and resonances given black male faces in U.S. culture and society. If blackface for Jewish men is a route to potency, for black men it's an emblem of masochism. This is the black mirror's double bind.

Just this sort of caste-inspired disparity lies behind the irony of Rogin's subtitle: *Jewish Immigrants in the Hollywood Melting Pot.* Any melting that occurred or occurs in the United States finds African Americans, as Rogin would have it, stuck to the bottom of the pot. In the broadest sense such negative pressure brought to bear on the reigning conceptual apparatuses of American liberalism— consensus nationalism, melting-pot exceptionalism, declarations of independence, and so forth—distinguishes *Blackface, White Noise* the way Rogin's memorable plotting of Melville's America through contemporaneous Marxian categories distinguishes his book *Subversive Genealogy: The Politics and Art of Herman Melville.* All the more interesting, then, that *Blackface, White Noise* should have provoked such a negative review in the pages of *Tikkun* by left historian Paul Buhle and cultural critic Edward Portnoy.[4] The review arises in part from scholarly disagreements and political/interpretive discrepancies, but its place of publication and certain of its emphases mark the response by Buhle and Portnoy (and Rogin's book) as skirmishes in what had by the 1990s become an unsettled rancor regarding the relations between blacks and Jews (very often the rancor erupted among Jews themselves). Far be it from goy-boy me to hope to soothe the raw nerve Rogin touched with his book, evidenced, for example, in the disavowal by some critics of what Rogin made of Neal Gabler's excellent study *An Empire of Their Own: How the Jews Invented Hollywood*, his account of Jewish assimilation—and American transformation—through the early film industry.[5] The point is not to soothe nerves anyway, but rather to acknowledge the sparks that fly and sores that open in the long revolution of cultural mirroring and interracial negotiation. As Rogin argues at length, it is politically bankrupt to close our eyes to this gnarled history—as Buhle and Portnoy do in their review, condescending to cultural historians (like Rogin) who deploy continental literary theory, dismissing *Blackface, White Noise* because it doesn't discuss more (left-wing) films, and rationalizing the unseemly racial tropes of such left-leaning films as Robert Rossen's *Body and Soul* (1947) and Carl Foreman's *Home of the Brave* (1949) as—without evidence—the best that was "possible at the time of their production." "The Jewish capacity to see non-whites as sufferers like themselves," they say, "is still not gone—not by a long shot"; Rogin is too obsessed with blackface crimes. Such left-wing-of-the-possible arguments, to say nothing of this overinvestment in Jewish benevolence (and suffering as the only hinge of solidarity), seem a desperate attempt to prop up interethnic bridges at any cost.[6]

It's fair to say that cultural historians exploring such ethnoracial intersections over the last two decades have discerned an intractable antinomy of mirroring and misprision—evident in most attempts to represent the posture of Jewish or Italian or Irish performance in the orbit of black culture, right down to the Buhle and Portnoy review. The examples of (and arguments for) intercultural solidarity and amity are as partial and particular as those of exploitation are inevitable, given the uneven access to resources and public hearing on the part of African American performers over against even the most struggling new immigrants on their way to official whiteness. To think of the matter *as* an antinomy, then, strikes me as the best way to keep one's eyes open to surprise while leaning hard on culture industries structured in racial dominance. As scholars such as Stephen Steinberg, Adolph Reed Jr., David Roediger, Micaela di Leonardo, Matthew Frye Jacobson, and many others have observed, black-white ethnic relations have been overdetermined by the inequalities between new-immigrant mobility and access and the black immiseration and segregation on which it often depends, despite a long history of cross-racial interest and involvement (the inequalities themselves have not infrequently underwritten such interest and involvement). In the political realm alone, a black commitment to interracial struggle (in the NAACP and other organizations) has allowed whites partial oversight of African American affairs, while a corollary black involvement in Jewish, Italian, or other white-ethnic political initiatives is generally unthinkable. By the same token, black and white-ethnic "separatisms," as it were, are not analogous: black autonomy has usually been perceived as churlish and aggressive, while white-ethnic investments are felt to be sacrosanct, noble, and rootsy (and certainly off limits to black commentary). In light of such structures of dominance, Paul Berman's shallow psychologizing of black-Jewish conflicts as a product of the "narcissism of small differences"—one group's manufacture of a threatening "Other" out of a parallel group that is "Almost the Same"—falls quite short of the mark.[7]

Historically sensitive accounts of the messy ways racial formation occurred across the long twentieth century suggest why ethno-racial cultural antinomies have been so unyielding. The language of white "ethnicity" that we take so much for granted today is an ahistorical and indeed reifying abstraction, as Gwendolyn Mink, Jacobson, Roediger, and others have shown; by and large a post–World War II construct, it retroactively assumes the always-already whiteness of those eventually deemed worthy of the label and overlooks the vicissitudes of the latter's arduous construction. Although European immigrants would indeed later move on to official whiteness, they were upon arrival classified in strongly "racial" terms and languages—a category quite apart from "native" whites and not unrelated (but also not equal) to that of darker peoples. While African Americans, Asians, and Native Americans tended to be seen as "color races" and new immigrants were understood to be "nation races," as Reynolds Scott-Childress argues, the idea of race, however fuzzy and contested, nonetheless brought all these groups into conceptual proximity. For the first half of the twentieth century, nation-race groups lived "in between" the stark racial binaries of the United States, and I would argue that precisely this "inbetweenness," as Roediger terms it, threw immigrant performers into the arena of black culture even as it kept them on this side of the segregated divide, the very terms of the antinomy they could neither avoid nor circumvent. The bifurcated language of race instituted a felt closeness between the groups that binary racial codes at the same time disallowed. As Jacobson puts it, the "saga of European immigration has long been held up as proof of the openness of American society," with ethnic "inclusion," "mobility," and "assimilation" the standard on which the American ideal is deemed to work. "But this pretty story suddenly fades once one recognizes how crucial Europeans' racial status as 'free white persons' was to their gaining entrance in the first place; how profoundly dependent their racial inclusion was upon the racial *ex*clusion of others; how racially accented the native resistance was even to *their* inclusion for something over half a century; and how completely intertwined were the prospects of becoming American and becoming Caucasian. Racism now appears not anomalous to the working of American democracy, but fundamental to it."[8] Jacobson not only states one of the guiding assumptions of the present study, he gestures to the cultural contradictions we will see from *The Jazz Singer* forward.

Some primordial joining and jostling, then, compose the crossover dreamwork of new-immigrant engagements with "blackness." This is not the first time I have invoked dreaming and fantasy as analogues for and aspects of the cultural mirroring at hand; and if cultural products reveal the dreamwork of the social, as Michael Denning has it, it should come as no surprise that Freud is suggestive on one aspect of their political unconscious.[9] Freud's brief review essay "The Antithetical Meaning of Primal Words" (1910) recaps one emphasis of his *Interpretation of Dreams* (1900) even as it connects that emphasis to ancient or archaic languages. For Freud, famously, antithesis and contradiction do not exist in dreams, as they do not in certain ancient languages (his particular focus is Egyptian), and he is interested in the relation between the two domains. Dreams "show a particular preference," he writes, "for combining contraries into a unity or for representing them as one and the same thing." This is so much the case in dreams and ancient languages that any element, says Freud, can equally mean its opposite; devoid of negation, primal states of representation structured like language in the unconscious produce signifiers housing exactly opposed meanings. With every conception the twin of its opposite, Freud realizes as well that the relation between them, precisely their difference, is built into what manifests as a unity.[10] I am struck by the suggestiveness of such remarks for considering certain instances of white-ethnic cross-cultural dreaming, instances involving affects and performances of a primal inwardness or noncontradiction ultimately unhinged by the difference lodged at their heart. The discursive meeting ground of religion has historically been one chief arena of connection, African American cultures of the enslaved having made use of Old and New Testaments to voice their emancipatory desire in ways later played on by Jewish and Catholic entertainers from Jolson (who linked the "tear in his voice" with that of the sorrow songs mostly to further his secular ambitions) to Frank Sinatra (who in the 1940s did a version of "Jesus Is a Rock" with the gospel group the Charioteers) to Bob Dylan (especially late 1970s born-again Dylan, whose Grammy-winning calling card was the gospel song "Gotta Serve Somebody"). The churchly place of pharaohs and Israelites, exile and exodus, bondage and jubilee, salvation in the body of Christ, the Bible turned antiphonal in African American cultural forms, has been a rich source of crossover call-and-response, the biblical paradigm a sort of primal Word in Freud's sense. The more modern(ist) church of show business itself, the primordial move pioneered by *The Jazz Singer*'s cantor-to-be Jakie Rabinowitz through his new incarnation as Broadway star Jack Robin, has been another such fertile ground of mirroring, as we shall see, not least because of its fraught relationship to worship for post-observant Jews with an eye on the entertainment main chance (like the Warner brothers and Al Jolson) and its welcoming embrace of the Sunday-morning performance skills that black entertainers brought to the party. The antitheses don't go away, they just seem more or less to harmonize: this is the often-problematic gambit of white-ethnic identifications with and representations of African American culture.[11]

The Jazz Singer, and *Show Boat* too, have gotten a just share of attention, but there is also, and equally in step with my purposes, *The Green Pastures,* both Broadway play (1930) and Warner Brothers film (1936), a religious fable featuring key episodes from the Bible with black actors in every role from God to Adam.[12] It comes in the wake of *The Jazz Singer* and is in a way its inverse: in the first, the Warners use "blackness" via blackface to move its Jewish makers away from an Old World / Old Testament ethos into mainstream entertainment culture; in *Green Pastures,* they use an all-black cast to stage biblical tales that saddle African Americans with a rather archaic brand of Afro-Christian spirituality. The ethno-racial twinning is seamless but works once again to exploit and condescend to the black image. Jolson himself was interested in and for a time contemplated purchasing the rights to the play so that he could play its central figure of De Lawd (who had been played by black actor Richard Harrison on stage), an eventuation averted only when the producers turned him down. As Arthur Knight observes, this very possibility is self-consciously parodied in Jolson's film *Wonder Bar* (1934) and its lengthy blackface finale song, "Goin' to Heaven on a Mule."[13] As goes the parody, so went the original, with black southerners (figured as children learning the Bible) imagining a heaven populated with black folk like themselves and a Lawd who seeks (though not in precisely these terms) to turn the sinful ways of southern life into the upstanding and respectable values of the New Negro. There are no external enemies, only the wayward nature of black Americans themselves. The Hall Johnson Choir, Broadway actor Rex Ingram, vaudevillians Eddie ("Rochester") Anderson and Ida Forsyne, and dozens of others mounted a black version of Old Testament fall and ultimate deliverance. To paraphrase Donald Bogle, Adam and Eve are a muscular bronze man and his coquettish mate; Cain is a rough-and-ready no-account and his high-yaller gal, Zeba, a high-strung strumpet; Moses becomes a clever conjurer; and Noah is a gregarious Tom complete with top hat and raincoat. Heavenly paradise is an everlasting fish fry. The fallen world is replete with exemplary black sinning—drinking, gambling, knife-play, fornication, murder, the whole coon-show array—from which Anderson's Noah and his ark must steer a new way. The Moses story of exodus ("Let de Hebrew chillun go!") liberates African Americans from the bondage of Pharaoh ("Don' you know de Hebrews is my slaves?"), who looks not a little like Marcus Garvey. Babylon is in essence the Cotton Club, from whose clutches an invented character called Hezdrel (Ingram) must lead his people, who teach De Lawd (also Ingram) to be a more merciful God. Black deliverance comes with a turn to the New Testament and a vision of the Crucifixion. The film presents southern folk belief as something like the last repository of U.S. spirituality, and in this it doubly exploits its material, making black Americans the bearers of U.S. folk life—they are both perfect sinners and perfect believers, a genuine American peasantry. The black press offered more than a few stinging rebuttals.[14] If *Green Pastures* calls on Jewish-black connections by way of the Old Testament, it does so in order to frame, control, and finally distance or disavow that connection—the difference harbored in its primal noncontradiction; the religious faith modernism eroded and made naïve can still be accessed by the back door. Paying forward the late nineteenth-century vogue of Jubilee Singers by giving the Hall Johnson Choir's spirituals an airing, the film twists these performances into a vision of infantilized reverence.[15] The fight to regain paradise is not without specific political resonance, but it unfolds in terms that recall Mark Twain's reliance on blackface sentimentalism.

Fast-forward thirty years to that cunning Mel Brooks sortie, *The Producers* (1968), which would pull back the curtain on the manipulations and calculations behind such imaging, producing, and controlling on Broadway and in the movies. It was to be mirrored in turn by Spike Lee's *Bamboozled* (2000), and the relations between the two, as Susan Gubar has shown, are instructive.[16] Like the mirroring at work in *Green Pastures,* shuttling from the Brooks to the Lee film suggests the convergences but also the imbalances inevitably at work—imbalances well realized by and in some sense built into the stories of the respective filmmakers. Working entirely with campy parodies of Jews and Nazis, *The Producers* would seem to be operating far afield from the present context; but I discern something of a Jolson joke at its heart, a nicely self-conscious moment in what is already a quite self-conscious context. Max Bialystock (Zero Mostel), a once-great Broadway producer and now a has-been schlemiel, is reduced to cadging checks for his next production by operating as a gigolo to rich old widows. His accountant, Leo Bloom

(Gene Wilder), hits on the idea that an oversubscribed flop would allow them to retain the money that an already oversubscribed mediocrity would not. Thus is born the sunny Nazi musical, *Springtime for Hitler: A Gay Romp with Adolph and Eva at Berchtesgaden,* a show too heinous not to fail. Instead the plan backfires and the show is a huge hit, which takes them to the brink and ultimately to jail (where they mount a new show, *Prisoners of Love*). *Springtime*'s audience, at first genuinely appalled, is won over with the appearance of lead actor L. S. D., Lorenzo St. DuBois (Dick Shawn), as a sort of hipster love-child Hitler. His blackvoice jive talk ("Hey man . . . I *lieb* ya, I *lieb* ya baby, I *lieb* you. Now *lieb* me alone") and bluesy numbers ("Adolph and Eva") are the pivot: blackface without the blackface puts the satire across, it's a hip joke now, and the show is a rave. It is true, as Gubar observes, that Nazi lampoon throughout the film devolves on a queering of Aryan pretense to übermasculinity; from a limp-wristed L. S. D. to campy director Roger De Bris to *Springtime* writer Franz Liebkind's transparent crush on his former Führer, same-sex desire is used to top the master race. But blackface is deployed, for once, as an ironized vehicle of audience attraction. Whiteness here is not the desire accessed through the blackface mask, as in the long tradition from which Mel Brooks emerged, but, in Nazi form, the ludicrous enemy.

Such mutations were amplified first in Brooks's race-conscious *Blazing Saddles* (1974), which paired Gene Wilder with Cleavon Little, and then in the Arthur Hiller film *Silver Streak* (1976), a showpiece for Wilder and Richard Pryor. In the latter, Wilder plays book editor George Caldwell, who gets caught up in a complicated murder plot while on the titular cross-country railroad train; himself accused of the murder, George escapes and steals a police car containing Pryor's Grover T. Muldoon, and the two become associates in fugitivity. Attempting to elude the cops and reboard the Silver Streak in Kansas City, George and Grover repair to a men's room to work up a blackface disguise for George. As Scott Saul has demonstrated, this scene, written originally as standard racist fare, with Grover affirming the legitimacy and hilarity of cooning, was radically reconceived by Pryor at the eleventh hour: no longer a vehicle of fun at Pryor's expense, the shoe polish Wilder uses to black up becomes a self-reflexive critique of the blackface tradition itself.[17] In its original

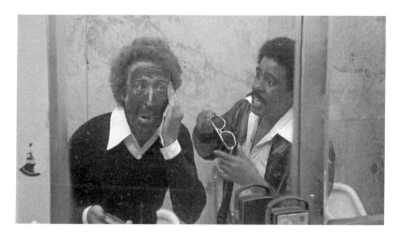

Fig. 4. Gene Wilder and Richard Pryor in *Silver Streak*, 1976, 20th Century Fox

form, the bit has a blackfaced Wilder successfully passing as black; in the final version, a black passer-by and Pryor himself crack wise at the get up, and the joke is on the whites and the cops, for whom even a pitiful disguise is good enough to pass. As Saul writes, "In the script, the blackface is a goof that Grover Muldoon embraces; in the scene Richard plays, it's a ruse Grover unmasks."[18] Pryor engineers the scene in every sense. When George hesitates to put on the shoe polish, Grover snaps, "What? Are you afraid it won't come off?" Turning half-blacked Wilder full face into the mirror, Grover quips that "Al Jolson made a million bucks looking like that." Pryor *makes* the Jew black up, again—a melancholic rem(a)inder of a tradition not yet dead; a bleak joke at the expense of whites who still adore the counterfeit; a homosocial gambit that results in an affectionate exchange of masks (Grover gives George his jacket and shades as well) that in no way erases the difference between them. The mirror sustains no illusions here: as Saul concludes, Grover schools George on how easy it is to don a caricature, and how heavy it is to bear the weight of one.

Bamboozled, however, will later indicate that while all these turns are salutary, they are also quite partial. (I am reminded in this connection of stalwart Hollywood director Alfred E. Green doing *The Jolson Story* [1946] and then following that up a few years later, as though in a logical progression, with *The Jackie Robinson Story* [1950].) *Bamboozled* works in self-conscious homage to *The Producers,* as though to exhibit the ultimate asymmetries between them. Its industry vet looking for a loophole flop is Pierre Delacroix (Damon Wayans), a television producer who chafes at his token status, the substandard fare he is forced to produce for "the idiot box," and his boorish wigger overseer, Dunwitty (Michael Rapaport), who boasts that he is blacker than Pierre. In order to induce public outrage and get him released from his contract, Delacroix and his sidekick Sloan (Jada Pinkett Smith) hit on their version of *Springtime for Hitler*: *Mantan—The New Millennium Minstrel Show,* complete with two brilliant black performers, Womack (Tommy Davidson) and Manray (Savion Glover), in blackface. The show is a whopping success. Before Lee's film goes off the rails with a moralizing critique of selling out and a *Network*-style plot featuring black militant rappers the Mau Maus, who kidnap Manray and execute him on live television, it is extremely incisive in its depictions of minstrelsy as a kind of general condition, quite apart from mediated television representation. If blackface minstrelsy and its afterlives are (still) all about copping black style à la Dunwitty, black minstrelsy labors under the weight of this history of appropriation and its resulting ideologemes. Everyone in the picture is a kind of minstrel. Before they become television stars, Manray and Womack dance on a shingle for money like antebellum street minstrels; Manray auditions by jumping up and dancing on Dunwitty's desk as though it were an auction block; sniffy, Ivy League–educated Delacroix is a kind of Zip Coon dandy (a second-order minstrel routine, given Damon Wayans's role in creating and starring in the early 1990s neominstrel television program *In Living Color*); the Mau Maus themselves are presented as authenticity-hungry neominstrels. *The New Millennium Minstrel Show* is a hit because a Jim Crow imaginary still reigns. Yet, with regard to the earlier Brooks film to which *Bamboozled* alludes, the symmetry of and in the mirror of caricature breaks down. Several scenes of Manray and Womack blacking up in the mirror before their show depict truly sickening and moving moments of self-alienation, all the more so because their performances are so powerful. What was camp in *The Producers,* and anyway mostly with Nazis as the butt of the joke, is here unavoidably cast in the tragic mode. In the show,

the Roots appear as the Alabama Porch Monkeys; there are frequent forays on plantations and in watermelon patches; characters
are arrayed in coon and buffoon clothes. The conceptual frame of
Bamboozled comes from a painting of the same title by Michael Ray
Charles (cf. Fig. 1), an artist working in a scabrous signifying tradition that includes Robert Colescott, Carrie Mae Weems, and Kara
Walker, all of whom in one way or another suggest the continuing
influence of minstrelization on both black and white life. Not "self-
hatred" or mere self-doubt but psychic (when not literal) dismember-
ment, shit-stained hurt, the violence of self-destruction, the loss of
a self to doubt—abjection born of white dominance is the threat. As
Delacroix's father, Junebug (played by Richard Pryor's old friend,
Paul Mooney), drunkenly advises, "Keep 'em laughing." *Bamboozled*
is compellingly clear on just how painful the joke is.[19]

It is clear as well on the ethno-racial entertainment politics
that reach back into the early years of the twentieth century. The
choice of Michael Rapaport as boss Dunwitty is rather precise in
this light, even though it puts a Jewish actor in WASPface (or at
any rate gives him an unspecified ethnicity). In this church of show
business, primal joinings of Jew and black finally cannot help but
fracture; for all the mirroring, the image is off. And yet: *Bamboozled*
carries a final title dedicating the picture to Hollywood writer Budd
Schulberg—screenwriter, producer, novelist; nephew of famed agent
and producer Sam Jaffe; part of the first corps of World War II servicemen to liberate the Nazi camps; author of *What Makes Sammy
Run?* (1941), a novel of one man's hustle from the Lower East Side
to dog-eat-dog Old Hollywood; writer of Andy Griffith's starring role
in *A Face in the Crowd* (1957), another self-reflexive tale of the ruses
of power in the culture industry. Schulberg also, in the wake of the
1965 Watts riot, launched the Watts Writers Workshop, an attempt to
galvanize writing among the South Central LA dispossessed, which it
did, lasting into the early 1970s. The mirror, there, for just a moment,
gave rise to freedom dreams.

LET US HEAR THIS DYNAMIC RESOUND in some pop musical locations, where these antinomies are no less intractable. White-ethnic
pop singers and band leaders, fronting milieus in which Catholi-

cism or Jewishness is variously in play, are on the choral front lines. Not least because of the vestigial or adoptive black church practices at work in much of their music, they enter a scene of mirroring in which two faces appear, and not just by way of the interventriloquial situation at hand, black voices commingling with white and white thrown into a domain of what Stefano Harney and Fred Moten term black study.[20] Antiphony, you might say, here becomes unison. Primal noncontradiction is doubly unsettled in crossover call-and-response (the unsettling of soloist by collective and of white-ethnic lead by black sidekicks and backups). The cross-racial play in the acoustic mirror is the primal connection and its displacement, the mirror's uncanny disturbance, the doubling that is and isn't, sometimes tilting into approximation and appropriation and elsewhere summoning more genuine impulses.

Bruce Springsteen has never really tried to dance (that amusing old video for "Dancing in the Dark" aside), or for that matter sing, like one of his soul mentors, not even Smokey Robinson, whom he has said he has in his head when he writes his songs. But his sometime messianic complex has a model, and that model is most certainly James Brown—as Springsteen has remarked in interviews and in the speech he gave inducting U2 into the Rock and Roll Hall of Fame in 2005. Not really in his musical style or song structure, which have so thoroughly come to convey and speak to the idea and audience of the white rustbelt working class (or its Dust Bowl–cum-post-Fordist folk variants, as on the albums *Nebraska* [1982], *The Ghost of Tom Joad* [1995], and *Devils & Dust* [2005]). And not, obviously, in band makeup, although, as the joke goes, at any Springsteen concert (post-1975), the black people onstage outnumber those in the audience (because there's one on stage). But, as Joel Dinerstein has definitively argued, as a model for live soul ritual, as a methodology of performance and stagecraft and show pacing, as the very template for the sweaty redemptive four-hour show by the hardest-working white man in show business, J. B. was the mothership.[21] The only bemusing thing, really, is how such a lengthily elaborate 1970s soul performance paradigm—closer to Sly Stone than the Rolling Stones, with its secular transposition of the gospel impulse to bring down the spirit to greet and exorcise ordinary pain, its preaching to and on behalf of a community of souls upraised through ritual barings of collective emotion—came to read as white classic rock.[22] From "Tenth Avenue Freeze-Out" to "The Rising," with a raft of others before, in between, and after, sublimated soul-revue sermons first to last.

If Clarence Clemons was always the symbolic centerpiece of this gambit, he was also, *for this reason,* the symptom of its limitations.[23] I don't mean his saxophone playing necessarily (though, along with David Sanborn, he came close to ruining the instrument's power as a pop instrument in the 1970s, playing the same damn broadside in song after song). It is, rather, that in the context and drama of the E Street Band, Clemons was reduced to exactly a signifier—the supplement, perhaps, of what was repressed from the band's frontal attack. Think back to the beloved cover of *Born to Run,* with Bruce and Clarence doing their best Huck and Jim, Clarence the reliable shoulder on which the (then) skinny little white guy leans for soul support; even there, *even there,* Clarence is on the back of the record: you have to open it up to see the whole picture! The interracial brothers-in-soul bond that defines the band's aura, played out everywhere in little dramas such as the way the sax solo on "Born to Run" answers Bruce's words of love (the tenor roars in hard upon them, the love as much between Bruce and Clarence as between Bruce and Wendy), was of course codified long ago on "Tenth Avenue Freeze-Out," that sketch of the redemptive formation of band brotherhood so often used to climax the band's shows. But this allegorical achievement, of a black man joining and completing and therefore *making* the band, is an always-already (here they are, playing for you) that is at the same time a not-quite-yet, since it has to be played out and reaffirmed night after year after decade (and now after life). But for Christ's sake, *Dave Matthews* had three black guys in the band; how redemptive was it, really, to string out the Clarence thing? Isn't this at best an embarrassing holdover from an earlier time, when every white band had its one black member as a showy embrace of racial unity? A hollow celebration of cross-racial amity that works mostly at the level of symbolism, especially since the horn itself played less and less a part in the music after the early 1980s? In the 2007 song "Girls in Their Summer Clothes," Springsteen updated this dynamic, only to make plain again its contradictions in his lines about Shaniqua.[24] A surprise, this: not Rosalita, not Wendy, not Mary, not even Candy, but Shaniqua, a new turn in Springsteen lore.

Who is Shaniqua? Shaniqua is the waitress who, deep into the song, refills the coffee of "my poor Bill"—the song's aching, adrift, possibly ex-military, and presumptively white protagonist—and in doing so maybe saves his life. A fine moment of connection and breakthrough as far as it goes, but once again it's a black donor facilitating white spiritual transformation.

Similar things attend the late 1970s born-again Bob Dylan of *Slow Train Coming* and after, trying to cross specifically into a black Pentecostalism modeled for him by backup singer / lovers like Helena Springs, Clydie King, and lots of others too, above all Carolyn Dennis (whom he married and fathered a child with in the mid-1980s). Primal connection, ventriloquism, the marriage of heaven and hell approximately—which of these *didn't* get an airing in this period of Dylan's work? One gets the sense that Dylan himself understands something of this from his winking reference to it on *Modern Times*'s "Thunder on the Mountain": "I was thinkin bout Alicia Keys, couldn't keep from cryin / When she was born in Hell's Kitchen I was livin down the line [that would be January 1981, so yep] / I wonder where in the world Alicia Keys could be"—or as Dylan told *Rolling Stone* he realized after playing with Keys at the Grammy Awards, "There's nothing about that girl I don't like."[25] Gettin' busy being born-ready is baked into *Slow Train*'s "Gotta Serve Somebody." You're not going to mistake Dylan for a gospel singer there, but I think you do hear him reaching for the right master (embodied in the women behind him). Asked for her thoughts on this moment in Dylan's life, singer Maria Muldaur said: "I think he [dated] some of these black girls because they didn't idolize him" (not least, she avers, because "they had no idea who he was"). "They were real down to earth and they didn't worship him. . . . [They are] strong women who would just say, *cut off your bullshit.*"[26] Dylan undoubtedly found this refreshing, perhaps baptismally so (despite the lack of black folk at his shows); another way to hide, to circumvent being Bob Dylan, offstage but also on, where his backups already knew the answer to the question they sent him to ask. Carolyn Dennis reportedly helped hire the singers who would back him, one of whom was Louise Bethune, who had sung with the Shirelles and the Crystals, so, back to from before where he started. Dylan would have these women do his hair (required hairspray and a certain arrangement, it

seems); he would get them up for wee-small-hours harmonizing sessions. He wanted to fade into them, as the song goes, a move perhaps
most winningly rendered in the choral japes and overall vocal design
of *Knocked Out Loaded*'s "Brownsville Girl," that Wild West opus
with echoes of border ballads, gospel music, Dust Bowl sagas, Hollywood movies, and Sam Shepard plays (Shepard cowrote it). A "Series
of Dreams," as Dylan would say, seconding Freud, where nothing
comes up to the top, everything stays down where it's wounded, opposites attracting in embattled unison.

Better, perhaps, to turn to Laura Nyro and her early 1970s
work with Labelle (Patti Labelle, Nona Hendryx, and Sarah Dash).
Bronx-born Jewish Nyro, née Laura Nigro (truly, you cannot make
up this kind of thing), was already plenty black(face)-identified by
the time she recorded her album of girl-group and Motown covers
Gonna Take a Miracle (1971)—with Gamble and Huff at Sigma Sound
in Philadelphia, too, a full four years before David Bowie got there to
record *Young Americans* (1975) (which by analogy would make this
album Nyro's *Young Americans* and Bowie's covers album *Pin Ups*
rolled into one and prior to both). Startlingly precocious, Nyro's
late-1960s albums (*Eli and the Thirteenth Confession, New York Tend-
aberry, Christmas and the Beads of Sweat*) and songs from "Wedding Bell Blues" to "Stoney End" to "Eli's Coming" to "Stoned Soul
Picnic" were already widely influential and widely covered before
Gonna Take a Miracle's ars poetica celebrated her sources (miracle
as in Smokey Robinson). The album opens with a cover of the Shirelles' "I Met Him on a Sunday," segueing seamlessly into a Marvin Gaye
composition recorded in 1970 by the Originals, "The Bells." Met him
on a Sunday—church again—missed him on Monday, found him on
Tuesday, dated him on Wednesday, kissed him on Thursday, he didn't
come Friday, so I said bye-bye on Saturday. One of the many things
that's just so great about this performance is the way it splays the
song's "I" across white and black singers, adducing a sisterly collective that as one metes out Saturday's kiss-off. It's another dream of
noncontradiction, this time courtesy of the Shirelles, even as you notice the varying timbres and approaches to note and phrase—a less
kind way of saying which is that you always know exactly when Nyro
comes in—and the fact that it is Nyro who gets the key narrative
lines, "met him," "kissed him," dissed him. The cumulative effect of

Gonna Take a Miracle's homage is to displace or to acknowledge the displacement of white star-sovereignty by the traditions it is heir to and by the context of sisterly study brought to bear by Labelle's support and intervention. There is no call to order as the record begins because all you can do is join what is already in progress, as Harney and Moten would have it. It's an uncanny mirroring because so *hamish,* but then again Labelle was already intent on their own crossing over—the "Voulez-vouz coucher avec moi ce soir?" of the song "Lady Marmalade" doubling as their own pop-aesthetic credo. If not exactly a performance of archival melancholia as Daphne Brooks has described it by way of Amy Winehouse—with "best black Jew" Sammy Davis Jr. serving as her Labelle—Nyro's is certainly a self-conscious playing with the voice's mediations, the allusive and finally elusive character of its racial provenance.[27]

A somewhat less self-conscious instance of such mediations and mirrorings involves Sammy Davis in another context, that of the Rat Pack.

IN 1965, Frank Sinatra turned fifty. In a Las Vegas engagement early the next year at the Sands Hotel, he made much of this fact, turning the entire performance—captured in the classic recording *Sinatra at the Sands* (1966)—into a meditation on aging, artistry, and maturity, punctuated by such key songs as "You Make Me Feel So Young," "The September of My Years," and "It Was a Very Good Year."[28] Not only have few commentators noticed this, they haven't noticed either that Sinatra's way of negotiating the reality of age depended on a series of masks—blackface mostly, but also street Italianness and other guises. Though the Count Basie band backed him on these dates, Sinatra deployed *Amos 'n' Andy* shtick (lots of it) to vivify his persona; mocking Sammy Davis Jr. even as he adopted the speech patterns and vocal mannerisms of blacking up, he maneuvered around the threat of decrepitude and remasculinized himself in recognizably Rat Pack ways. We know of the enormous influence black jazz musicians generally and Billie Holiday in particular exerted on Sinatra's style; by the mid-1960s, Sinatra's Italian accents depended on an imagined blackness both mocked and ghosted in the exemplary performances of *Sinatra at the Sands.*

Sinatra sings superbly all across the record, rooting his performance in an aura of affection and intimacy from his very first words ("How did all these people get in my room?"). "Good evening, ladies and gentlemen, welcome to Jilly's West," he says, playing with a persona (habitué of the famous Fifty-Second Street New York bar Jilly's Saloon) that by 1965 had nearly run its course. Where the Basie band is concerned, though, this intimacy completely depends on the mediations of *Amos 'n' Andy*'s Kingfish, imitations of whom punctuate his between-songs patter. The Jersey sons of Hoboken and Red Bank, respectively, greet each other in the alienated language of minstrelsy in a context, nonetheless, of real musical rapport (have a listen to "One for My Baby"). Indeed, blackface, or blackvoice, is exactly turned to the account of interracial connection on Sinatra's part; minstrelsy here becomes the lingua franca of black-Italian musical kinship. This isn't as crazy as it might seem today—plenty of black people found *Amos 'n' Andy* funny, even if, as Amiri Baraka put it long ago, they never confused its characters with themselves. And if there is now a nostalgic African American vogue of reclaiming minstrelsy, for example, critic Margo Jefferson's embrace of *Amos 'n' Andy* in the pages of the *New York Times,* it's also true that interracial interaction has for the last 200 years been mediated through the culture industry's languages of race.[29]

Still and all, *this is 1966.* One is reminded of this abruptly when, in riffing on Dean Martin's drinking habits, Sinatra quips: "I would say, roughly, that Dean Martin has been stoned more often than the United States embassies." Bombs were dropping on North Vietnam early in 1965; massive antiwar activism had materialized; the Student Nonviolent Coordinating Committee had revolutionized the civil rights movement. And Sinatra is making like Jolson in front of another of the great geniuses of twentieth-century music, Count Basie. "I hope that you're having an enjoyable stay here in Las Vegas, and also hope that you have been fortunate. . . . I can't say the same for Mr. Basie and myself, because we run into a streak of baaaad luck. Sunday we went up to da Grand Canyon and it was *closed!* And last yee-ah, we invested a bundle of money in a pumpkin farm and den dey called off Halloween! And when I told dat to Sapphire, she said you goin' around wid dat bum again, dat's what's the matter with you!" Sinatra's New Frontier charisma is deeply compromised by these turns. As though to keep hold of a street credibility attenuated by success and demanded by the interracial context, Sinatra goes lowbrow in an astonishing extended monologue humorously describing his life and career. You can even hear the band laughing. Don't get me wrong: who would want a sanitized situation of "antiracist" sincerity here? And yet the Rat Pack's mascot role, taken up by Sammy Davis, comes to this. (One doesn't forget, either, that when in 1957 Louis Armstrong spoke out against President Dwight D. Eisenhower and Arkansas governor Orval Faubus regarding the outrages in Little Rock, Sammy did his part to shut Pops down, criticizing Armstrong for playing before segregated audiences.)[30] The interesting thing is that what is disavowed in the figure of Sammy Davis (Sinatra jokes that Davis has been booked for a long engagement at the Sands—"just to clean") comes roaring back in Sinatra's own voice. I mean the inhabitance of a black male body—Kingfish, to be sure, maybe Billy Eckstine too, but in any case an imagined persona simpatico with the rocking band sharing the stage. "Run and hide," says Sinatra at one point as the band gears up into overdrive, "run and hide."

Doing so ironically, but predictably, affords Sinatra the street Italianness perfect for the threatening surroundings—outside as well as onstage. The long monologue at the center of *Sinatra at the Sands* clarifies the stakes here, its movement of mind, facts of feeling, and intimate urgencies. At once affecting autobiography and low shtick, this twelve-minute set piece is every bit as cunning and calculated as Sinatra's singing. It's a narrative of up-from-Hoboken that nevertheless lays claim to the working-class arena in which Sinatra was raised—"the qualms and traumas of life"—and which suffuses his mature persona, however polished that might be. Sinatra's father, in Sinatra's telling a Rutgers English major, is rendered as Kingfish in dagoface; his son's crisp diction, the way he has of biting off phrases and clinching words, owes everything to immigrant English—weird English, Evelyn Ch'ien calls it[31]—immigrant English subsumed, transformed, and at some level disavowed. The disavowal comes in Sinatra's insistence on "class," as in his remark about the ongoing renovation of the Sands Hotel. It comes as well in his shunting of what there is in him of the father's voice onto blackface, its equal and opposite number.

But it's the singer's advancing age that I think most accounts for the surge of blackface all across *Sinatra at the Sands*. Note first the following. Hard upon a crack about Sammy comes a remark about his own age, as though the two were somehow linked in Sinatra's mind, the body's advancing age, and perhaps Sammy Davis too, portending a compromised potency that I would argue is resolved in the blackface mirror. As ever, blackface is the realm of white fun, and combined with the Vegas pleasure dome of broads and boozing, both of which Sinatra heavily boosts in his stage patter, it offers access to a reaffirmed masculinity facing the hard realities of fifty years on Earth. It's worth saying that even blackface is sublimated in the exquisite swing of certain indelible moments, for instance the hard-luck song "One for My Baby." Saying so, though, doesn't mean Sinatra's hard-bitten persona isn't floated on the wings of racial desire. The relationship of persona to masquerade is vexed and complicated, and thinking about it with regard to Sinatra is useful since the persona seems so sui generis—three o'clock in the morning, no self-pity about the hard knocks, drink in hand, an adult singer for other adults, as Gary Giddins once remarked.[32] Basie's restraint and economy are the perfect foil for this act, which makes clear how much the persona abuts cross-racial masquerade. If only because the *Amos 'n' Andy* bits are so outrageous and laughable, Sinatra's singing persona seems all the more refined. It may well be, though, that the two masks have more in common than we thought.

Thomas Ferraro has argued precisely this in a fabulous essay, "Urbane Villager."[33] The dichotomy between the crass Jersey boozer and the classy singer of American standards is false, as it is between the racially challenged jokester and the swinging vocalist. Why, then, do writers routinely tout Sinatra's civil rights commitments, which are indeed there in the record—think of Sinatra's Popular-Front anthem "The House I Live In" (1945), or his refusal to stay in segregated hotels without Sammy Davis Jr.—while making no attempt to link these with the problematic performative politics that produced the Rat Pack?[34] I don't think you can excuse stage practice by way of the star's offstage persona. Bruce Springsteen is closer to the mark in hailing Sinatra's "deep blueness": "while his music became synonymous with black tie, good life, the best booze, women, sophistication, his blues voice was always the sound of hard luck and men late at night with the last ten dollars in their pockets trying to figure a way," a structure of feeling that for me encompasses not only

Sinatra's classiness and working-classness both but also his general indebtedness to canons of African American swing, the embrace of which Sinatra was all too aware of—hence his handling of it through blackface.[35]

Sinatra was always singing to his mother, John Gennari has forcefully argued.[36] She was the social-psychological root of his relation to his audience—hence its intimacy but also, Gennari suggests, its crisis of masculinity, always on display. Dino, Dean Martin, was the *real* gangsta; Sinatra was the mama's boy. Mammissimo, it's called, and it returns Sinatra to a primal scene every time he sings— to a mammy. Sinatra is always in a kind of masculinist drag. And it's this drag act—Frank Sinatra, an American, one of the roughs, a cosmos—that requires just a little help from his black friends.

"IN THE SAME WAY AS SINATRA, her closest male counterpart in terms of popularity and influence, Streisand brought a theme to her songs," writes Neal Gabler. That theme was more or less herself. "No matter what song she was singing, they were all 'Streisand-ized.'" The key to this, Gabler suggests, lay in the fact that she did not try to disguise her ethnicity in her diction; she always sounded Jewish.[37] This is so much the case that, as with Brooks's *The Producers,* blackness is until her 1970s work almost entirely sublimated: her strategy was to make Jewishness cool. If she drew for her effect in part on vaudeville coon shouters such as Sophie Tucker and Fanny Brice, her move was to make unconventional ethnic beauty the new black—as though to blow away entirely the remnants of Al Jolson, to refuse the lure of whiteness afforded by the black mask. And this she does, until 1971, when she turned away from the American Songbook to more contemporary sounds, not least Laura Nyro's "Stoney End," her first number-one single since 1964's "People." The retrieval of certain of Streisand's signature stylistic features by Amy Winehouse (Egyptian eyeliner and beehive hairdo, not vocal approach) brings out some of this blackness-turned-brassiness. In many respects Streisand's is the least conflicted two-faced mirroring in this chapter because when she looks in the mirror (as she does in a great many of her films, from her first all the way to *The Mirror Has Two Faces*), it is hard to make out anyone else.[38]

When Barbra Streisand emerged in the early 1960s with a persona equal parts Judy Garland and Fanny Brice, she produced something not seen since around 1910, where I began: a propulsive, even violent white-ethnic appropriation of popular American (which is to say significantly "black") song that was nothing if not political. This is hard to remember from here, after all of her ill-advised contempo gambits, her lame duets with too many third-raters, her films' cringe-inducing narcissism, her sodden arrangements of the worst the culture industry has to offer. What's bad about her has always been inseparable from a certain pleasure in her work—namely, an extremity of self-love, a *necessary* self-love perhaps, that amounts to a colossal drama of musical vulnerability and will pulled from the primordial racial mix of American music. Streisand approaches everything in the vein of the tour de force, as though hitting the note and overdoing the color were a matter of life and death—the voice as will and idea. This tends to induce a frisson of embarrassment at precisely those moments when she comes across as most moving, most defiantly Jewish, or most melodramatically involved in a lyrical-emotional dialectic of desire and loss. Our cringing is part and parcel of Streisand's achievement.

Who else has had the audacity to act out the simple desperation of our drive for recognition, and the talent and wit to pull it off? The titles of her television specials alone tell the story: *My Name Is Barbra* (1965), *Color Me Barbra* (1966), *The Belle of 14th Street* (1967), *A Happening in Central Park* (1968) (er, namely, that she performed there), *Barbra Streisand . . . and Other Musical Instruments* (1973), *Funny Girl to Funny Lady* (1975), *Barbra: With One More Look at You* (1976), on and on, up to *Barbra Streisand: Timeless* (2000) and well beyond. Narcissism is the *point,* and if it's embarrassing, she can take it. Consider, for one early example, 1963's "Cry Me a River"—the very first song on her very first album. The sense here of Lotte Lenya shaking hands with Bjork ought to give us a sense of Streisand's radicalism in its moment, however continuous she seemed with Broadway convention (listen to the almost Johnny Rotten–esque way she careens beyond the boundaries of the song at the end of "Lover, Come Back to Me"). As Armond White has written, Streisand "went at these songs as if to destroy them—or at least their middle-class, respectable, hierarchical culture—in order to make this art form

her own. . . . She scaled the edifice of showbiz (carving her own im-
primatur) with nothing like respect for the form, just reveling in
music and emotion and the chance to be different."[39] The political
stakes of this aesthetic project, moreover, are perfectly in tune with
the emotional drama of "Cry Me's" persona—a two-front strategy
with major musical consequences. Her self-assertion in song and in
song history almost unhinges the whole thing, and in an exemplary
rock 'n' roll way. Take another key example, "Second Hand Rose." "Pi-
anaa," "poils," "noive": if the inspired nasality doesn't convince you
she's not just playing this for novelty, then how about that last pun
on "avenue"—the Yiddish "nu"? Hey Mr. Arnstein, here I am: "Don't
Rain on My Parade" begins where "Cry Me" ends, which is saying
something.

There's a lot of weather in Streisand's music—"Soon It's Gonna
Rain," "Right as the Rain," "When the Sun Comes Out," "Like a
Straw in the Wind," "Where's That Rainbow," "Don't Rain on My
Parade," "On a Clear Day," "A Piece of Sky," "Autumn," "Kiss Me in
the Rain"—even "Cry Me a River" and "Evergreen" have something
of an environmental cast. Perfect for the cyclonic emotions and rock
'n' roller-coaster psychic tempests Streisand's songs enact. But perfect, more importantly, for an artist who's never really been able
to split off the object-world from her inner struggles. This world-
conquering self-inflation goes down easy in a male artist like Bob
Dylan; why does it appear unseemly when the singer is a woman?
Female *ressentiment,* because in Streisand's case it seems so *formally*
biting relative to the show-tune tradition from which it stems—in
contrast to which, Dylan's liberties were already embedded in the
blues and Guthrie veins he worked—in this case carries a major
abrasive force. This is why, as Robert Christgau remarked several
decades ago, Streisand usually ruins pop songs that devolve upon a
gentle poignancy or irony.[40] Willful narcissism is an "unprestigious"
or "ugly" feeling, as Sianne Ngai might term it, and it is key to Streisand's claim on her material, and our attention.[41] Streisand *owns*
the intensity of envy with which she approaches the world; look at
me, she says, forget about you; I'm the weather itself! It's mortifying,
but it's not false. And while I'm celebrating its critical or "negative"
force, I don't want to suggest that it is easily recuperable: it's a highly
equivocal thing, as off-putting as it is thrilling. Like the rain.

Shooting so high that at any moment it might be brought low, Streisand's persona, for all its amplitude, is defined by its vulnerability, its blues—one part of her long-standing appeal as a queer icon. She so much wants to be loved, and wants so much of it, that pain and longing always lurk in the shadows. Here again Streisand's strategy works at the level of both song and career; her tales of desire stalked by failure, disappointment, or abandonment become little allegories for the industry stakes of an obnoxious Jewish girl from Brooklyn with a fascinating nose. She stayed too long at the fair and couldn't find anybody to care; her daddy never could have known / she'd be successful and yet so very much alone. This eager heart of hers is singin' lover where can you be? He comes at last; love has its day; that day is past; he's gone away. She cried a river and now it's his turn; somebody's raining on her parade; all her stuff is second-hand. Looking for salvation, looking for love, she goes down the Stoney End, though she never wanted to go. Even though she's miserable since she fell for him, she can't get him out of her heart. It's raining, it's pouring, her love life is boring. Memories may be beautiful and yet what's too painful to remember she just chooses to forget. All this, plus you don't bring me flowers anymore.

Indeed, one reason Streisand may be so often reviled is that she's seen as owner of the phallus, not just its partner. Hence the gigantic, robotic Mecha-Streisand of *South Park* fame, or all the talk about her extensive sexual conquests, from Omar Sharif to Bill Clinton. But the music makes clear, I think, how uncertain a proposition this is and how desperate is her claim on self-possession. In Streisand's hands this redounds to a primary, necessary narcissism: Streisand's overarching, sometimes overreaching, vocal ambitions. These are often fulfilled and often stunning, but they come at the expense of not only her dignity but ours as well. The pleasure of her major melodramas and minor tantrums comes by definition in the unrespectable *outwardness* of the emotions she objectifies. One just isn't supposed to find oneself so goddamn charming or important. The effect of such a musical gambit, I would argue, is to bring shock or commotion to the listener and thereby, as has been said of everything from the Kantian sublime to Barthesian *jouissance,* transform a threat to the system into libidinal pleasure. Her world-historical overearnestness (think "People" or "Send in the Clowns"), to say

nothing of the intensity of her jokey self-regard (think the whole of
What's Up, Doc?), suggests a primal envy: in Melanie Klein's sense,
"the angry feeling that another person possesses and enjoys something desirable"—from, say, the pop-song canon to a never-ending
string of goy-boy toys—"the envious impulse being to take it away or
spoil it."[42] Streisand's music is all about the breathtaking nakedness
of this impulse, with hardly a thought, in her best work, about trying
to conceal it. Our pleasure in the "spoils" of Streisand's career therefore moves in a realm beyond "the pleasurable in [a] narrow, culinary,
bourgeois sense," which is exactly what's guilty about it.[43]

Guilty is the title of Streisand's 1980 duet album with Barry
Gibb, a partner to whom she returned for her album *Guilty Pleasures*
(2005). In Streisand's music as elsewhere in life—this may be what
she was put on the planet to show us—there is no pleasure that *isn't*
guilty. This is less the pleasure of racial appropriation than of sheer
self-assertion, though appropriation is unavoidably there in Streisand's soft-rock and disco maneuvers, as it is in certain of Streisand's
unrecognized epigones—Stefani Joanne Angelina Germanotta, say,
Lady Gaga, another queer icon, who appeared in blackface on the
cover of *V* magazine and whose teamwork with Beyoncé (the song
and video for "Telephone" [2010]) and others makes her, with Amy
Winehouse, Joss Stone, Lily Allen, and many more, yet another
"daughter of Al Jolson," in the words of Kandia Crazy Horse, a tradition of women singers involved for at least a century now in what
Daphne Brooks terms "sonic blue(s)face performance."[44]

THE TWO-FACED-MIRROR double bind has been virtually the
grand theme of the band Steely Dan. In their defining decade of the
1970s especially (and to a lesser extent in the wake of their 2000 re-
grouping), Donald Fagen and Walter Becker have been consistently
and cleverly alive to the caste-based usages and disparities driving
their own band's jazz-, funk-, and R&B-derived music. In many of
their songs, cowriter and lead singer Fagen seems to be channeling
Michael Rogin's work on blackface Jews before the fact; in some
ways he was there first. Fagen and Becker, after meeting as students
at Bard College, became New York Brill Building songwriters near
the end of a remarkable tradition going back to Jerry Leiber and

Mike Stoller in the early 1950s and including Doc Pomus and Mort Shuman, Burt Bacharach and Hal David, Neil Sedaka and Howard Greenfield, Carole King and Gerry Goffin, Barry Mann and Cynthia Weil, Jeff Barry and Ellie Greenwich—one music-industry equivalent, in other words, of Neal Gabler's Jewish Hollywood. If this tradition helped boost black careers from those of Big Mama Thornton to the Drifters to Dionne Warwick to Aretha Franklin, its songwriting practices also borrowed liberally from African American musicking, vaudeville, chitlin' circuit, R&B, and the rest (and fantasies thereof—according to Kenny Vance of Jay and the Americans, the great Jerry Leiber would coach vocal groups by slinking and dancing around the office, transforming himself into "that guy that he wanted them to imitate. I had never really seen anybody break character like that. I had never really seen anybody transform himself into a black guy.").[45] Leaving the Brill Building behind, their group named after the strap-on dildo in William Burroughs's *Naked Lunch*, their first album (*Can't Buy a Thrill*) titled after a line in a Bob Dylan song, Fagen and Becker came on with extreme hipster self-consciousness, their crystalline arrangements an almost Adornian "immanent criticism" of the Los Angeles music industry and its racial rigors from which they subsequently emerged. As Living Colour guitarist and Black Rock Coalition cofounder Vernon Reid put it in conversation with Greg Tate,

> Steely Dan is the manifestation of the white Negro made rock, made jazz, made pop. . . . In their aesthetic they're masters of the kind of crafty bad-is-good linguistic doublespeak realized in their blues . . . the ultimate jaded-hipster / post-beatnik clique whose songs are an oblique catalog of obsessions, twisted lives, the pleasures and dangers of underground economics. They probably have the most hit songs devoted to a life of crime outside of hip-hop in pop. They also chronicle a kind of noirish disillusionment with the romance of the American ideal: like Bogart playing Philip Marlowe, or Otis, "Sitting on the Dock of the Bay"; forever brokenhearted and forever haunted. Their song "Any Major Dude" is about a more experienced hustler having the compassion to share the dark knowledge

any hustler would. . . . The fact that there's so much about the American racial dynamic in their music is a great gift.

Rightly lauding the band's subtle, sly, self-deprecating, and world-weary humor, Reid locates the ethos of "hustlers who are running out of time" that so often provides their songs' subject matter but that also perfectly describes their unavoidably racially opportunist creators—and they know it. They continually make light of their own immersion in that opportunism; from *The Royal Scam*'s "Kid Charlemagne" (1976): "You are obsolete / Look at all the white men on the street"! Hence Reid and Tate's assessment of Steely Dan as the "redemption of the white Negro."[46]

The band has gone to honorable lengths to be as scathing at their own expense as possible (one of their best post-2000 songs is called "What a Shame about Me"). One example among many: the title song from the album *Pretzel Logic* (1974) is cast in a relatively straightforward blues format, rare for a band notoriously fond of intricate and arcane chord changes and arranger's tricks. "I would love to tour the Southland," announces the singer (two times per blues form), "In a traveling minstrel show";

> Yes I'm dying to be star and make them laugh
> Sound just like a record on the phonograph
> Those days are gone forever
> Over a long time ago.

Reversing the logic of mechanical reproduction, invoking a history of racial / mechanical mimicry from minstrelsy to the record we're listening to, the band consigns it all to a history they know was far from over a long time ago. Verse two concerns Napoleon, lonely still on that hill, another long-gone figure unless he brings to mind Richard Nixon in 1974. "They say the times are changing but I just don't know": finally coming out and doubting outright a historical logic closer to pretzel than arrow. In appropriated blues form, on a record featuring a Duke Ellington cover ("East St. Louis Toodle-oo"), a riff stolen from Horace Silver (on "Rikki Don't Lose That Number"), and a tribute to Charlie Parker ("Parker's Band"), these lines come off as extremely self-knowing, essentially theorizing the predicament the band enacts. "Deacon Blues" from the album *Aja* (1977) is the other chief white-Negro anthem, with its protagonist's decision to

> Learn to work the saxophone
> I'll play just what I feel
> Drink Scotch whiskey all night long
> And die behind the wheel.

Other variations on this theme include *Gaucho*'s "Babylon Sisters" (1980), in which a going-down-slow louche lizard drives with a pal out Sunset Boulevard to the coast for commercial sex with young black women, and, a personal favorite, "Haitian Divorce" from *The Royal Scam*. Babs, a white woman estranged from her new husband, takes a trip to Haiti to get away; she's there for the party, and party she does when she sees "Charlie with the lotion and the kinky hair." After a tearful reunion with hubby back in the United States, a baby comes along but grows "in a peculiar way":

> It changed, it grew, and everybody knew
> Semi-mojo
> Who's this kinky so-and-so
> Papa go.

The Haitian divorce predicated on a cross-racial jones is amusingly underscored by an intentional musical solecism—the song is written not as a Haitian compas or merengue but in reggae form. Well before that later noble crew the Beastie Boys, the Dan were sampling sounds in ways that blew back in their white-ethnic faces: fun with deconstruction.

Semi-mojo: what we might think of as one of the finest and funniest characterizations of artists caught up in new-immigrant antinomies of attraction. The antithetical force of primal mirroring always throws things a little off; for all the revealing symmetries that buttress such solidarities, the results are most often just a bit more partial. Cross-racial identification and collaboration born of shared marginality too often amount to eating the Other.[47] The mirror is convex, its reflection always skewing the image, the gazers' visage looming larger than that of their object of desire. The most self-conscious of these artists know this and make that knowledge part of the act. The rest don't even make it to the semis.

CHAPTER 4

HOUSE OF MIRRORS

The Whiteness of Film Noir

IN THE FINAL MOMENTS of Edward Dmytryk's *Murder, My Sweet* (1944), the police offer private dick Philip Marlowe (Dick Powell) the priceless jade necklace Marlowe has at last recovered for his wealthy client. The chief object of mercenary desire in the film and therefore a figure for the corruption and deceit of its dramatis personae, the necklace also suggests an Oriental(ist) languor whose fruits could now be all Marlowe's. Marlowe declines: "No thanks," he says; "it's wrong for my complexion." We are given to understand "complexion" first and foremost in the moral sense; Marlowe has beaten the forces of greed and graft that threaten to swamp him no less than the roués, quacks, idle rich, and petty mobsters by whom he is surrounded. In another and equally pressing sense, though, Marlowe has remained true to a racial physiognomy, that of whiteness, which indexes his pristine soul.

Film noir—"black film," as French critics first dubbed it in 1946—has long fascinated observers with its interest in darkened frames and darkened lives. But the specifically racial means of noir's obsession with the dark side of 1940s American life has been virtually ignored. Perhaps this should come as no surprise: raced metaphors in popular life are as indispensable and invisibilized as the colored bodies who give rise to and move in the shadows of those usages. Yet not to call attention to film noir's fairly insistent thematizing of spiritual and cinematic darkness by way of bodies beyond the pale is to persist in a commonsense exploitation enacted by black-and-white films (running from roughly the early 1940s to the middle 1950s) stressing the unwholesome predicaments of whites and accepted by a rich subsequent history of commentary on them. No less than the white-ethnic entertainment traditions I have outlined, indeed part and parcel of them, Hollywood noir deepened a practice of screen mirroring by which racial tropes and the presence of African Americans shape the sense and structure of U.S. cultural products that on the face of it have nothing to do with race.[1] The informing presence in the American imaginary of racial difference, which amounts to little less than a constitutive condition of cultural articulation, not surprisingly suffuses a cinematic mode known to traffic in black hearts and minds. At a moment when bold new forms of black, Chicano, and Asian activism and visibility confronted resurgent white revanchism and vigilantism, film noir's relentless cinematography of chiaroscuro and moral focus on the rotten souls of white folks constantly though obliquely invoked the racial dimension of this figural play of light against dark. Here the black mirror throws back such a supremely critical and subversive portrait of postwar white selfhood, such a corrosive and charged picture of interracial imbrication, that it must finally be disavowed. The black mirror is in turn the vehicle of that disavowal. The entire genre plays like the crashing house of mirrors that concludes Orson Welles's *The Lady from Shanghai,* and I think Welles knew it.

Criticism of film noir since the 1940s has variously sensed the form's uses of otherness. In the French critical notice that brought "film noir" into our vocabulary, that otherness is chiefly moral or psychosocial—a preponderance of crime, violence, obsession, and guilt—the "dark" side of the white Western self.[2] Nicholas Ray's *In a Lonely Place* (1950), for one, associates its protagonist Dixon Steele (Humphrey Bogart) with all of these, though his actual culpability is left in some doubt. The Stateside burst of critical activity on noir in the late 1960s and early 1970s, which brought the form firmly into the orbit of American critical allure, took for granted this emphasis and began to expand on its innovative stylistic expressions.[3] Paul

Schrader went so far as to claim that noir was characterized primarily by its emphasis on visual style. First noting the hardened sociopolitical mood of the 1970s that precipitated an embrace of noir's thematic affinities (8), Schrader acutely observes the peculiar cinematic attack 1940s films made on their own political moment: "[*film noir*] tried to make America accept a moral vision of life based on style. . . . *Film noir* attacked and interpreted its sociological conditions, and, by the close of the *noir* period, created a new artistic world which went beyond a simple sociological reflection, a nightmarish world of American mannerism which was by far more a creation than a reflection" (13). In Schrader's account, the stylistic recurrence in noir of night scenes, shadows, oppressively composed frames, odd angles of light, actors dwarfed by overly prominent surroundings, complex chronologies, and the like (11) is itself a negation of the corrupt society responsible for producing this corrosive cinematic response. Given a social prod, in other words, noir comes back with style. Although the world of noir is bleak, stylistically it is (as Richard Poirier once called American literature) a world elsewhere; we confront it in forms that transcend its perils. What Schrader calls film noir's "shades of black" are strategies of artistic othering meant to surmount the cynicism, meaninglessness, and psychosis that they nonetheless portray.

If the blackness of style is seen here as a kind of clear-eyed, panicky refuge—which only extends earlier critics' celebration of noir's bringing the dark to light in what Mike Davis calls noir's "Marxist cinema *manqué*"[4]—many critics have on the contrary seen the frightening "other" side of American life portrayed in film noir as crucially reliant upon the villainous and villainized women to be found there. E. Ann Kaplan's collection *Women in Film Noir* first established the way in which the faithless, ruthless women in noir exemplify and perform the dark deeds that signify the underside of the self that upstanding men must refuse in the interest of self-preservation.[5] Female power is the quite apparent crime these women represent, and noirs typically require that power to be renounced, compromised, or destroyed. Noir men like Walter Neff (Fred MacMurray) in Billy Wilder's *Double Indemnity* (1944) often fall prey to them, thereby succumbing to the "darkness" noir firmly associates with feminine wiles. The feminist critique of noir constitutes the most far-reaching account of the self's partitioning (into good/masculine and evil/feminine) in this run of American films, and without it our understanding of noir would be impoverished indeed. My own work follows in its tracks, and since the processes of identification and disavowal that I will explore here usually involve an overlapping series of gender and racial feelings, feminist work on noir has already begun to ask the sorts of questions whose answers, I believe, require a racial component. My purpose is to ask why, as yet, no one has challenged the association in these films of the self's and society's darkness with a racial dimension and why that dimension in the form of striking black appearances on film has seemed merely marginal, local, insubstantial. Even Joan Copjec's collection *Shades of Noir,* which specifically attempts to place noir within more specific urban and political topographies, does not trouble the racial unconscious of noir possibly at work in its very title.[6] The opening pages of Manthia Diawara's contribution to the Copjec anthology—on the way noirs by current black directors work classic noir's codes to their own purposes—have a clear sense of the racial metaphorics of noir's "shades," but this sort of analysis is not undertaken between the volume's covers.[7]

Diawara rightly remarks the interanimation of noir's stylistic, moral, and implicitly racial concerns. "[A] film is *noir* if it puts into play light and dark in order to exhibit a people who become 'black' because of their 'shady' moral behaviour" (262). The slippage in Diawara's own exact epigram—"black" racially or morally?—clues us into the ease with which racial mirrors are both literalized and dissipated; or rather, since both racial and moral senses here are metaphorical, it shows us how elusive yet coherent is the metaphorical character of racial definition; such slippages indicate, then, the ready use-value and real centrality of racial tropes despite their emanation from the margins of white texts and Caucasian lives. In this the figurations of race work like most important features of the psycho-symbolic domain; as Peter Stallybrass and Allon White have written, the "most powerful *symbolic* repertoires" of bourgeois societies are situated at their "borders, margins and edges, rather than at the accepted centres"; they reprocess, displace and condense, perform the labor of the signifier on the social formation's boundary-defining events, materials, and relationships and thrust them to the center

of its socially symbolic narrative acts; there are no simple correspon-
dences or one-to-one relations here.[8] And indeed the apparent
marginality of racial Others in the postwar U.S. social formation
(whatever their absolute centrality to the latter's labor and culture)
might encourage us to dismiss any seemingly racial associations in
film noir as merely coincidental, tricks of demography, the ruses of
metaphor, when in fact such metaphorical ruses and the presence of
black, Asian, or Mexican bodies confirm the central symbolic significance of color to the black-and-white world of many noirs, which re-
volve upon a racial axis that exerts great force at more key moments
in more films than can easily be written off as exceptions.

Whether it is the racialized dramas of interiority in such films
as Wilder's *Double Indemnity,* Delmer Daves's *Dark Passage* (1947),
Robert Rossen's *Body and Soul* (1947), George Cukor's *A Double Life*
(1948), Orson Welles's *The Lady from Shanghai* (1948), Max Ophuls's
The Reckless Moment (1949), or Ray's *In a Lonely Place;* the black,
Asian, and Mexican urbanscapes and underworlds of Dmytryk's
Murder, My Sweet, The Lady from Shanghai, The Reckless Moment,
Rudolph Maté's *D.O.A.* (1950), or Welles's *Touch of Evil* (1958) (the
self-conscious endpoint of noir and its racial tropes); the hysterically racialized family romances of Michael Curtiz's *Mildred Pierce*
(1945), Charles Vidor's *Gilda* (1946), *The Reckless Moment,* Otto Preminger's *Angel Face* (1953), Fritz Lang's *The Big Heat* (1953), and
others; or any of a number of minor reliances and major subtexts, the
troping of white darkness in noir has a racial source that is all the more
insistent for seeming off to the side. Film noir is replete with characters of color who populate and signify the shadows of white American
life in the 1940s. Noir may have pioneered Hollywood's unprece-
dentedly merciless exposure of white pathology, but by relying on
race to convey that pathology it in effect erected a cordon sanitaire
around the circle of corruption it sought to penetrate. Film noir res-
cues with racial idioms the whites whose moral and social boundaries
seem so much in doubt. "Black film" is the refuge of whiteness.

Double Indemnity

"No visible scars—till a while ago, that is": Walter Neff's account
of himself at the start of *Double Indemnity* refers us not only to the

gunshot wound administered by femme fatale Phyllis Dietrichson (Barbara Stanwyck) but again to the "complexion" of a man so scarred by his own deceit, violence, and cunning and so fully immersed in blackened cinematic compositions that his darkness threatens to manifest itself on his very skin. And, indeed, in a very stylish conceptual move Neff's shoulder wound bleeds through his suit jacket little by little throughout his voiceover flashback so that the stain, which appears black onscreen, grows larger with Neff's deepening involvement in passion and crime. Secluded after hours in the darkened Pacific All-Risk Insurance Company office building tended almost wholly by black janitors and custodians, Neff now inhabits the racial space *Double Indemnity* constantly links with his dark deeds.

Neff's adulterous partnership with Phyllis Dietrichson has from the beginning taken the form of a passage out of whiteness. Phyllis lives in a "California Spanish house" built, Neff surmises, in the mid-1920s, a moment of racial exoticism and primitivism perfectly appropriate to Phyllis's darkling designs. When Neff first sees her she's been sunbathing, and this historically relatively new white interest in fashionable self-othering, together with the redoubtable signifier of Phyllis's anklet or "slave bracelet," makes even more necessary the cosmetic masquerade of Phyllis's attempt, as she puts it, to get her "face on straight." Already the open visage of LA is consigned to the realm of mere appearances and masks, which hide the unwhite portents of no good. This diagnosis is clinched by the cut from this scene to the office of Pacific All-Risk's claims manager Barton Keyes (Edward G. Robinson), who is in the act of sniffing out Greek American Sam Garlopis's fraudulent insurance claim (he's torched his own truck—a foretaste of the "blacker" attempts at fraud to come). Garlopis's Greekness suggests his potential for moral lapse as his duplicity defines his excessive ethnicity; showing him the door, Keyes gives Garlopis a mock-naturalization lesson in how to turn the handle and open it. Moral rot is quite unself-consciously aligned with nonnormative Americanness in *Double Indemnity,* giving rise to a seemingly uncontrollable profusion in the film of ethnic, national, and racial signifiers, from English soap to Chinese checkers. By the time Neff says of his voiceover confession to Keyes that he is "not trying to whitewash myself," we know exactly what he means.

Perhaps he knows the attempt would be futile. Hasn't Keyes described Neff's job of salesman, by contrast to his own managerial brainwork, as a species of lowbrow "monkey talk"? And after Neff strangles Mr. Dietrichson from the back seat of Phyllis's car, doesn't he find himself under a great (literally blackening) shadow of vulnerability, the one that hobbles on crutches into the opening frames of the film? Isn't this compounded by his ultimate failure to put up a convincing "impersonation" (as Keyes calls it) of Mr. Dietrichson's Stanford-educated whiteness in faking the latter's accident? When Dietrichson's daughter Lola—herself a paragon of whiteness carrying on a dangerous, proscribed relationship with one Nino Zachetti, whom Lola meets clandestinely at the superbly patriotic (and parodic) corner of Vermont and Franklin Streets—begins to suspect Phyllis and her own erstwhile paramour Zachetti (ethnicity will out) of plotting her father's (not to mention her mother's) death, Neff takes her, by now unsurprisingly, to a Mexican restaurant to literally seduce her into silence. Such a figural crossing of the border perfectly conveys *Double Indemnity*'s sense of the iniquity to which Neff has sunk. Neff himself is now a moral resident of Phyllis's Spanish house.

There is no greater index of this fate than Neff's two alibis for the murder of Dietrichson. The first is the black garage attendant, Charlie, whom Neff visits in the parking garage to establish his whereabouts before exiting (by the service stairs Charlie himself presumably uses) to execute his plot. Phyllis consciously schemes on this basis, suggesting Walter take advantage of being "surrounded" by black domestic strangers. The second is the Westwood Jew, Lou Schwartz, whose name derives from the Yiddish word for "black" and whose status as another of the film's resident Others helps secure Neff's uncriminal whiteness while suggesting Neff's moral fall. Indeed what interests me about Neff's alibis is that they throw a critical light on the way white selfhood makes exploitative use of boundary-defining nonwhites even as they register the dark depths of Neff's spiritual condition. The character and color of Neff's excuses precisely indicate his moral otherness, his guilt. The same is true at the very end, when a black janitor, spotting a trail of blood on the floor, calls Keyes over to the insurance company to finger Neff in his office, the black presence here an embodiment of the outer darkness to which Neff has traveled and perhaps the visible sign of his guilt returning midconfession to indict him. It is no accident that Neff at the end wants to escape across the Mexican border.[9]

Film noir is a cinematic mode defined by its border crossings. In it people fall from (g)race into the deep shadows new film technologies had recently made possible. With the help of technical innovations such as the Norwood exposure meter (which for the first time could take a weighted average of light from all directions rather than a single direction), faster film stock, photoflood bulbs that permitted better location filming, antireflective lens coatings, and the like, film noir found a world in the dark.[10] The moral and visual passage into "shadiness," conjoining as it does states of psychological and social definition with the actual look of white skin on screen, almost by definition has a racial analogue in the American context; and it is for this reason that any understanding of the postwar U.S. cinematic apparatus—which, as Stephen Heath puts it, "hold[s] together the instrumental and the symbolic, the technological and the ideological"—must involve its racial economy.[11] Racial borders are invoked and implicated in social and representational ones, analogizing easily with and even providing a conceptual framework for Americans gone afoul of actual and cinematic laws. Hollywood lighting conventions demonstrate this multiplex drama of transgression. Richard Dyer has suggested that the lighting of white big-screen icons (such as Lillian Gish) has given their ethical purity a racially particular form, most especially in black-and-white film. Associations of worth and whiteness are by now so naturalized as to pass beneath conscious notice, and Hollywood has always exploited them. Commenting on the racial import of the brightly lit star, Dyer writes: "She is more visible, she is aesthetically and morally superior, she looks on from a position of knowledge, of enlightenment—in short, if she is so much lit, she also appears to be the source of light."[12] Filmic translucence—the people on screen literally have light shining through them—is aligned with spiritual hygiene, provided the people on screen are white. And it certainly helps if they are men, too, given the always available equation of radiant femininity (Rita Hayworth in *Gilda* [1946]), or at least a blonde wig (Barbara Stanwyck in *Double Indemnity*), with the entrapments of desire. But with the advent of noir even the women were mostly cast into blackness, living, like the men, in shadows that suggested their racial fall from Hollywood lighting conventions no less than they mimicked the moral transgressions onscreen. Notably, the exception to this rule in *Double Indemnity* is the innocent Lola, whose glowing white face at one moment evidently enchants Walter Neff in his condition of moral disrepair. More typically, the intensely shadowy scenes featuring Phyllis and Walter that plot and punctuate the film, from the drinks Walter makes in the gloom of his kitchen to their post-killing kiss in a shadow that bisects their heads to their final meeting in the near-total darkness of Phyllis's house, confirm their departure from social as well as stylistic norms.

Noir's crossings from light to dark, the indulgence of actions and visual codes ordinarily renounced in white bourgeois culture and thereby raced in the white imaginary, throw its protagonists into the predicament of abjection. Noir characters threaten to lose themselves in qualities that formerly marked all the self wasn't and that now unsettle its stable definition. Antisocial acts of lawlessness and passion, deceit and recklessness signify the state that, according to Julia Kristeva, makes borders irrelevant, repression inoperative, and the ego an Other.[13] Stable demarcation (moral, visual, racial) replaced by fluidity, straying, "going all the way to the end of the line" (as *Double Indemnity* has it), noir's abject selves meet the world without boundaries—no mere moral failing, since it involves disturbances around the disavowal of the mother in the formation of (principally masculine) gender definition and of the racial Other in the formation of white self-identity. The two converge in the opening shadow of Walter on crutches: his wounded manhood the result of Phyllis's duping control and finally the bullet she puts in his shoulder; his "blackening" the outcome of actions he is willing to perform for thrills, passion, and cold, hard cash. Thus does Neff say of his abject state after the murder that his "nerves were pulling me to pieces." Likewise, Phyllis's "black" widow role in several respects represents the film's worst white male nightmare: the former nurse of Dietrichson's first wife—an occupation resembling other of the service occupations in the picture, from the black office custodians to Charlie the garage attendant to the "colored woman" Walter says cleans his apartment—Phyllis mothers her charge badly enough to "accidentally on purpose" kill her (as Lola says) before becoming

Lola's evil stepmother and Dietrichson's scheming wife. It must indeed be said that Phyllis is so typical of 1940s Hollywood women that her boundary-loss, endangering poor Walter's own, is hard to perceive as abjection. And yet the illicit pleasures, fantasies of omnipotence, and thoroughgoing "rottenness" she inspires (as she herself says) are those attributes most imagined to have a black as well as female source. As Slavoj Žižek has observed, the formation of selfhood in white Western societies requires the remanding of the unspeakable powers of enjoyment—pleasure is by definition illicit and rotten—which are imagined to be the special privilege or province of racial Others and whose experience or return, therefore, threatens the white self girded by specifically racial negations.[14] *Double Indemnity*'s attempted escape from the iron cage of respectable morality that is the prime benefit and lure of whiteness reckons the racial component of its unrespectable pleasures. Villainizing the desires that drive the narrative, utilizing racial codes implied in moral terminologies and visual devices, film noir preserves the idea of whiteness its own characters do not uphold.

Why, other than the pathological social formation of white interiority, might this contradiction have been present in films of the 1940s? As many historians have observed, the decade's civil rights activism presaged the better-remembered struggles of the 1960s. A. Philip Randolph's massive March on Washington movement against discrimination in the wartime defense plants, begun in 1940, motivated Franklin Roosevelt to issue an executive order outlawing discriminatory hiring practices by defense contractors and to establish the (ineffectual) Fair Employment Practices Committee. In 1941 black Ford workers at River Rouge threw their weight behind the United Auto Workers, forcing the company for the first time to sign a union contract. The ranks of the NAACP began to grow in tandem with rising black political and economic desires—over half a million African Americans migrated out of the South between the opening up of defense hiring and the end of the war—and in 1943 the Congress of Racial Equality (CORE) was founded. The "double V" campaign endorsed by many black newspapers and civil rights organizations sent up the cry for a double victory over racism at home as well as fascism abroad. Hollywood itself felt the heat in 1942 when its major studio heads met with the NAACP's Walter White and agreed to reshape black movie roles in accord with the new times; this was the period of *Cabin in the Sky, Stormy Weather, The Negro Soldier, Crash Dive, Sahara,* and *Bataan* (all 1943). Lest we underestimate the white hostility toward this surge of activity, however, it is well to note, for instance, that at the same moment black noir writer Chester Himes was racebaited from the studios (Jack Warner proclaimed, "I don't want no niggers on this lot") and spent the war years working in defense plants, writing in *If He Hollers Let Him Go* (1945) and *The Lonely Crusade* (1947) of what he later termed the "mental corrosion of race prejudice in Los Angeles."[15]

In the long, hot summer of 1943, such militant disgust with unbending American racism took to the streets. Urban insurrections erupted in Harlem, Detroit, and twenty-five other U.S. cities. These were often labeled "zoot suit riots" because the black and Mexican youths so attired (in defiance, it might be added, of the War Production Board's rationing of cloth) were convenient targets of attack for the white servicemen and police whose violence often sparked such street combat. Pathologizing accounts of zoot subcultures were embraced as a means of defining the civilized self, as in Kenneth Clark's 1945 study of what he called the "zoot effect in personality" (published in the *Journal of Abnormal Psychology*). Writers from Ralph Ellison to Chester Himes to C. L. R. James and others grasped the political urgency of apparently trivial squabbles over sharkskin; meanwhile the LA City Council voted to make wearing zoot suits a misdemeanor, facilitating the easy arrest of Mexicans and blacks. The concurrent ordeal of the Sleepy Lagoon trial, in which seventeen pachuco zoot suiters were convicted of and imprisoned for murder under extremely questionable legal circumstances (they were later released and the charges dismissed after the protests of the Sleepy Lagoon Defense Committee, with whom Orson Welles was allied), secured the image of the Mexican juvenile delinquent, sparked fears of internal subversion by a foreign conspiracy (the prosecution insisted on the "Oriental," pre-Columbian source of the Mexicans' "total disregard for human life"), gave rise to "Li'l Abner" creator Al Capp's widely read and virulent "Zoot-Suit Yokum" comic strip in which a zoot suit manufacturers' conspiracy is happily thwarted (perhaps inspiring a *Los Angeles Times* caricature of Japanese premier Tojo in a zoot), and symbolized the beginning of the Chicano movement in America. Meanwhile, as is well known, hysteria about the yellow peril and the internment of the Japanese in California completed this picture of panicked whites in dubious battle.[16]

As one key contribution to our understanding of this period has put it, race displaced class as "the great, unsolved problem in American life."[17] Noir responded to this problem not by presenting it outright but by taking the social energy associated with its social threat and subsuming it into the untoward aspects of white selves—a mirroring that produced a sharply critical gaze even as it deflected social malignity onto dark Others. The "dark" energy of many of these films is villainized precisely through the associations with race that generated some of that energy in the first place. Film noir is in this sense a sort of whiteface dreamwork of social anxieties with explicitly racial sources, condensed on film into the criminal undertakings of abjected whites. This may explain two otherwise random or unremarkable matters in *Double Indemnity*. The first is Nino Zachetti's portrayal as a juvenile delinquent, a UCLA dropout dallying with both Phyllis and Lola and liable at any moment to boil over with hotheaded anger (as he does when he finds Neff has given Lola a ride to meet him downtown—Zachetti's natural setting). He might as well be wearing a zoot; what we have instead is his ethnically marked name. Zachetti may be a mask (anarchist or fascist either one) for fairly legible social anxieties afoot in the United States of 1943. The LA zoot riots occurred in June; *Double Indemnity* started filming there in September. The second matter is the site of Neff and Phyllis's faking of her husband's death, the Southern Railroad observation car. The train, not least because of the active leadership by A. Phillip Randolph of the Brotherhood of Sleeping Car Porters, was in the popular imagination associated with its black caretakers, the redcaps, Pullman porters, and cooks who serviced railroad lines across America.[18] Randolph, recall, had used his power to desegregate the defense plants in 1941. Now *Double Indemnity* only follows James M. Cain's novel in placing the train at the center of Phyllis and Walter's plot; but the scene in which Walter mimics Dietrichson's death prominently features several black railroad workers, both sentinels and servants of the racially marked space of the coach; and not one of these workers, interestingly, casts an identifying look at Neff's face as he boards the train. *Double Indemnity* seems to suggest again the importance of black help in marking off the white self—hence their aid in this alibi—even as the black attendants betray Walter Neff's criminality by their very presence. Neff has chosen the perfect place to evince his "black" heart.[19]

Double Lives

Rarely are the raced double lives of noir protagonists made as plain as in George Cukor's *A Double Life* (1948). Actor Tony John (Ronald Colman), who has great difficulty leaving his stage roles in the theater, takes on the part of none other than Othello. He is reluctant at first because he knows he will as usual get too involved in the character; but the shadowy glimpses he catches of himself in mirrors and dark plate glass (which make casual use, by the way, of noir's links between dark lighting and blackness) convince him there's an Othello somewhere inside him. This is perhaps intimated early on when Tony says that becoming ambitious as an actor meant "tearing myself apart, and putting myself together again, and again," papering over who knows what inner life and preconscious rages. These come out as the play's run continues. Tony falls into a romantic intrigue with a waitress, Pat Kroll (Shelley Winters), whom he chokes to death Othello-style when he becomes jealous of the affair he suspects between his former wife Brita (Signe Hasso) and the play's publicity agent. (The racial underpinnings of this crime are stressed, if unconsciously, when Pat, in response to Tony's raving about all the assumed nationalities he carries within him, says: "I got mixed blood too.") The publicity agent's decision to link the unsolved murder to their production of *Othello* presses on the substantial interpenetration in *A Double Life* not only of art and reality but of black rage and white crime, particularly given that it is Tony's violent rage when he hears of this scheme that helps reveal his misdeed. Carrying the theatrical metaphor fully into the world, the police arrange to have a waitress disguised as Pat confront Tony, his horrified response to which confirms his guilt. Wandering the black streets in his blackened state, Othello's expos'd: Tony impales himself on a knife during his character's final speech and dies, like Othello, of the uncontrollable rage released by his alter ego.

Usually the presentation is a bit more oblique. Delmer Daves's *Dark Passage* (1947), for instance, plays cosmetic changes on *Double Life*'s conceit. Vincent Parry (Humphrey Bogart) has been wrongly imprisoned for murdering *his* wife and escapes from San Quentin. Although the film is interested in exonerating Parry, it nonetheless saddles him with a complexion he must leave behind because it is recognizable. We don't see Parry/Bogart's face for over an hour into the film because its pivot is the cosmetic surgery that results in Bogart's face and the chance at a redemptive new life. The suspicious, as-good-as-guilty "true" visage is invisible to us, either not shown within the frame or (of course) heavily shadowed; the key taxi ride that will lead Parry to the plastic surgeon who transforms his mug is indeed a striking instance of "blackening," as Bogart sits in a deep, localized shadow. For all intents and purposes, that is, Parry is guilty, and, moreover, his new face does nothing to keep blackmailers and conniving snitches off his back. Parry's "true" complexion only goes underground, first submerged under the emphatically white bandages that help heal his post-op face and then under the face so naturalized as Bogart's. Against the film's wishes, perhaps, and despite our glimpse in a newspaper photograph of Parry's old face, we can't help feeling like there's something *under* there, waiting to manifest itself, or continuing to cause the ongoing difficulties from which Parry has so much trouble extricating himself. When Parry and his newfound sweetheart, Irene Jansen (Lauren Bacall), escape to Peru, one gets the idea that this exigency was quite necessary and, given the territory and its racial associations in noir—the Mexico of Robert Mitchum and Jane Greer's illicit love in Jacques Tourneur's *Out of the Past* (1947), for instance, or the implicit Latinizing of Glenn Ford through his close association with Uncle Pio (Steven Geray) in *Gilda*'s Argentina—quite fitting.

The racialized interiors of whites in extremis erupt most tellingly in such key texts in the noir series as Max Ophuls's *The Reckless Moment* (1949), Nicholas Ray's *In a Lonely Place* (1950), Rudolph Maté's *D.O.A.* (1950), and Robert Aldrich's *Kiss Me Deadly* (1955). *D.O.A.*'s Frank Bigelow (Edmond O'Brien) has only a few days of life left to discover who it was that poisoned him with iridium. His

Fig. 5. Humphrey Bogart in deep shadow, *Dark Passage*, 1947, Warner Brothers

search leads him back to a jazz dive featuring heaving, sweating black musicians—the bar where a masked unidentified stranger had dropped the lethal dose in his drink. Cast into the roles of both detective and victim, Bigelow is animated as well as, eventually, suffocated by a substance whose source is thematically proximate to blackness. (George Marshall's *The Blue Dahlia* [1946] activates similar ideas with its nightclub's jukebox "monkey music.") *Kiss Me Deadly* is perhaps the most typical in its casual exploitation of racial tropes; the inner states and plot predicaments of detective Mike Hammer (Ralph Meeker) are conveyed at crucial moments through black characters and counterparts. The film opens with Nat King Cole on Hammer's car radio singing "I'd rather have the blues than what I got"—a lyric that will later reappear in a low moment of Hammer's trajectory. The song portends the depths to which Hammer (and for that matter the postatomic world of the film) will be plunged, and it is amusing that Hammer feels he has to flick it off as he approaches a police roadblock, the Law beyond whose barricades he himself will cross as a man of the "jungle," in the film's phrase. Hammer's whiteness may contrast with the Greekness of his yammering friend Nick, who runs around hysterically, salivating over nice sports cars and shouting "Va-va-voom" like the automobiles with which the so-called grease monkey is literally identified before he is murdered by having one lowered, crushingly, onto his chest. Yet despite these intermittent differentiations that confirm Hammer's racial stature—not to mention one in which a seductive mob moll named Friday tempts Crusoe Hammer—Hammer is figured as black at significant moments in the narrative. At a time of crisis Hammer loses himself in, of all things, a black lounge, where a woman sings "I'd rather have the blues than what I got" while Hammer drowns his sorrows to such a degree that he has to be carried in all his abjection out of the club. What's more, the climactic scene where Hammer fights the mobsters who have drugged and caged him in a bedroom plays out against the radio broadcast of a boxing match we can only guess is the one involving black boxers whose venal promoter, Eddie, Hammer had earlier visited in search of information. With some wit, but with little sense of the racial stakes, Aldrich stages Hammer's big fight as a black one, occurring on the other side of the barricade to which Hammer routinely travels yet from which he can always somehow return. Something of this dynamic is at work in Robert Rossen's richer boxing noir *Body and Soul* (1947), which, for all its sympathetic interest in the interracial relationship of Charley Davis (John Garfield) and Ben Chaplin (Canada Lee), makes Charley's success dependent on his difference from Ben—or as Michael Rogin puts it, "Charley tries on, to free himself from, Ben's role."[20]

In a Lonely Place is more complex in its racialized suggestiveness. The cranky, hard-drinking, and, it is rumored, disturbed and violent Hollywood screenwriter, Dixon Steele (Humphrey Bogart), invites a warm and quick-witted hat-check girl back to his place so she can narrate to him a bestselling novel from which he is supposed to craft a script. She is apparently open to romance but Steele sends her away in a taxi, whereupon she is murdered and Steele presumed the murderer. His alibi comes in the form of Laurel Gray (Gloria Grahame), with whom he quickly becomes involved and with whose aid and comfort his writing recovers its power. His jealousy and temper, however, make her uneasy, and she begins to suspect his involvement in the murder; Steele's volatility increases as he senses her doubts. Laurel tries to leave the day of their wedding, when Steele finds her and nearly chokes her to death. At this moment the police call with the news that the hat-check girl's killer has been discovered, but all that has transpired between Steele and Laurel has doomed their relationship. Two crucial moments in this drama, both seemingly en passant and innocuous, go to the heart of Steele's situation. The first occurs when Steele, upon hearing of the hat-check girl's death, decides to send flowers but doesn't want to take them himself to her funeral. So he asks a black man spraying down the sidewalk in front of a florist if he will deliver two dozen white roses. This would appear not only to alleviate Steele's feelings of guilt (with white roses) but to implicate by association the black man in a crime Steele may sense he is perfectly capable of committing. The anonymous black figure signifies Steele's dark past relationships with women, whom we're told he's beaten and otherwise abused; Steele atones by sending his black double with white (and whitening) flowers. The second such moment is when Steele and Laurel go to a club where they are serenaded by a black chanteuse (Hadda Brooks), who mediates white heterosexual desire *Casablanca*-style—with Grahame and a black woman forming an equal and opposite homosocial bond from that of Bogart and Sam in the film of eight years before. The unnamed singer expresses Laurel's love for a man whose volatility may well kill it. If guilt and the capacity for violence are figured through Steele's deal with the black man, the fond hopes raised and then dashed by Steele's obsessive love are intimated in a black woman's song. I would argue that Steele's love for Laurel is indeed a failed search for his own innocence; she is after all his alibi as well as his lover, and when she espies his dark underside, Steele loses everything he originally sought in her. It is interesting to learn, then, that the working title of the film was *Behind This Mask*.[21]

There is also, incidentally, an odd moment of Hollywood self-consciousness located in a quip by Steele's agent, Mel Lippman (Art Smith), who softens the blow in telling Steele he doesn't like the latter's filmscript by saying: "But then I'm the one who told Selznick to drop *Gone With the Wind!*" Here the Jew references his good racial taste—no plantation tradition for Lippman—while acknowledging what Michael Rogin reads as the Jewish role in black exploitation onscreen from *The Jazz Singer* (1927) forward, including *Gone With the Wind* (1939). In also equating Steele's script with *GWTW*, Lippman inadvertently highlights Steele's racial usages in *Lonely Place* itself.

The Reckless Moment departs in an important sense from these films because it uses a black figure to present the forbidden aspects of a white woman's life and thus complicates its implicit racial exploitation. The film tells the story of well-positioned Lucia Harper (Joan Bennett), who, in the absence of her traveling husband and in an attempt to keep her daughter Bea from being implicated in the accidental death of a suitor (Bea hits him with a flashlight to stave off an attempted sexual assault and he pitches over a railing), hides the body she has discovered on the nearby beach. Soon, however, blackmailers inform Lucia they possess love letters from Bea to the suitor, Darby, that they're sure the police would want to see. Martin Donnelly (James Mason), one of the blackmailers, falls in love with Lucia and tries to protect her, ultimately killing his partner in blackmail though he is wounded in the fight. He leaves with his partner's body before Lucia can stop him, and at this point Lucia and her black maid Sybil (Frances Williams), whom we have seen several times around the house, follow Donnelly with Sybil at the wheel. They find Donnelly at the scene of his wrecked car, dying but not before he can confess to both of the killings and exculpate Lucia's daughter. The role of Lucia's maid Sybil is another fine illustration of a black character occupying the margins brought on to do major thematic work. Lucia's "recklessness"—her independence and incipient adulterous desire for Donnelly as well as her self-sacrifice in the effort to protect her daughter—is figured succinctly by her maid, the perfect black mirror. Not only does the black woman whose very name calls up cliché notions of penetrating wisdom divine the desire for Donnelly from which Lucia shrinks and expresses it for her ("I always liked him," she says); she also stands as a black double for Lucia's descent into reckless self-sacrifice, the only role we see Sybil play in all her table-setting and assiduous caretaking. Sybil's commanding the wheel at the picture's climactic moment (Lucia curses her failure of autonomy earlier, saying "I should've driven my car") is the fullest expression of Lucia's agency in love and trouble—completes that agency, rounds it out, and makes it plainer than it is respectable for a white woman to do. That is, the maid here is a figure not of aversive lampoon but of sympathetic identification, and the sympathy encompasses the interracial friendship as well as the female power and mobility for which Sybil finally stands as much as Lucia does. For all that, however, Sybil's gifts of knowing and action, which manifest Lucia's own plot and cement white and black female solidarity, nonetheless exile the black woman from the womanhood so brightly depicted at the film's end, when white suburban Law—the law-abiding harmonious family telephoning long-awaited Daddy on Christmas—has been, however ironically, restored.

What such films appear to dread is the infiltration into the white home or self of unsanctioned behaviors reminiscent of the dark figures exemplified in the 1940s and early 1950s imaginary by zoot suiters, pachucos, and Asian conspirators. In this, they firmly support Elaine Tyler May's thesis that the postwar family was invented as a bulwark against this sort of dread.[22] And, though the films constituted a corollary invention, what they apparently cannot do is completely shove these figures out of the picture, though noir may stave off their most fearsome shapes or place them in a safely removed elsewhere. Many films, *The Reckless Moment* included, imagine a dark underworld that is out of sight and (usually) downtown—thus when Lucia is scheduled to meet in a bus station with the blackmailer Donnelly, one shocking frame has their conversing faces suddenly obscured by a working-class Chinese man's face in the very close foreground, as though to suggest what's out there and what, too bad for both of them, has crept *in here*. Or there is the Chinatown to which Elsa Bannister (Rita Hayworth) tries to escape in the last section of Welles's *The Lady from Shanghai* (1948), a film that, for all its interest in narrating ethnicity (from Welles's "Black Irish" O'Hara to the various national and ethnic descents of his sailor associates to the abused black maid Bessie to Arthur Bannister's "Manchester Greek" mother to Elsa's own sojourn in China), is not above playing stereotypes for a laugh, as during the trial scene when two Chinese women in the courtroom, speaking sotto voce in their native tongue, break it off when one blurts "You ain't kiddin'!" Chinatown and Elsa's Chinese gang herald the darkness of L.A.'s would-be El Dorado and summon as well the ghastly nature of Elsa's fatal plotting—though the famous final scene in the Chinese funhouse displays how easy it is for such racialized corruption to gnaw at the hearts of whites split (by the iconic funhouse mirrors) into dissociated parts and then completely shattered when the mirrors are shot to bits. As Welles's O'Hara puts it, all these dark souls were "chewing away at their own selves." For his part, Marlowe in Dmytryk's *Murder, My Sweet* (1944) refuses the temptations of this encroaching underworld of Asian erotic enchantments (the Asian dancer in the Coconut Beach Club at whom thug Moose Malloy takes a long look) and Asian styles of adornment (the jade necklace, Ann Grayle's subtly Orientalist makeup). But they have certainly laid claim to the gruesome crew by whom he is surrounded. From Peter Lorre's feminized Far Easterner Joel Cairo in John Huston's *Maltese Falcon* (1941) to Jack Palance's diseased and rat-like Blackie in Elia Kazan's *Panic in the Streets* (1950), noirs populate a sinister subterranean milieu with roving racialized phantoms.

The great fear, indeed, is that racial Others, far from residing comfortably downtown, keep coming back into white lives in film noir. Untoward behavior and its seemingly inevitable racial echoes indelibly mark the white homes—and films—for which race typically exists somewhere else.

Domestics and Domesticity

This return of the oppressed is clear enough from the foregoing examples, but it is on spectacular display in films anxious to narrate the fate of the white family. *Murder, My Sweet,* like several important noirs, depicts with varying degrees of self-consciousness a specifically racial deviance at the center of the domestic sphere. The film opens with the reflection of a dark phantom in Marlowe's office window; turning around, Marlowe discovers its source in (still fairly dark) Moose Malloy (Mike Mazurki), who speaks with what sounds like a Mexican accent and whose suit looks suspiciously zoot-like. Moose is in search of the similarly ethnically resonant Velma Valento, and takes Marlowe to the bar Florians—which, because of some burned-out neon, has become, appropriately, "Forins"—to locate her.[23] This plot cross-cuts the one in which Marlowe tries to recover a lost jade necklace for some wealthy clients, Mr. and Mrs. Grayle. The circle of people revolving around Mrs. Grayle is rotten in ways already suggested by their lust for jade, but a quack psychoanalyst, Amthor, delves deep into Mrs. Grayle's past and predictably finds much with which to blackmail her. As Mrs. Grayle admits, "I haven't been good, not halfway good." Finally, since, as Marlowe says, "I had to know how the jade figured," he convenes all the parties in the Grayles' beach house only to discover, in a furiously doubled racial whammy, that Mrs. Grayle *is* Velma Valento. And to think Marlowe nearly succumbed to her seductive come-ons! In the storm of bullets that ensues, Marlowe escapes with scorched eyes that come too close to a firing gun, this near-castrating close call externalized in the eye patches he wears during his movie-long voiceover flashback and the implicitly mixed-race predicament of the Grayle family implicated in its demise.

Mothers, wives, and lovers are typically abjected in noir, but their symbolic racialization clinches the genre's sense of immanent familial dysfunction. Otto Preminger's *Angel Face* works an interesting twist on this scheme, since it literally places a bickering Japanese couple within the home they serve and whose topsy-turvy gender relations they evoke. The Japanese wife, who, it is alleged, has become "too American" and so no longer obeys her husband, is the counterpart of daughter of the house Diane Tremayne (Jean Simmons), who takes too much power into her hands and finally kills her father and stepmother by—significantly—tampering (like a mechanic) with their car. *Angel Face* laments a putative postwar loss of innocence; Diane's real mother was killed during the war (there goes the nuclear family), and Diane's villainized discontent, which finally eventuates in the auto-death (in both senses) of Frank Jessup (Robert Mitchum) and herself, signifies an America mired in Orientalized triviality, female usurpation, and domestic war—for all of which the rancorous Japanese couple stands as a perfect figure. The Japanese wife hasn't become too American; the Americans are turning Japanese.

But it is Michael Curtiz's *Mildred Pierce* (1945) that perceives this sort of threat most compellingly. Mildred (Joan Crawford) determines to win her daughter Veda's love by affording her all the available luxuries, and when this desire is stymied by Mildred's husband, Bert, Mildred leaves him. Her departure, for which alone (as Pam Cook has rightly argued) she is demonized, sends her into a dizzying narrative space of female autonomy and ultimate defeat and punishment.[24] Mildred takes a waitress job to provide financially, but when Veda finds out about it she is scornful and wounding— which goads Mildred into plans to open her own restaurant. The restaurant is wildly successful—former boss Ida (Eve Arden) now comes to work for her, and Mildred's initial investment blossoms into a whole chain of restaurants—though the success depends on the help of Monte Beragon (Zachary Scott), a mysterious roué whom

Mildred marries. Unthrifty Monte ultimately bankrupts the chain of restaurants and seduces Mildred's daughter Veda to boot. Mildred catches them together and Monte disavows his interest in Veda, whereupon Veda kills him; Mildred attempts unsuccessfully to take the rap. What interests me about this rise and fall of an independent woman is that her trajectory is shadowed at every step by her black maid Lottie (Butterfly McQueen), who figures the proletarian fate Mildred is driven to beat and whose disabling likeness suggests Mildred's darkest dread. Lottie is the kitchen worker who always lurks somewhere inside Mildred, less the representative of hard labor Mildred is perfectly willing to perform for her own interest than of the "nigger work" this labor echoes. Hence Veda's joke when she discovers her mother's waitressing: she has Lottie don Mildred's work uniform to wear about the house. The two women are versions of each other. At one key moment their mirrored lives are suggested by Lottie's remark that the opening night of Mildred's restaurant feels like her own wedding night, which overlays as it distinguishes the two women's trajectories. Not surprisingly, then, Mildred increasingly uses Lottie for the differentiating purposes of household adornment, as a sort of failed mistress of the house who puts on ridiculous airs. Even in this device, however, one sees the parodic likeness between the women amid the instituted difference.

This ambiguity in the meaning of Lottie (all that Mildred has left behind or her hidden double?) is overdetermined by the resonance of "gypsy fortune teller" Beragon. (On one occasion, in one of the film's many racist cracks, when Ida speaks of Beragon's "big brown eyes," Lottie, bustling in the background, mistaking the remark as a reference to herself, says "Beg pardon?") He is a strange sort of raced creature—his lineage, which he says includes Spanish and Italian blood, is made the subject of fascination and discussion—now close within the family circle as Mildred's husband. His counterpart is Mildred's other daughter, Kay, whose memorable little "gypsy dance" perhaps indicates her danger to the family and therefore presages her death. Beragon's racial aura is in some sense aligned with his profligacy, and it is joltingly played on in the striking scene where we see him kiss Veda. This kiss, a nearly incestuous one, is yet portrayed as its opposite, as a kind of interracial seduction, with Beragon hovering in full shadow over the virginal

Veda, the metaphorics of interracial sex hardly submerged at all in the lighting of the scene. It is an extraordinary moment, and it raises the question of just what the racial crime is here. Is it mere racial mixing, or is the racial Other living much closer to home, within it, part and parcel of the incestuous act which might seem diametrically opposed to the racial threat from outside but in fact only accesses it? There's an Other in the house. Thus when Monte is killed, Mildred is not automatically restored; on the contrary, the brilliant final scene, in which Mildred and her first husband walk out into the light of day past two washerwomen scrubbing the floor on their knees, suggests that the hard labor and its racial dimension she seems to have left behind is not distant at all but are, as it were, part of the frame.

The question arises as to why a Marxist cinema manqué at a time of left-liberal high tide in Hollywood would fall so readily into dubious racial devices. To be sure, good racial intentions abounded. Edward Dmytryk and Adrian Scott conceived of their anti-anti-Semitic picture *Crossfire* (1947) as a frankly "heroic" measure (as Scott put it in a memo to RKO) to stop "anti-semitism and anti-negroism," a casual linkage that is interesting in itself (Scott references the lingering anti-Semitism after the war as well as anti-black rioting). The Sleepy Lagoon Defense Committee, which featured a variety of screenwriters, directors, and actors (I have mentioned Welles, who was joined by Rita Hayworth, Canada Lee, Ring Lardner Jr., and others), was perhaps the most intense organized antiracist initiative of the time, but there were also projects such as the UAW-sponsored antiracist cartoon film *The Brotherhood of Man* (1947) and the occasional civil rights noir (Joseph L. Mankiewicz's compelling *No Way Out* [1950], or Robert Wise's politically interesting but cinematically dull *Odds Against Tomorrow* [1959]). However, not only did the House Un-American Activities Committee's hearings on Hollywood cut into left enthusiasm after 1947, the studios began to retreat from liberal race pictures such as *Gentleman's Agreement* (1947), *Pinky* (1949), and *Home of the Brave* (1949); RKO, for example, backed out of a plan to allow Scott and Dmytryk to make a movie about black life. And needless to say, black stereotypes and foolish bit parts persisted undisturbed both out of noir (e.g., Disney's *Song of the South* [1943]) and in (Anthony Mann's otherwise honorable *Border Incident* [1949] contains a pair of thuggish Mexican goofs), and would probably have done so without either the blacklist or studio complacency. As Larry Ceplair and Steven Englund write:

> The radical screenwriters were like so many Penelopes: in the daytime, at the office, they unraveled the efforts of their evenings and weekends as political activists, for the movies they wrote reinforced the reigning cultural ethos and political-social order. No Communist (or, for that matter, liberal) screenwriter, of course, would have agreed to write an obviously anti-black, anti-Semitic, or anti-brotherhood script, but then Hollywood turned out very few movies which were so blatantly racist that they offended accepted social definitions and values [*sic*]. Racial and ethnic stereotypes abounded in every writer's scripts, however, as did the myths of democracy, justice, material success, etc., which were intricately interwoven into the film genres which dominated in Hollywood.

This latter point, it seems to me, is the key one, not only for the Hollywood left but for all of noir's creators. Racial dominance was so built into Hollywood industrial and generic norms that a new cinematic mode built on human corruption and darkened compositions created, as an almost inevitable by-product, a new intensity of racialized imaging—an intensity undoubtedly overdetermined by a climate of felt social decline, cultural degradation, moral brutality, and spiritual defeat: what Joseph Losey, one of noir's left directors, called "the complete unreality of the American dream." In this sense, left-liberal perceptions of decline harmonized with center-right ones in imagining white selves cast into a nightmarish world of otherness and racial aliens.[25]

Us as Them

The oft-stated view of Orson Welles's *Touch of Evil* (1958) as film noir's epitaph makes sense also because of its brilliant playing with the notion of white border crossings. Welles demonstrates an awareness in *Touch of Evil* of everything I have tried to argue about film noir's sense of the intimate proximity of racial Others to American national identity and its hysterical (if unconscious) attempts both to use and to exile them in portraits of white corruption. In Welles's counternarrative, the Law comes in the form of Mexican Mike Vargas, whose nemesis is the bloated, criminal, white police detective Hank Quinlan (Welles). That Vargas is played in brownface by none other than ur-American Charlton Heston—Charlton Moses, as Edward Said once called him in reference to his part in the blockbusting film of two years earlier, *The Ten Commandments* (1956)—wittily communicates his not-white and yet not-quite-Mexican status with which Welles teases our perception of justice's racial tropes.[26] Vargas's brownness curiously (and, I think, purposely) oscillates in and out of focus as we forget and remember that this is after all Charlton Heston, undermining fairly definitively the simple demarcation of whiteness and its equation with the Good. The film takes internal and external border-construction as its very theme; Vargas is newly married to a white woman (Janet Leigh), and the two are seen walking across the Mexican border into the United States at the film's start (in one of the most heralded long takes in cinema history).[27] Does America's designation of "us" and "them" adequately parse moral distinctions between right and wrong, the film asks us, and it mixes up the racial clues we might use to answer the question. Quinlan's attempted framing of Vargas and other Mexicans only cements our sense of Vargas's moral purity and exposes the processes of projection and abjection that would pin white criminal activities on dark bodies and deploy them as racial metaphors for white crimes. When, after crossing the border, Vargas and his wife, Susan, kiss for the first time in, as Susan says, "my country," the bomb explosion that tellingly interrupts their forbidden kiss is a self-conscious turn away from black films of racial marking and disavowal.

4

CHAPTER 5

WHITE LIKE ME

Racial Trans and the Culture of Civil Rights

My first afternoon as a Negro was one of dragging hours and a certain contentment.

—John Howard Griffin, 1961

AT THE START OF A JOURNEY into the "night side of American life," which would furnish the material for his *Black Like Me* (1961), John Howard Griffin strikes up a relationship with a black shoe-shine "boy."[1] Griffin, a white investigative journalist turned black by medical treatments, sunlamp sessions, and black stain, asks for lessons in the ways of Negro life. The shine man, Sterling Williams, "promised perfect discretion and enthusiastically began coaching me." "'You just watch me and listen how I talk,'" says Williams. "'You'll catch on'" (27). Apparently he does catch on, for Williams soon certifies Griffin's racial transmutation. "Within a short time [Williams] lapsed into familiarity," Griffin writes, "forgetting I was once white. He began to use the 'we' form and to discuss 'our situation.' The illusion of my 'Negro-ness' took over so completely that I fell into the same pattern of talking and thinking. It was my first intimate glimpse.

We were Negroes and our concern was the white man and how to get along with him" (28).

Though seemingly at odds with the politics that define the tradition of blackface minstrelsy, Griffin's six-week performative stunt and the noirish narrative that issued from it comprise one of its more notable sympathetic instances. It is as though noir's oblique racial figurations and occasional commitment to civil rights narrative had taken a U-turn and plunged full force into blackness (a film version of Griffin's book was to appear a few years after). No disembodied affair, the ventriloquizing or indeed purloining of black and other cultures has often taken the form of a homosocial dance of white men and black, though female performers have also gotten in on the act, reworking the terms of homosociality and summoning the specter of sexuality that male exponents have mostly attempted to repress. Whether blackface performers' fascination with enslaved singers and dancers, Carl Van Vechten's mimicking and brokering of Harlem Renaissance writers, white-Negro Norman Mailer's coverage of Muhammad Ali, pretty much everybody's engagement with Barack and Michelle Obama, or other examples unto infinity, white men's intercourse with black men has been fraught with masculinist rivalry as well as "compromising" desire, while white women's forays into cross-racial mimicry, from vaudevillian Sophie Tucker to journalist Grace Halsell (author of *Soul Sister,* a white woman's version of *Black Like Me*) to comedian and singer Sandra Bernhard (especially but not only her one-woman show and film, *Without You I'm Nothing*), have tapped a long vein of fantasy about black women's sexuality and location within the sex/gender system. These performances have injected potent fantasies of the black body into the white Imaginary—and thence into the culture industry. In thus giving shape to the white racial unconscious, such scenarios actually found the color line even as they witness the latter's continual transgression. Griffin's "We were Negroes" is the perfect summation of this dynamic: renegades together on the "night side," Griffin and Williams enact a racial encounter that is both age-old and implicitly affirming of the Berlin Wall they have momentarily agreed to scale.

Griffin's example still has its adherents—Gerald Early and Nell Irvin Painter, for example, who testified to its importance fifty years after the fact, perhaps echoing Stokely Carmichael's long-ago avowal that Griffin's work was indeed important—for white people.[2] It so set the tone for white engagement with the politics of race in the 1960s that we ought to pause to consider its broadly influential structure of feeling. *Black Like Me* took the available materials of white cross-racial interest and used them to new ends; it is the crucial historical switchpoint between a racist history of cooning and a new politics of sympathy. And while the cooning still hasn't gone away, the book inaugurated an enduring liberal civil rights template that captured the imagination of Halsell, for one, and reemerged as late as 2015 in the form of Washington State NAACP head Rachel Doležal, who was revealed to be a white woman passing for black.[3] Why and under what circumstances does such a practice occur? My assumption is that blackface is a charged signifier with no coincidental relationship to the racial politics of culture in which it is embedded. Why, we might ask, this literal inhabiting of black bodies as a way of interracial solidarity in cultures of civil rights activism? Griffin's civil-rights-era contemporary Leslie Fiedler famously argued in *Love and Death in the American Novel* (1960) that white male U.S. writers have been continually possessed by the idea of two men, one white and one dark, alone together in the American void, Ishmael and Queequeg, Huck and Jim, Kirk and Spock, Dre and Eminem, who apparently fulfill a white need to be "Negroes" together. The historical fact of whites literally assuming a "black" self, the eternal and predictable return of the racial signifier of blackface, is one performative analogue of this, and I would argue that it began and continues to occur when the lines of "race" appear both intractable and obstructive, when there emerges a collective desire (conscious or not) to bridge a gulf that is, however, perceived to separate the races absolutely. Griffin's *Black Like Me* and the other instances exemplify this structure of feeling, whether in their earnest antisegregationist politics or more derisive garden-variety but still obsessive attempts to try on the accents of "blackness" in fraternity stunts and celebrity Halloween parties.[4] Blackface acknowledges a racial relationship that to whites seems neither satisfactory nor surmountable; this acknowledgment owes in turn to perceptions of "race" and its signifiers that we would now term "essentialist." To black up is to express a belief in the complete suturing together of the markers of blackness and the black culture, apparently sundered from the dominant one, to which they refer.

Today neo-blackface performance is all around us, usually (but not always) without the blackface—race thus detached from culture visibly but still in many ways sutured to it invisibly.[5] Blackface reifies and at the same time trespasses on the boundaries of "race." This doubleness is highly indicative of the shape of American whiteness.[6]

The historical formation of whiteness has received exemplary scholarly inquiry over the last two decades or more. Accounts of white cultural expropriation and travesty, however, have too little discerned the way the liberal imagination generally is informed by just such mirroring and fantasy. *Black Like Me,* as I noted in my first chapter, and as Glenn Ligon has illustrated, offers something like the ground zero demonstration of this fact, particularly its extraordinary mirror scene, to which I will return. (Not for nothing is the study of Griffin by his friend Robert Bonazzi, who married Griffin's widow, titled *Man in the Mirror.*) Even white liberalism could not exist without a racial Other against which it defines itself and that to a very great extent it takes up into itself as one of its own constituent elements. By way of several instances in the history of imaginary racial transformation, I want to look at some American constructions of whiteness—in particular this curious dependence upon and necessary internalization of the cultural practices of the dispossessed. My chapter title implies that Griffin's *Black Like Me* is precisely misnamed, that what Griffin uncovers in his trip through the black South are the contours of straight Caucasian maleness. But to engage this and other post–World War II racial trans texts cast in the form of middlebrow nonfiction social commentary and personal reportage, we must acknowledge the American racial and sexual histories and cultural products that implicitly structure them. By this I mean nineteenth-century blackface performance and other similar artifacts, but I mean also and more variably the transitioning from one racial or sexual category to another, a process in which sex / gender identity is deeply implicated. In examining the racial unconscious of American liberal whiteness, I assume the close connection between it and sex / gender formation. Reaching for the Other in oneself addresses an internal colonization whose achievement is fragile at best and that is often exceeded or threatened by the gender and racial arrangements on which it depends. The contradictions of racial liberalism, as in the case of Mark Twain, under-gird white self-making even as they unsettle the terms of social and legal custom.[7]

I WILL NOT TARRY long over testimony from white nineteenth-century blackface performers, but some of it is richly suggestive. Ben Cotton claimed that he would sit with and study black men on Mississippi riverboats: "I used to sit with them in front of their cabins, and we would start the banjo twanging, and their voices would ring out in the quiet night air in their weird melodies. They did not quite understand me. I was the first white man they had seen who sang as they did; but we were brothers for the time being and were perfectly happy."[8] "Brothers for the time being" is an inadvertently contemporary self-description for those who seek, however briefly, to pass as black (indeed it echoes the title of Alisha Gaines's study of the phenomenon, *Black for a Day*). To be a brother for the time being has usually been a bohemian rhapsody, the desire of minstrel men, jazz heads, funk followers, white rappers, and other cross-cultural savants. From Dan Emmett to Mezz Mezzrow to Eminem and beyond, there is a clumsy courtship of black America, a fantasy of living on the outside or down low.[9] Encounters with black folk— slave or dancer or vendor or music-maker—have given bohos their access. T. D. Rice allegedly used an old black stableman's song and dance in his first 1830s "Jim Crow" act. Dan Emmett, founder of the first 1840s blackface band, learned to play the infantry drum from a man nicknamed "Juba"; dancer Frank Brower learned his dances directly from black men.[10] Sometime blackface songwriter Stephen Foster no doubt had contact with black wharf workers and boatmen in his hometown of Pittsburgh, but according to his brother he experienced black church singing firsthand through a family servant, Olivia Pise, "member of a church of shouting colored people."[11] A century later, Jewish jazzman Mezz Mezzrow so thoroughly crossed over into the world of black musicians that he felt his lips, his hair, and his skin had undergone a racial transformation.[12] Greek bandleader, musician, and songwriter Johnny Otis identified as black across a fifty-year career playing with and promoting musicians including Big Mama Thornton and Jackie Wilson.[13] Like many of the above artists, the man who would become rapper Eminem, Marshall Mathers

III, has made much of the way his debased class status threw him into the company of African American friends and performers.[14] These white Negroes launched a pattern inherited, rather against the odds, by civil rights stalwarts no less than their culture-industry counterparts.

"Born theoretically white, we are permitted to pass our childhood as imaginary Indians, our adolescence as imaginary Negroes, and only then are expected to settle down to being what we really are: white once more," as Leslie Fiedler once wrote of "theoretical whites."[15] There is something to the idea that dominant codes of U.S. whiteness, particularly but not only white masculinity's embroilment in fantasies of black masculinity during the onset of pubescence, carry a melancholic remainder of racial otherness. Hence the "achievement," the racialized laboring, the performativity, the self-impersonating, as I will suggest below, of being "white once more." If blackface performance reproduced or instantiated a structured *relationship* between the races, racial difference itself, as much as black cultural forms, this difference was as internal as it was external. To assume the mantle of whiteness, the evidence seems to say, is not only to "befriend" a racial Other but to introject or internalize its imagined special capacities and attributes. The Other is "already in us," a part of one's (white) self, filled out according to the ideological shapes one has met in one's entry into the culture. The (racial) splitting of the subject actually makes possible one whole area of white desire, the contours of white fantasy—but it also ensures that the color line thus erected is constantly open to transgression or disruption.[16]

This is the combined vigilance and absorptive cross-racial fascination of North American whiteness, and it underlies white liberalism no less than white racism. Deviser of boundaries, "raced" signs, and practices by way of an engagement with the Other, the blackface performer or crusading white-Negro heir, in Julia Kristeva's words, "never stops demarcating his universe" not despite but because they have opened racial boundaries and confines to fluidity (8). This holds as true for those who seek to pass as it does for those who are loath to stay long (if at all) on the Other side of the line: Mezz Mezzrow's autobiography, for instance, is nothing if not anxious to solidly confirm his "Negro" bonafides, not least through jive expression (right down to an appended jive glossary)—which only makes him seem all the more anxiously white. The abjection so redolent of pre-oedipal archaism is reactivated amid the guilty pleasure of white-to-black trans, but it is masked with a racial logic. More than a little of this dynamic appears to be at work in the case of Rachel Doležal. If "whiteness" seems generally or at least putatively to depend upon the renunciation of enjoyment, the body, an aptitude for pleasure, with the Other seen as especially gifted in this line (with regard to food, music, bodily exhibition, and sexual appetite), Doležal's upbringing was by her account quite forcibly renunciatory. Her severely strict rearing by fundamentalist Christian parents put her in search of something better, which she found first in her adoptive black siblings and then black college friends and mentors, and later her (now ex-) husband; she went on to enroll in an MFA program at Howard University. Organizing her enjoyment and self-definition through the Other whose identity she herself assumed, Doležal not only accessed a new relation to the world but took it upon herself to push for African American civil rights, ultimately as head of the Spokane chapter of the NAACP, perhaps cleansing herself of the guilt of transitioning but in all respects apparently earnest in the effort of demarcating her universe, disavowing with fervor her appropriation even while enacting it. This is rather precisely the mixed erotic economy of American whiteness.[17]

If this structure has meant, for one thing, that the dispossessed become bearers of the dominant classes' "folk" culture, their repository of joy and moral passion and general revivification, one of the less recognized shapes of that revivifying has come in white access to sympathetic identification with black dispossession. Whether it precedes or follows a dominative logic of pleasure, an identificatory white antiracism in blackface guise is in fact its twin. This perhaps explains Doležal's feeling of being home at last upon racially crossing over, and her embrace of the rearranged kinship structure by which she has more or less adopted two of her parents' four adopted black children as her own. And according to Doležal, it all began with black hair: braiding her black sister's hair, then having hers done in various black-styled braids and weaves, she pursued her inner blackness through the pleasures of bodily expression. Much has been made of Doležal's having sued Howard while a student there for discriminating against her whiteness, which makes her turn to black seem all the more opportunistic. To my mind, there is hardly any contradiction here: both moves are underwritten by white privilege, both seek recognition from her chosen people.[18]

Doležal's position on her adopted blackness rather amusingly aligns with Walter Benn Michaels's arguments about the incoherence of racial identity. Michaels has long scored social-constructionist arguments for being tacitly biologistic; passing is logically impossible, according to Michaels, because you can't "secretly" be your former race once you pass if race is in fact a social construction: you just are your new racial definition, with no blood residue about it.[19] Michaels would logically have to consider Doležal to be as black as she regards herself. It is indeed essentialist to remind her she is white—which is why antiessentialism is not really the point. Doležal and Michaels both disregard the desperately uneven historical pressures, the burdens and opportunities inequitably distributed to white and black, in the formation of racial regimes, no matter how "false" the category of race may be; these pressures cannot be readily circumvented either by breezily casting off whiteness or by newly shouldering blackness, nor can they be reduced to tidy syllogisms. True, Doležal crossed over not for fame or money but for inner peace as well as social justice and race leadership; in this, she suggests, she is trans, not unlike Caitlyn Jenner (though Doležal doesn't push the analogy), and such commentators as Melissa Harris-Perry (on MSNBC), Kareem Abdul-Jabbar (in the *New York Times*), and scholar of passing Allyson Hobbs (ditto) have come variously to her defense. Doležal does ironically encapsulate in one body a long NAACP history of white patrons/allies and black race leaders. But this performance of identity is not so easily decoupled from the legacy of blackface. In assuming the privilege to speak for and as a black woman, she is nothing if not, at least in part, white once more.[20]

NORMAN MAILER'S "THE WHITE NEGRO" (1957), an extended riff whose mythologies are as telling as its analysis, is the garish post–World War II advertisement for this pose—freedom dreams, hipster division. As none other than Norman Podhoretz observed in 1958 of the white-Negro discourse of which Mailer's essay was the centerpiece: "I doubt if a more idyllic picture of Negro life

has been painted since certain southern ideologues tried to convince the world that things were just fine as fine could be for the
slaves on the old plantation."[21] Not a postdating or mere continua-
tion of antebellum racial cross-dressing but its genealogical legacy,
this postwar discourse—Mezzrow, the Beat writers, Elvis Presley's
early career, Mailer's hipster, Griffin's *Black Like Me,* and others—did
(in all its racial "modernity") reproduce the obsessions of certain
nineteenth-century *northern* ideologues but in racially sympathetic
form. To the extent that these obsessions weren't wholly continuous
with the dominant culture in the ensuing years of protest, they returned as farce in the late 1960s: Elvis's 1968 comeback TV special,
Grace Halsell's *Soul Sister* (1969) (Griffin's second-generation simula-
crum), and, in a crowning blow (to which I will return), Melvin Van
Peebles's *Watermelon Man* (1970)—in which Godfrey Cambridge in
whiteface plays a suburban racist who wakes up one morning to find
himself turned black. The steady backbeat of this trope and of white
Negroism generally since then—the movie *Soul Man* (1986); black-
folk-filled music videos and performances from Madonna to Miley
Cyrus; Lee Atwater's blues Republicanism and Bill Clinton's Elvis
ticket; Quentin Tarantino movies and white-Negro parodies (e.g.,
Malibu's Most Wanted [2003]); Vanilla Ice, Robin Thicke, and Iggy
Azalea—is as bewildering in its ubiquity as in its ideological vari-
ousness, but these instances and countless others only confirm the
original template.[22]

Mailer's piece codifies the renegade ethic of male sexuality conceived out of and projected onto black men—and always driven by a
rather transparent eroticizing of them—that informs the more than
metaphorical racial romance underlying one construction of American whiteness: "Knowing in the cells of his existence that life was
war, nothing but war, the Negro (all exceptions admitted) could rarely
afford the sophisticated inhibitions of civilization, and so he kept for
his survival the art of the primitive, he lived in the enormous present,
he subsisted for his Saturday night kicks, relinquishing the pleasures
of the mind for the more obligatory pleasures of the body, and in his
music he gave voice to the character and quality of his existence, to
his rage and the infinite variations of joy, lust, languor, growl, cramp,
pinch, scream and despair of his orgasm."[23] Mailer and other male
white Negroes inherited an affective paradigm whose self-valorizing

marginality and distinction require a virtual impersonation of black manhood. It is revealing that while the liberatory preoccupations of Mailer's existential errand are inexactly calibrated with either Griffin's *Black Like Me* or Elvis Presley, the shape of this white mythology looks pretty much the same in all cases. Its resonance is, for instance, succinctly articulated in white guitarist Scotty Moore's gleeful remark to Presley at one of the mid-1950s recording sessions in which Elvis first found his voice: *"Damn,* nigger!"[24] Nelson George has observed that Elvis was the historical referent Mailer missed in limning the "white Negro." Bringing to the stage the sort of "symbolic fornication" that for whites denotes "blackness," his hair pomaded in imitation of blacks' putative imitation of whites, Elvis illustrates the curious dependence of white working-class manhood on imitations of fantasized black male sexuality.[25] By the time of Presley's 1968 Christmas special, when after several years of tame movies and ho-hum singing he roared back in black leather on network television, trying desperately to recapture his audience, the doubled structure of the show intimated a familiar sublimation of the white-Negro racial deployment. Broadway productions of Elvis numbers (Elvis had not yet entered his Vegas period) alternate with an unplugged circle of Elvis and fellow musicians getting raw. In these latter scenes the black leather of his outfit defines the ambience; it refuses to slip from your mind; Presley himself remarks upon how hot it is. Particularly in a show dedicated to proving how foreordained and irrelevant is all the music since Elvis's early triumphs (stage patter at one point has Elvis damning with faint praise "the Beatles, the Beards, and the whoever"), its "blues" portions appear to mediate (against all odds and despite the artist's intentions) what had been going on in the streets by the time it aired in late 1968. That is to say, the split show structure suggests the meaning of the suit and the "blacker" performances: they are the "unconscious" of the production numbers—white as the whale—that surround them. In the leather-suited takes, and in cross-racially empathetic songs (however maudlin and embarrassing) such as the following year's "In the Ghetto," Elvis reveals his reliance even for resurrection upon "blackness." His enduring stature as one of *the* icons of white American culture, a fulfillment of the dubious potential augured by the comeback special's production numbers, clinches the necessary *centrality and suppression* of "blackness" in the making of American whiteness.[26]

Black Like Me turns this structure into social criticism. While Griffin has blacked up to beat his forebears, his is not a story of passing. He has only spotty interest in what black people think of him; his concern is with whites and how they will treat him in his adopted state. Whiteness is his standard: " 'Do you suppose they'll treat me as John Howard Griffin, regardless of my color—or will they treat me as some nameless Negro, even though I am still the same man?' " Griffin asks some friends, among whom, incidentally, are three FBI agents (10). It is the position of "nameless Negro," not member of any community one might care to name, that interests Griffin, and he does encounter his share of white aversion and aggression. He passes less into a black world than into a "black" part of himself, the remissible pleasures of abjection, triggered or enabled by white distaste and desire (some of which is his own—he speaks of the idea of turning black as having "haunted" him "for years" before undertaking his effort [7]). What he goes on to uncover are the contours of blackness *for whites:* contours he has externalized and thus indulges in his very disguise.

This racial logic underlies Griffin's whole enterprise. In revealing ways, *Black Like Me* is complicitous with the racial designs it sets out to expose. Griffin seems only dimly aware, for instance, that his disguise *is* an externalization, and yet there is evidence that his imagination of "blackness" colors him before his blackface does. Early on, pondering the dangers of his experiment, Griffin is gratified to find his wife ready, while he is gone, "to lead, with our three children, the unsatisfactory family life of a household deprived of husband and father" (9). That this is an unconscious reference to the reactionary construct of the female-headed black family soon to be terminally mythologized in Daniel Patrick Moynihan's "The Negro Family: The Case for National Action" (1965) is indicated by Griffin's other mentions of the sadly depaternalized black family—as in "[The black man's] wife usually earns more than he. He is thwarted in his need to be father-of-the-household" (90; see also 42). Even when Griffin is still white, that is, he is "black" inside; it is this part of his "makeup" that he explores in *Black Like Me.*

One need not look far for the sources of this concern in Griffin's text. Early in his days of blackness, Griffin, for reasons that appear as unclear to him as they do to us, walks down his hotel hallway in the early hours of the morning (he can't sleep) to the men's room. There he encounters two black men, one in the shower and the other naked on the floor awaiting his turn. Griffin writes that the waiting man "leaned back against the wall with his legs stretched out in front of him. Despite his state of undress, he had an air of dignity" (19). This rather anxious (and certainly cliché) assurance to the reader has its counterpart in Griffin's remark to the man: "'You must be freezing on that bare floor, with no clothes on'" (20). As if things weren't bare enough all around, the waiting man "flick[s] back the wet canvas shower curtain" and implores the bather to let Griffin wash his hands in the shower. (A nearby sink has been discovered to have no drain pipe.) Griffin hastily interjects:

> "That's all right, I can wait," I said.
> "Go ahead," he nodded.
> "Sure—come on," the man in the shower said. He turned the water down to a dribble. In the shower's obscurity, all I could see was a black shadow and gleaming white teeth. I stepped over the other's outstretched legs and washed quickly, using the soap the man in the shower thrust into my hands. When I had finished, I thanked him. (20)

Clearly the driving force here is the simultaneously fascinating and threatening proximity of black male bodies, beckoning, stretching, thrusting. If the accident of the scene's having occurred is not revealing, Griffin's retrospective mapping of it surely is. Moments like this put Griffin in the position of racial voyeur, allow him to confront the "shadows" of the white Imaginary. As with his tutorials with the shine man, Sterling Williams, their result is to encourage Griffin to prophylactically identify with black men; "I fell into the same pattern of talking and thinking," he says of Williams (28). Whether or not as a defense against interracial homoerotic desire, Griffin in any case mentally assumes and impersonates—one might almost say he "masters"—the position and shape of black maleness. Poised in his disguise between white subject and black object, Griffin enters "blackness" according to the dictates of white desire.

This indeed emerges from the many pages that are taken up with conversations a hitchhiking Griffin is forced to have with white men who pummel him with questions about his sex life. "There's plenty white women would like to have a good buck Negro," says one (86); another, a young man "who spoke with an educated flair" (86), opines that Negroes "don't get so damned many *conflicts*": "I understand you make more of an art—or maybe *hobby* out of your sex than we do" (87). This particularly scholarly driver eventually asks Griffin to expose himself; refused, he remarks: "I wasn't going to do anything to you. . . . I'm not a queer or anything" (89). Griffin's despair at such a predictable turn of events disguises the homosocial nature of the dialogues. For in these conversations, white men's interest in black male sexuality is mediated by but also identifies them with the white women black men are supposed to crave. In other words, the voyeuristic urge to expose the black man's body in congress with a white woman is quite cognate with fantasies of the forbidden coupling of black and white men—a coupling, after all, that Griffin has in effect been engaged in. These car scenes merely reiterate the shower scene, and implicitly place Griffin in the white male driver's seat as well as in that of the black passenger. Griffin's conscious distaste permits him both to distance himself from the debased discourse of which he is structurally the victim (the walking black penis that forms the object of white male desire) *and* to engage in that obsessive discourse through the pleasures of impersonation.

Leaving to one side *Black Like Me*'s stated intent of showing for the first time what it was like to be black in the segregated South—as though plenty of black-authored books had not investigated that predicament already—Griffin's text can be read as a story of what happens when this sexualized racial unconscious of American whiteness is not kept suppressed or partitioned. It is all very well to fetishize black male bodies, as Griffin does above and also when he remembers seeing black dockworkers in Mobile "stripped to the waist, their bodies glistening with sweat under their loads" (99). But it is quite another thing, Griffin finds, to inhabit a black body. The famous scene before the mirror that reveals his blackness to him for the first time reduces Griffin to total self-negation:

> Turning off all the lights, I went into the bathroom and closed the door. I stood in the darkness before the mirror, my hand on the light switch. I forced myself to flick it on.

In the flood of light against white tile, the face and shoulders of a stranger—a fierce, bald, very dark Negro—glared at me from the glass. He in no way resembled me.

The transformation was total and shocking. I had expected to see myself disguised, but this was something else. I was imprisoned in the flesh of an utter stranger, an unsympathetic one with whom I felt no kinship. All traces of the John Griffin I had been were wiped from existence. Even the senses underwent a change so profound it filled me with distress. I looked into the mirror and saw reflected nothing of the white John Griffin's past. . . . My inclination was to fight against it. I had gone too far. I knew now that there is no such thing as a disguised white man, when the black won't rub off. The black man is wholly a Negro, regardless of what he once may have been. I was a newly created Negro who must go out that door and live in a world unfamiliar to me.

The completeness of this transformation appalled me. It was unlike anything I had imagined. I became two men, the observing one and the one who panicked, who felt Negroid even into the depths of his entrails.

I felt the beginnings of great loneliness, not because I was a Negro but because the man I had been, the self I knew, was hidden in the flesh of another. If I returned home to my wife and children they would not know me. They would open the door and stare blankly at me. My children would want to know who is this large, bald Negro. If I walked up to friends, I knew I would see no flicker of recognition in their eyes.

I had tampered with the mystery of existence and I had lost the sense of my own being. This is what devastated me. The Griffin that was had become invisible.

The worst of it was that I could feel no companionship with this new person. I did not like the way he looked. Perhaps, I thought, this was only the shock of a first reaction. But the thing was done and there was no possibility of turning back. (15–16)

"White skin," to play on Frantz Fanon, is here obliterated by "black mask"—a possibility only available to someone who imagines skin color in the way Griffin apparently does, as completely constitutive of identity and entirely divisive of the races. The "newly created Negro" fears he has gone too far: "the black man is wholly a Negro, regardless of what he once may have been," an almost purely incoherent sentence that justly captures Griffin's extreme disorientation (16). Any sense of Du Boisian double perspective that chances to emerge—for instance, Griffin remarks that he "became two men, the observing one and the one who panicked"—melts away under the feeling of being "Negroid even into the depths of his entrails" (16). Fantasy here returns as frightening fact. What Richard Dyer calls the "hysterical boundedness of the white body" has been transgressed; while Griffin appears not to believe in the moral superiority of whiteness, he yet cannot let go of its powerful, life-preserving fixity: as he says, his inclination is to fight against his new reality.[27] Griffin's disorientation is true to Lacan's account of the mirror stage, though it produces a distorted one; his response reveals the (b)lack upon which whiteness depends but disallows an idealization of the mirror image that might heal the lack once and for all. He pitches into some Dantesque zone of lonely exile. Confronted with a "black" self-image, Griffin simply empties out the self. In what is most likely an allusion to Ralph Ellison—itself an authorial mirroring—Griffin writes: "The Griffin that was had become invisible" (16). Yet the Griffin that had become invisible can only be prior mirrored Griffins; it is that mediated image Griffin looks for but doesn't find; the mirror here fails to reproduce some earlier, even foundational, mirror. Which is to say that, even if unconsciously, Griffin here both snatches his whiteness from the teeth of its self-administered death *and* realizes the status of "the Griffin that was" to have been always already a fantasy of white plenitude. Whiteness is likeness, like-me-ness, specular and self-impersonating; to identify with it *is* it; that is what it is. No wonder Griffin's vertiginous response to its loss.

We ought, at this moment of crisis, to briefly look at *Watermelon Man,* which, nine years after *Black Like Me,* alludes in turn to Griffin's travails. *Watermelon Man*'s white protagonist, Jeff Gerber, awakes in the middle of the night, stumbles to the bathroom, looks in the mirror, and experiences precisely Griffin's sense of self-negation upon learning that he has become black. In the first part of the film, Gerber (Godfrey Cambridge) is a jocular though devoted racist whose compulsive engagement with "blackness" undergirds or buttresses his whiteness. He exercises while singing blackface tunes ("Jimmy Crack Corn") and stages imaginary boxing bouts with Muhammad Ali ("You're a credit to your race," he says to an imaginary Ali). The film gives body to this fascination by way of Gerber's ongoing sarcastic banter with three black men: a bus driver, an elevator operator, and a lunch-counter waiter (played, in a stroke of casting genius, by an aged Mantan Moreland—the perennially frightened sidekick from the Charlie Chan movies). Disdainful of the black urban insurrections on television that constitute the film's soundtrack, yet everywhere dropping into "black" dialect and other "black" affectations, Gerber reveals that white supremacy has as one of its constituent (if unconscious) elements an imaginary closeness to black culture.

His sudden turn to black is thus both a logical and a scarifying one. Transfixed before the mirror, Gerber is at first frightened; he then hysterically acts out his subject/object split. He shadowboxes in the mirror the imaginary Ali he has now become; chants "How now brown cow"; robs his mirror image at gunpoint; drinks some milk; gets an idea and looks down his pants (but "that's an old wives' tale," he says); soaps himself; and "proves" by his bridgework that the man in the mirror is really himself. The frenzied shifts in subject-position, from white to black to white again, point up what Van Peebles is ultimately after in the film—a Fanonian state-of-the-race address on black self-hatred. Posed against *Black Like Me,* it offers, in other words, a perspective on the status of black masculinity apart from white male fantasy.

No simple affirmations are forthcoming, though. Much of the impact of *Watermelon Man* stems from its implication that the identities of both white and black men owe a heavy debt to a sort of displaced minstrelsy. Lamenting his new color, Gerber cries that his kids won't love him anymore, won't understand: "Wait till I get down on my knee and I sing 'Mammy'!" The inevitable Jolson joke is actually a rather complex figure in this context. Surely it suggests a Gerber in blackface, referring once again to the obsession with blackness. But it also puts a *black* Gerber in blackface, lays a burden of white-filtered black images on his shoulders. As in Fanon, Gerber undergoes the self-othering attendant upon blacks in the West and devalues and ridicules his race accordingly. Soon Gerber is tracking down all the skin lighteners, hair straighteners, facial molds, and milk baths he can find. If as a white man he had wanted to be black, and dedicated many hours under the sunlamp to attain it, as a black man he wants just the opposite. No wonder Negroes riot, he says—the facial creams don't work.

Ultimately a simple attention to the facts of everyday life forces him to sympathize with the black militants and then become one. In fantastical form, then, Gerber experiences the transmogrification into "blackness" that the film perceives black Americans generally to have experienced in the 1960s. Meanwhile Gerber's blackness comes between him and his wife, Althea (Estelle Parsons); she leaves and takes the kids to her mother's home in Indiana. The primal scene of the interracial marriage bed is crucial as well to the climax of Griffin's *Black Like* Me—but in light of *Watermelon Man* it carries a very different meaning. For Melvin Van Peebles's *Watermelon Man,* the way out of black racial mimicry or minstrelsy is into a militant blackness; its consequence is a refusal of desire for the white woman's body. (Jeff Gerber's chief moment of black self-understanding, a foretaste of the gender politics of Van Peebles's *Sweet Sweetback's Baadasssss Song* [1971], occurs as he stares into the mirror of a black bar; a top-less black female dancer is visible above his head in the mirror; two white detectives conduct a vice raid in the corner.) Conversely, for John Howard Griffin, the way out of the threatening sexual return of black manhood (his own included) is into a despairing liberal white-ness; its consequence is a retreat to the politics of minstrelsy.

This is interesting because author Grace Halsell, as Baz Dreis-inger convincingly observes, pursues a mild form of sex tourism with black men once she undergoes her racial change. Having sought out Griffin and gained his approval, she tans and medicates to turn her skin darker, which (but why only then?) awakens her interest in a number of black male intimates and bed-mates. Her *Soul Sister,* Dreisinger rightly argues, is as much an account of second-wave sexual liberation as it is one of liberation from whiteness.[28] A presi-dential aide in the Lyndon B. Johnson White House, Halsell departs to sojourn in Harlem and the South as a newly created black woman. She concludes her experiment when a white southern employer tries to rape her, but before then she is party to revelations both similar to and quite gender-specifically different from Griffin's. Homosocial links come in the form of white women complaining bitterly and shamelessly about the sexual inadequacies of their husbands, and the employer desperate for "some black pussy" is far more aggressively violent than Griffin's sexual interlocutors. Meanwhile, a friendly pimp assumes she is a sex worker and tries to turn her out. As Halsell writes, "I, as a white woman, have never seen eyes so full of lust and greed as I have as a black woman looking into the faces of white men who want to possess me. . . . Always, as a black woman among white men, I have felt they considered me as in-season game, easily bagged, no license needed." Thus are the disturbing passions of white maleness and the constrictions of black femaleness revealed to a white woman who realizes her desire for black men. If this account too winds up recentering whiteness, it is notably less invested in policing its boundaries. It is no surprise that the company of black men should now seem so appealing and consoling.[29]

This is just what Griffin's book finds so hard to countenance. At a pivotal moment, under a great deal of stress, beset by racist harassers and black self-haters, Griffin finds himself alone in a Hattiesburg rooming house contemplating his family. He spots some old film negatives on the floor; they are "blank." Griffin imagines a prior occupant having had them developed only to find them wasted. This negating of the negative is meant to be a kind of self-portrait of Griffin in extremis. The image does echo a remark Griffin earlier makes about "the world of the Negro" appearing to him as "a blank" (12); the lexical similarity of "blank" and "black" and their unfortunate metaphorical association in Griffin's mind (from negatives to Negroes) help Griffin to articulate his experience of self-cancellation. This glossing of the situation is, however, at odds with what happens next. Immediately after he spots the blank negatives, he tries to write to his wife: "No words would come. She had nothing to do with this life, nothing to do with the room in Hattiesburg or with its Negro inhabitant. . . . My conditioning as a Negro, and the immense sexual implications with which the racists in our culture bombard us, cut me off, even in my most intimate self, from any connection with my wife" (68). The page before him remains "blank" (68). Griffin means this as self-conscious, antiracist lament; the image he uses to describe himself under the reign of "blackness"—blankness—accords with the uncitizenly debasement he has wanted to experience. Yet I would suggest that he is himself actively suppressing the definite shape of (his) black manhood. For here and elsewhere, Griffin perceives the "immensity" of black men to be anything but blank. Indeed the "blank" page seems to loom for Griffin as a terrifying plenitude that must be sabotaged; its intimation of interracial sex, we note, "cut [him] off." Intoxicating if imagined, the fantasized black interlocutor is far too threatening as he rises up between white husband and wife. Griffin, haunted by a return of the racial repressed, in effect plumps for reifying or policing the color line. One suspects that the reason his family constantly feels so distant, why there is an absolute separation of self and other in the mirror, is because the transgressive racial pleasure Griffin everywhere imagines, and which he attempts to inhabit in his crossing of the line, must finally remain unbidden or refused. The flat film version of *Black Like Me* (1964) starring James Whitmore as Griffin employs as one of its central cutting devices a highway's broken center line in motion, no doubt emblematic of Griffin's travels and transgressions. It appears that to cross the line is to encounter one's imagined Other head-on, throwing whiteness into jeopardy.[30]

Or into self-mimicry. As I say, one result of all this is that whiteness itself ultimately becomes an impersonation. The subterranean components of whiteness that so often threaten it require an edgy, constant patrolling. If *Watermelon Man* too easily leaves Jeff Gerber in a black, deminstrelized zone, his selfhood no longer routed through white fantasies of blacks, *Black Like Me* throws John Griffin back into a whiteness that has been decisively disrupted and must be shored up. At the end of Griffin's book, the citizens of his hometown try to run him out: "But I felt I must remain a while longer. . . . I could not allow them to say they had 'chased' me out" (155). This final imitation of white manhood, Griffin's righteous "last stand"—conceptually indistinguishable, as Richard Slotkin has shown, from notions of hegemonic whiteness and symmetrically opposed to the ending of *Watermelon Man*—is the goal toward which his text has tended.[31] "White like me" names the internal division, the white self impersonating itself, that the black mirror is supposed to both afford and conceal but here does not.

CHAPTER 6

TAR BABY AND THE
GREAT WHITE WONDER

Joni Mitchell's Pimp Game

Tar baby and the Great White Wonder
Talking over a glass of rum
Burning on the inside
With the knowledge of things to come
There's gambling out on the terrace
And midnight ramblin' on the lawn
As they lead toward temptation
With dreamland coming on

—Joni Mitchell, "Dreamland," 1977

J. D. SOUTHER TELLS THE STORY of a day in late 1977 at record producer Peter Asher's house. Souther was introduced by Asher and his wife, Betsy, to a thin black man with huge sunglasses and a big mustache. His name was Claude, and Souther concluded he was a pimp. He was decked out in dark pants, white vest, and white jacket, his Afro tamed down by a fancy chapeau. Claude didn't say much as the group, which also included guitarist Danny Kortchmar, made small talk.

After a short while, as Sheila Weller recounts the episode in *Girls Like Us: Carole King, Joni Mitchell, Carly Simon—and the Journey of*

139

a Generation, "Claude took off his hat. And then he took off his *wig.* Claude was *Joni,* in blackface. Souther and Joni had been lovers, but he hadn't recognized her under the costume. This was her new alter ego, a character she would imminently name 'Art Nouveau,' her 'inner black person.'" Mitchell has often repeated what she says will be the first line of her autobiography: "I was the only black man in the room."[1]

Mitchell pulled this stunt more than once. A candid snapshot by famed rock photographer Henry Diltz not long ago surfaced showing Mitchell at bassist Leland Sklar's 1976 Halloween party in full Art Nouveau regalia. Sklar's annual party was a mainstay of the closely knit southern California musical star system, and it was curious, says Diltz, to see this unfamiliar face at the affair.

> Everyone thought it was someone whom someone else knew: "Is that guy your friend?" "I thought he came with you." I was taking a picture of my wife—we went as pirates—and this guy happened to be in the background.
>
> I can't remember how this person's true identity came to be known, but it wasn't until an hour or two into the party that we figured out he was Joni Mitchell—she dressed herself up that way to see if she could fool all her friends, and she did. She was a dear friend of everyone in that room, and no one got it. Joni was very into observing street life—pimps and hookers, and characters like that—so she could write about it. She was fascinated by that side of life. . . .
>
> Joni was proud she was able to pull this off.[2]

Such cagey acts of everyday performance art are of interest not least for the way they produce an offense against intimacy, registered in Diltz's vaguely miffed tone: Mitchell was proud to pull this off in the midst of friends and ex-lovers who should have known better. It's more than worth asking what she was trying to prove. The pose is hardly unprecedented, and its appeal hasn't yet departed, as Daphne Brooks observes in her rousing critique of Amy Winehouse as a "retro-soul Jolson in a dress." Brooks proposes that Winehouse's "real innovation" is that she "created a record about a white woman wanting to be a black man—and an imaginary one at that."[3] If Joni, as she did on so many other counts, got there long before, she also did it in a more corrosively sociological vein, uncannily reminiscent of John Howard Griffin and Grace Halsell, evincing her inner pimp in her music and her everyday life to make sense of the scene in which she found herself, which as she knew meant the "star-maker machinery" of the 1970s southern California culture industry. Something of a (Saskatchewan) spy in the house of its pimps and pirates, she "observed" its rather different "street life" in a guise at once undercover and all too racially revealing—of it as much as of her. She was after all the only black man in the room.

As the 1970s began, Joni Mitchell was at the center of the Laurel Canyon singer-songwriter aristocracy, penning such countercultural anthems as "Both Sides Now," "Big Yellow Taxi," "Woodstock," and "The Circle Game." She was the blond damsel with a dulcimer, crowded by other laureates of female autonomy such as Laura Nyro, Carole King, and Carly Simon, not to mention industry stalwarts such as David Crosby, Neil Young, Jackson Browne, and Graham Nash, but her early songs were quickly covered by other artists, and her albums *Ladies of the Canyon* (1970) and *Blue* (1971) established her unusually liberated musical, lyrical, and political intelligence. Mitchell's following albums *For the Roses* (1972), *Court and Spark* (1974), *The Hissing of Summer Lawns* (1975), and *Hejira* (1976), if not indeed several subsequent records, constituted a period of sustained brilliance that, while certainly appreciated today, still has not gotten its full critical due. Always restless in her search for new sounds, even at the cost of her pop audience, Mitchell by the end of the decade had produced a concept album about jazz great Charles Mingus—the culmination of a gathering fascination across these years with African American culture and her relationship to it. The nadir (or maybe just the pivot) of this fascination came with Mitchell's appearance in blackface drag—as Art Nouveau, or Claude the pimp—on the cover of her 1977 album *Don Juan's Reckless Daughter.* Mitchell here doubles, even triples herself (she appears as a little girl in First Nations costume on the cover's back), an insistent mirroring she deployed again in the 1980 concert film *Shadows and Light,* where during a song about bluesman Furry Lewis the face of her Art Nouveau is superimposed over her own. The mirror becomes literal in a short film she did around this moment titled "The Black Cat in the Black Mouse Socks," one of nine female-authored contributions commissioned by producer Barry Levinson for a cinematic compendium called *Love* (1980).[4] Dressing up as Art before the mirror, surrounded by manifold accoutrements of "blackness" (a hustler's manual, bling, a boombox playing Miles Davis), Mitchell attends a Halloween party and meets up with a former lover. With a couple of notable exceptions, Mitchell's decade-long plunge into black culture has more or less mystified most commentators, despite the professed admiration for her work by artists including Prince, who recorded a fabulous cover of "A Case of You"; Q-Tip ("Joni Mitchell never lies," he intones on Janet Jackson's 1997 song "Got Til It's Gone," which samples Mitchell's "Big Yellow Taxi"); and Herbie Hancock, whose fine 2007 album *River: The Joni Letters,* featuring Mitchell compositions sung and played by a variety of performers, won two Grammy Awards.

Greg Tate long ago remarked upon Mitchell's "black" and even "hip hop" sensibility and attitude, "not a parrot, a pirate, or a parody." Kevin Fellezs counts Mitchell a defining figure in a field of male musical influences on the formation of jazz-rock fusion. Miles Park Grier has undertaken the most sustained study of Mitchell's blackface drag and the way it afforded the artist a way out of the singer-songwriter pigeonhole and into the ranks of the male rock canon.[5] I am interested in the way Art Nouveau's black mirror gave Mitchell the unlikely but provocative critical leverage she needed on the presumptively white and male 1970s L.A. social and musical scene. Mitchell's employment of backing jazz musicians; race-driven songs like "The Jungle Line," "The Boho Dance," "Furry Sings the Blues," and "Dreamland"; Beat garb like the beret she sports on the cover of *Hejira;* romantic relationships with black men like percussionist Don Alias; and, ultimately, her collaboration with Mingus form a revealing chapter in 1970s pop life, not to mention the cultural history of Los Angeles. Operating in a notoriously racist and segregated L.A. cultural scene, at the height of the post-Watts-riot "urban crisis," and amid a climate of race-war fantasy and fact (most obviously in the mind of Charles Manson and in the Hell's Angels' murder of a black man at Altamont), Mitchell left the folkie retreat of Laurel Canyon and, as it were, came down into the streets in imaginary cross-racial identification (the streets were those of Bel Air, but

Fig. 6. Cover of Joni Mitchell, *Don Juan's Reckless Daughter*, 1977, Warner Music Group

hey). Working with Mingus, himself from Watts, and formerly a pimp to boot, Mitchell walked some way out of whiteness; but given that *Mingus* (1979) was her least satisfying album of the decade—Robert Christgau rightly called it a "brave" but failed experiment—I mean to ask here what cognitive gain comes with her mix of interest in, identification with, and appropriation of black sounds and styles.[6] In a cultural domain known for its hideous racial entailments, Mitchell's valiant move certainly shows the limits of any merely individual attempt to undermine whiteness, but it curiously afforded a telling perspective on one ambitious woman artist's ascendancy, at a high pitch of second-wave feminism, in that weird new service industry to the American youth imaginary, commercial song.

Between 1963 and 1965, as Charlie Gillett long ago observed, the epicenter of U.S. pop music shifted from New York to Los Angeles: where records made in New York stayed at No. 1 on the charts for twenty-six weeks (to L.A.'s three) in 1963, by 1965 L.A.-made records had jumped to twenty weeks at No. 1 (to New York's one), and things stayed that way.[7] The political economy and social formation of Los Angeles are therefore key to understanding the consequences, and perhaps sources, of this westward drift. Eric Avila's *Popular Culture in the Age of White Flight* offers one notable account of the way in which the postwar L.A. dialectic of chocolate city and vanilla suburb (or canyon) came about. Hollywood, Disneyland (opened in 1955), Dodger Stadium (built in time for the 1962 season), and the Eisenhower-initiated, state-sponsored freeway system helped push-pull suburban/inner-city racial and class formations into being; midcentury L.A. was self-consciously made into a white or white-dominated city. As in other U.S. conurbations, housing in Los Angeles was concertedly racially redlined by a host of agencies and activities, not least among them the New Deal's Home Owners' Loan Corporation and Federal Housing Authority. Disney's choice of Orange County's Anaheim for the location of Disneyland certified the sanitized suburban ethos he meant to foster there. Dodger Stadium was set down atop a working-class Chicano neighborhood (Chavez Ravine) in an attempt by city fathers to "renew" the historic downtown area. Key to this entire cultural geography was the freeway, whose supplanting of an extensive, demographically diverse, public streetcar system cemented the new urban regime of privatized racially segmented living. (As California historian and activist Carey McWilliams put it in 1965, the "freeways have been carefully designed to skim over and skirt around such eyesores as Watts and East Lost Angeles; even the downtown section, a portion of which has become a shopping area for minorities, has been partially bypassed.") The figurehead for these developments, Avila observes, was Ronald Reagan, who aided the House Un-American Activities Committee in its quest for "subversive" influences in Hollywood, emceed the televised opening ceremonies at Disneyland, and appeared on live television to promote the building of Dodger Stadium. Reagan was governor of California from 1967 to 1975, precisely the years of Laurel Canyon musical hegemony.[8]

The Watts uprising in 1965 made spectacular protest specifically against the racial dimensions of this urban regime. Southern in-migration, particularly during World War II, had radically recomposed the city's demographics and geography; while whites settled in such locales as the San Fernando Valley, African Americans swelled the ranks of south-central L.A., the L.A. black population actually doubling in the munitions boom-time of the war years. This gave rise, for one thing, to the sounds of L.A.'s Central Avenue, with its crowds congregating in clubs like the Plantation, the Downbeat, and the Savoy. In his history of L.A. pop, *Waiting for the Sun,* Barney Hoskyns goes so far as to suggest we think of L.A., not Memphis or Chicago or Detroit or New Orleans, as the defining American R&B town.[9] (Even Motown was to migrate there in 1971.) The city was martially policed by an LAPD significantly shaped by white southern sensibilities; for this and other reasons, the L.A. black music scene had by 1965 been attenuated and supplanted by white pop reveling in one or another strain of endless-summer romanticism—this at a time when unemployment in Watts ran to a whopping 30 percent. In August these tinderbox conditions ignited when a motorcycle cop's traffic stop escalated into insurrection, resulting in thirty-four deaths, thousands injured, more than that arrested, and $40 million in damage over six days of pitched battle. L.A. songwriter Randy Newman later remarked, "I always felt that the race situation was worse here than anywhere," while Thomas Pynchon wrote in a now-famous 1966 piece that Watts was a "country which lies, psychologically, uncounted miles further than most whites seem at present willing to travel," the so-called L.A. scene "a little unreal, a little less than substantial," "a white Scene" with illusion everywhere in it, the Strip itself a puny enclave of unfulfillment.[10]

All of which is to say that mid-1960s Los Angeles became a racially segmented scene structured violently in dominance at the moment it emerged as *the* port of entry into the U.S. pop mainstream. The signature event of the British Invasion, for example, may have been the Beatles' 1965 show at Shea Stadium, but their label (before they formed Apple) was Hollywood's Capitol Records. The British Invasion, I would argue, is best understood as the invasion of Los Angeles. From the defining conceptual contributions to L.A. of Reyner Banham and Christopher Isherwood and David Hockney to the L.A.

presence of the Beatles and the Stones—1965's "Satisfaction" was recorded in L.A., not Swinging London—to the import of British pop sensibilities through teen shows like *Shindig* and *Where the Action Is,* UK minds and mentalities had very much to do with the West Coast's opening of "the doors of perception," as L.A. immigrant Aldous Huxley had it. The aforementioned Peter Asher, producer in the 1970s of such artists as James Taylor and Linda Ronstadt, had been the Peter of the British duo Peter and Gordon, known best for their 1964 hit "A World Without Love" (Asher's sister Jane had been a girlfriend of Paul McCartney). The organizing of youth as a pop collective in the late 1960s, that is to say, was very much a matter of a certain style of California dreamin'. The Sunset Strip was itself undergoing a perhaps Watts-emulating series of upheavals. The fall 1966 disturbances later depicted in the B-movie *Riot on Sunset Strip* (1967) were the Strip's answer to police repression in L.A. The scene was politicized not around race, however, but rather around youth leisure rights; in response to a business consortium's plan to replace Strip pop clubs with high-rises, youth revolted, with at least one massive march (featuring fixtures such as Peter Fonda, Dennis Hopper, and Sonny and Cher) and massive arrests. It is utterly symptomatic of this Strip scene that Stephen Stills's signature protest song of this moment, "For What It's Worth" ("Stop, hey, what's that sound / Everybody look what's goin' down"), is not about the Vietnam War, still less injustices across town in Watts, but instead the hassles on the Strip. The pop juggernaut fueled by revolting youth bore the decisive impress of L.A. white dominance.

In the wake of Watts, in other words, Laurel Canyon scarcely batted an eye. Buffalo Springfield; the Byrds; the Flying Burrito Brothers; Crosby, Stills, and Nash; Jackson Browne; Linda Ronstadt; the Eagles: among the ashes, find me any real engagement with race in the United States of the 1970s. Even for Neil Young, racism took place in "Alabama," not, say, Malibu. (I mean no disrespect to Young's brilliant songs broaching U.S. genocide and Native American extermination, among them "Cortez the Killer" and "Pocahontas.") A budding Laurel Canyon cultural historiography, including the books *Hotel California* by Barney Hoskyns and *Laurel Canyon* by Michael Walker, mimics and perpetuates this racial complacency.[11] When Joe Smith took over Elektra–Asylum Records from David Geffen in

1975, he worried that his blackest artist was Joni Mitchell—which is to say that alone of all the white L.A. crew, Mitchell was paying attention. Beginning with *For the Roses* (1972) and *Court and Spark* (1974), Mitchell used jazz musicians (albeit the fusiony bunch of Tom Scott's L.A. Express) for her backing band, and the inclusion of a cover of Lambert, Hendricks, and Ross's "Twisted" on *Court and Spark* marked the start of her own foray into jazz singing. By this time she had partnered up with jazz-identified drummer John Guerin, whose playing was key to the sound and shape of this music. But it is really with 1975's *Hissing of Summer Lawns* that Mitchell ventured self-conscious explorations of racial difference, blackness, and her own privileged whiteness (this was apparently Prince's favorite Joni album). From the celebration of rock 'n' roll in "In France They Kiss on Main Street" to the dissing of suburban whiteness in the title track, "Shades of Scarlet [as in O'Hara] Conquering," and "Harry's House," there's a new turn in Mitchell's work toward both social dissection and musical genre-jumping. "The Jungle Line," with its Burundi warrior drummers in the background, is a witty satire of white primitivism and exoticism—"safaris to the heart of all that jazz" by "those cannibals of shuck and jive"—including, I think, her own; not for nothing does the song depict a slumming Henri Rousseau, like Mitchell a painter, and another in a line of powerful men perfect for the singer's inveterate transvestism, as in the previous year's channeling of David Geffen in "Free Man in Paris."

The ars poetica of this strategy is "The Boho Dance," Mitchell's nod to Tom Wolfe. "Down in the cellar in the Boho zone / I went looking for some sweet inspiration, oh well / Just another hard-time band with Negro affectations," she sings. But she's way too smart to leave it at that: "I was a hopeful in rooms like this / When I was working cheap / It's an old romance—the Boho dance / It hasn't gone to sleep." Rich boho Joni with Negro affectations, she sure knows who she is. And yet there's self-congratulation here too in Mitchell's defiance toward bohemia, a certain self-satisfaction: Jesus may have been a "beggar, rich in grace," she sings, but Solomon—whom I take as Mitchell's figure for herself—"kept his head in all his glory." "It's just that some steps outside the Boho dance / Have a fascination for me." Conclusion? "Nothing is capsulized in me / On either side of town / The streets were never really mine / Not mine these glamour gowns." Joni is large, she contains multitudes, and she is forthright about the resulting contradictions.

Thus on one hand the ever-so-slightly self-parodic "Blue Motel Room" from the following year's *Hejira,* an amusing romantic moue sung like a road-weary blues mama crossed with Billie Holiday, and on the other the same record's "Furry Sings the Blues," as striking for Mitchell's sudden mimicry of bluesman Furry Lewis—during a visit, Lewis looks Mitchell in the eye and says, "I don't like you"—as it is for its rather withering self-portrait of Joni in Memphis longing to channel the souls of Lewis and W. C. Handy: "W. C. Handy I'm rich and I'm fey / And I'm not familiar with what you played / But I get such strong impressions of your hey day / Looking up and down old Beale Street." And then this, worthy of, even more self-scathing than, a Steely Dan tune: "Why should I expect that guy to give it to me true / Fallen to hard luck / And time and other thieves / While our limo is shining on his shanty street / Old Furry sings the blues." You've got to credit her honesty here, even if the cross-gender, cross-racial yearning is a trifle embarrassing. No question that Mitchell counts herself as one of the above "thieves." In other words, blackface or at least blackvoice has here become a not-altogether-negligible mode of racial self-awareness.

These moves are especially arresting given that *Hejira* was the record of an extended, meditational solo road trip Mitchell made in the wake of her short stint with Bob Dylan's Rolling Thunder Revue in 1975, the latter documented in Dylan's film *Renaldo and Clara* (1978). Rolling Thunder was a sort of vagabond carnival extravaganza with a constantly varying cast of performers including Joan Baez, Ronnie Hawkins, Ramblin' Jack Elliot, Sam Shepard, Allen Ginsberg, and many others; "Coyote," Mitchell's beautiful signature song of this period (the one she plays, for example, in Martin Scorsese's *The Last Waltz*), addresses with a wistful buoyancy her affair with Shepard.[12] Mitchell had any number of such liaisons and kept right at her business, which often involved conjuring art out of them; that was part of the point; that was very much the persona and one of the reasons she was so compelling, that she sang (as the song "Help Me" summarized it) about loving her loving but loving her freedom even more, even if it often meant pain and isolation. This persona also occasioned a certain queenly rancor toward Joan Baez on the

Rolling Thunder tour, alas, only one of the undermining forces be-
setting the tour's attempt to circumvent the star system by picking
up artists in whatever locales it visited (including off the street).
In any case, much of Rolling Thunder's importance to this period
of Mitchell's work comes in the benefit concerts the Revue did for
Rubin "Hurricane" Carter, the promising boxer convicted of murder
who occasioned one of Dylan's most famous mid-1970s songs, "Hurricane." Michael Denning has written of the benefit concert format
as an artifact specifically of what he calls the post-1973 Great Recession, and the agitation and performing on Carter's behalf, including a show at Carter's Clinton State Prison itself, incubated a
weird mix of activism, celebrity, and racial affect.[13] Carter himself
recounted one nasty episode in which Mitchell, after a poor reception at the prison, called him a "jive-ass nigger."[14] This postcounter-
cultural address to the state's carceral apparatus thus both reveled
in and foundered upon the white-Negro fantasies Mitchell had
for some time been skewering in her music. It thickens the context
for her subsequent exploration of such fantasies, as does the larger
political-economic context of the Great Recession, a context to
which I will return. Sexual freedom, female mobility, vested cross-
racial interests, the lures and snares of male power: all would be
condensed in the next turns of Mitchell's life and career.

It was at about this moment that Mitchell fell in love with Don
Alias. Stanley Crouch could have been describing Mitchell's relationship with Alias in his novel *Don't the Moon Look Lonesome* (2000), in
which a young blond South Dakota (Mitchell hailed from Saskatoon, just north) jazz singer's relationship with a black jazz musician
mixes crossover urgency with crossover's obvious limits. Mitchell
and Alias, an Afro-Cuban music specialist who worked with everyone
from Nina Simone to Miles Davis, had a deep but conflicted three-
and-a-half-year relationship, and Alias thereafter remained close to
her heart. His presence on *Don Juan's Reckless Daughter* helps give
that record its distinctive, bristling sound, and he commanded the
drum kit on the Shadows and Light tour. But Mitchell surely tested
his mettle; the gentle, onetime pre-med student was alarmed, for example, to find Mitchell's nude portrait of him, complete with hard-on,
suddenly hanging in the living room of their New York loft. She called
it a "testament to his sexuality"; he called it "an embarrassment."[15]

Alias insisted she repaint it, and she ultimately did, but Mitchell fought him every step of the way. This painterly investment in the black penis is of a piece with Mitchell's other racial and gender peregrinations, and it is the cover of *Reckless Daughter,* the music of this particular moment in her life, that sports Mitchell's Claude-the-pimp getup. The painting and the scuffle it occasioned are of interest for the race and gender reversals impacted there. The painting reverses the relations of looking by which hundreds of years of painted nudes have been structured; in assuming the male prerogative to look and to represent, there is something of the self-portrait in it; its figuration celebrates but also appropriates, exoticizes as well as owns, recapitulating her fantasy of her own black maleness. Having a black man, for Mitchell, came satisfyingly close to being one.

The turn to the pimp guise, then, however bizarre it might seem, does bring all of Mitchell's 1970s concerns together, and more besides: the question of sexual dominance and its emotional fallout, the attractions of male power, particularly black male power, and the matter of money—who has it, who is in a position to dispense it, and what it will get you in a recessionary economy nonetheless governed in part by the pop power machine. When you contemplate Joni as pimp, you realize that in her work the dialectic or conflict between women's romantic susceptibility over and against the desire for liberty and ambition, the pull of racial otherness and the street characters, including Rubin Carter, who seem to embody it, was all across the decade underwritten by a clear-eyed emphasis on cold, hard cash. "He was playin' real good / For free," goes the self-deflating "For Free," way back in 1970, on the same record, *Ladies of the Canyon,* that features the mythmaking "Woodstock" and the environmentalist whimsy of "Big Yellow Taxi." Mitchell was from the start able to offer withering critiques of her own willing place in the pop cash nexus. In so doing she offered up demystifying tales of what has been termed countercultural capital. Michael Szalay and Sean McCann, in their introduction and conclusion to a 2005 volume of the *Yale Journal of Criticism* entitled "Countercultural Capital: Essays on the Sixties from Some Who Weren't There," assailed the magical thinking and "merely cultural" thrust of much of the post-Woodstock generation's artistic and critical production, its disregard of, for example, what McCann calls "presidential government" (and they take me to task for the same tendency, incorrectly I might add).[16] Mitchell, I am arguing, always knew the "back to the garden" fantasy was precisely that. The song "Court and Spark," again, to take one of many examples, is structured in this fashion; though she falls in love with a deep soul who plays for "passing change" on the streets and in People's Park, she can't "let go of L.A./City of the fallen angels." The very cover of *Hissing of Summer Lawns* features Mitchell's painting of a very long snake in the suburban garden, Mitchell as Tom Wolfe again, while inside the gatefold comes a double-album-sized photograph of Joni luxuriating in her backyard pool! And *Hissing*'s "Edith and the Kingpin" is a tale of pimp and stable outright, making clear not only that the political economy of sex (as Gayle Rubin called it the year the song was released) is an economy structured in gender and financial dominance but also, and crucially, that pimp and whore are locked in an ineluctable codependency. As in—or better, as a version of—Hegel's master/slave dialectic, both parties realize themselves each through the other, need each other to exist "for themselves," might at any moment upend the balance of power that holds them together: "Edith and the Kingpin/Each with charm to sway/Are staring eye to eye/They dare not look away/You know they dare not look away." Mitchell's perhaps characteristic response: why not be both?[17]

A little backstory here. As David Yaffe has shown, a jazz-lore lineage of the pimp/whore dialectic extends back through such texts as Ralph Ellison's *Invisible Man* (1952), Billie Holiday and William Dufty's *Lady Sings the Blues* (1956), and most importantly for Mitchell, Charles Mingus's *Beneath the Underdog* (1971).[18] An L.A.-centric pulp pimp heir to such representations suddenly erupted in the late 1960s. Justin Gifford documents how the Los Angeles pulp publisher Holloway House almost single-handedly made available vivid, visceral stories of the pimp game in dozens of books by such writers as Iceberg Slim, Donald Goines, and many others.[19] By the early 1970s, blaxploitation film had emerged to throw such stories up on the big screen. Joni Mitchell seems to have keyed into the persona's usefulness in commenting on what Jean-Paul Sartre might have called her "situation" in the culture industry of her moment. Transmogrifying the pimp figure's South-to-North migration and defiant self-making into her own passage from Saskatoon to L.A. via Toronto and then Detroit—Joan Anderson became Joni Mitchell through her Detroit marriage to Chuck Mitchell, and Joni perhaps tellingly experienced firsthand Detroit's late-1960s "urban crisis" (though not the summer of 1967's Great Rebellion, by which time she had made her way to Greenwich Village)—Mitchell absorbed the pimp's stance and saw the logic of what Gifford calls a "pimp poetics." To wit, the pimp of Iceberg Slim's 1967 autobiography, Gifford argues, is a figure who adapts structures of white power and economic exploitation in order to achieve a radically individualized form of liberty: "Slim," an associate tells him, "a pimp is really a whore who's reversed the game on whores . . . a good pimp is like a slick white boss" (67). Which leads to the conclusion that pimping is not a sex game but rather a "skull game," all about ice-cold attitude and pile after pile of cash money (68). Floated by second-wave feminism but never feminist-identified, Mitchell bought into the radically individualized perspective of all this—a perspective purchased through the "star-maker machinery" she was tough-minded enough to analyze so clearly, and analyze so clearly because of her self-understanding as whore become pimp. If, as various critics have perceived, pimps and pimp writers both are service workers bound up in culture-industry protocols, Mitchell, I would argue, alludes in precisely this way to her own artistic practice. In this light, the great song "Free Man in Paris" comes to seem an act of pimp David Geffen being turned out by his friend, mack daddy Joni. Limning the pressures of the "star-maker machinery" on one of its own biggest operators, *she* hustles *him,* punks him into a character in a tune that *reads* him and that not incidentally made them both a lot of money. It's as though the best you could do in this crazy new exploding industry as a female artistic sole proprietor was aspire to hustle yourself, be your own pimp—that was Mitchell's implicit, and then explicit, claim.

Charles Mingus certainly understood himself this way in the political economy of jazz, as he makes elaborately, outrageously evident in his 1971 autobiography, *Beneath the Underdog,* a bulging, sprawling, brilliant mixture of self-psychoanalysis, sex manual, pimp narrative, and modernist character study that depicts Mingus, in whatever domain he chooses, always struggling to get a leg up, and over.[20] One of the great minds in jazz history, at once composer, arranger, bandleader, and bassist, Mingus called Mitchell out of the blue in the fall of 1978 with six new tunes he wanted Mitchell to write lyrics for. If Mitchell had dreamed that someday her pimp would come, this was it: Mitchell immediately devoured Mingus's autobiography and agreed to meet with him. The result was *Mingus* (1979), released shortly after Mingus's death at fifty-six from Lou Gehrig's disease.[21] In the album's liner notes, Mitchell writes about the experience: "It was as if I had been standing by a river—one toe in the water—feeling it out—and Charlie came by and pushed me in—'sink or swim'—him laughing at me dog paddling around in the currents of black classical music." The river is no longer frozen like the one Mitchell wished to skate away on in her famous 1971 song "River"; and pimped out or herself doing the pimping, little dog Joni swims in jazz, appropriating Mingus's voice and persona in songs such as "A Chair in the Sky," which riffs on Mingus's confinement to a wheelchair in the last months of his life. Mitchell here becomes one of what the song nicely terms "mutts of the planet"—an achievement that does not, however, preclude, and may even precipitate, some of the worst writing of her career to that point (it was to get much worse). The biggest payoff of black drag king Joni may be the discordant, angry guitar work on *Mingus*. But songs like "Sweet Sucker Dance" have an embarrassing tendency to claim ownership over Mingus's heart: "We're dancing fools/You and me/Tonight it's a dance of insecurity/It's my solo/While you're away/And shadows have the saddest things to say." And while Mitchell becomes white once more in her lyrics to Mingus's "Goodbye Pork Pie Hat," the slack, "Strange Fruit"-style lyrics meld Mingus and Alias into a single, iconic figure, and produce precisely the exoticism she lampooned just a few years earlier: "So the sidewalk leads us with music/To two little dancers/Dancing outside a black bar/There's a sign up on the awning/It says 'Pork Pie Hat Bar'/And there's black babies dancing . . . /Tonight!" This cul-de-sac of cross-racial identification played out equivocally in the Shadows and Light Tour that followed it, buttressed as it was by an almost entirely white host of backing jazz musicians, among them Mitchell veterans Alias and Jaco Pastorius as well as newbies Michael Brecker, Pat Metheny, and Lyle Mays.

If *Mingus* plays somewhat like a struggle for pimp supremacy, it also, like the whole pimp fantasy for Mitchell, gives new meaning to her idea of "both sides now," as Alexander Corey has suggested—Mitchell's oft-covered late-1960s song about love's and life's illusions. Traversing gender, racial, and class binaries, looking at them from both sides of the street, cruising between them as it were, Mitchell hits on the difference, or is it the sameness, of "being" and "having" the phallus, as Lacan's writings elaborate it. White woman and black man are twinned in the U.S. racial imaginary as threats to white masculinity—it's why their coupling is taboo, and perhaps why Mitchell wants to inhabit them both. The phallic investments of Mingus's autobiography might also have titillated her into this stance. As Corey puts it:

> When Joni Mitchell dresses up as the embodied possessor of the black penis, she is also drawing on her feminine ability to "be the phallus," which is her ability to turn the bodily allusion to the phallic symbol into the illusion of the phallus itself. It is a moment at which she triangulates a danger to white masculinity through simultaneous invocation of dangerous white feminine sexuality and a threatening black masculinity—a moment which may not have been fully realized, but perhaps a kind of opening or unanimated potentiality that resists the racial and sexual power structures that continued to govern American culture, albeit in a constantly shifting way. Castrating the white male comes from both sides; the white woman like Mitchell and the black man like, say, Eldridge Cleaver and Amiri Baraka.

Blackface drag is perfect for taking down or just surmounting white masculinist domination from "both sides now," a fraught way of negotiating the 1970s sex/gender system at the intersection of second-wave feminism and Black Power—a way, as Miles Grier writes, to criticize sexism as if it were racism against black men.[22]

California pimpin' in the Great Recession: in the words of Walter Sobchak (the John Goodman character in *The Big Lebowski,* another recessionary L.A. story), "at least it's an ethos." Walter's comic preference for Nazis over nihilists might seem uncomfortably analogous to Joni Mitchell's late 1970s moves. However outré and racially problematic, they at least offered a figural meditation on an artistic political predicament that she understood as such. Consider the alternative, which I'm sure she did. Succeeding Ronald Reagan in the California governor's seat was Jerry Brown, who famously cozied up to the Laurel Canyon firmament—figuratively in the case of artists like Jackson Browne and the Eagles, who did a benefit show in 1979 to raise funds for Brown's 1980 presidential run, and quite literally in the case of Linda Ronstadt, who for a time became his girlfriend. Compromised politics met compromised music in a small-*s* state imaginary that the Eagles' *Hotel California* all-too-easefully assailed: they did indeed check out anytime they liked, and sure enough they never did leave. Brown addressed recessionary times with a fiscal austerity that was widely seen as to the right of anything Reagan had overseen, and the musicians mostly did a lot of blow, shilling for it all and soundtracking late-1970s malaise. It was, in a way, a local version of what Michael Szalay examines in his study of the post–World War II American novel *Hip Figures,* which argues that the figure of the hipster, imagined above all in Norman Mailer's "The White Negro," was key to the postwar formation of the Democratic Party, clinched in the figure of "hipster president" John F. Kennedy but compelling in various guises beyond his life and example.[23] To be In, as Mailer had it, was to be in tune with the forces of history, out of office or in. It was no doubt difficult to dissent from this vibe in the late-1970s California pop-political landscape, so it was not nothing in this context for Joni Mitchell to ask, essentially, and with respect to race and the cash nexus, who's zoomin' who? Especially at a moment when the Bakke decision threatened to reverse significant aspects of affirmative action, and when the antitax revolt of Proposition 13 began to lay the groundwork for a national version of such revanchism. As Mike Davis argued in *Prisoners of the American Dream,* the groundwork for the Reagan 1980s was pioneered in California.[24] Black drag-kinging the pimp gave Joni Mitchell purchase on several contexts and conundrums at once, and in a state whose politics would come to define the federal apparatus across the decades to come. It wasn't pretty, and it's hardly defensible, but as she put it in the song "Shadows and Light": "Every picture has its shadows / And it has some source of light / Blindness, blindness and sight."

Coda: For the Roses

Edwardsville, Illinois, summer 1979, the Shadows and Light Tour: my friend Tom Byrne and I snuck backstage after seeing the show, filing in behind VIPs strolling into a little hut behind the outdoor festival stage. I was twenty and utterly starstruck. We were suddenly in the intimate presence of the band, several musicians including Jaco Pastorius and Michael Brecker gathered around an upright piano, Joni sitting regally in a wicker chair. She had gotten that late-1970s perm, blond kink, black and blond, as Greg Tate has it. She greeted us warmly and casually and in doing so left us tongue-tied. Courteous and almost courtly, she asked us about ourselves, and when she found out that I play drums she called Don Alias over and introduced us: tongue-tied again. She recounted her enjoyment of her recent musical moves, particularly playing with Pastorius, and way too soon people started to split. Joni spontaneously offered us the good-luck flowers that had been sent over by the record company—I still have the note that came with them. It reminded me of her acid irony about the business in "For the Roses"—"And now you're seen / On giant screens / And at parties for the press / And for people who have slices of you / From the company." And then I was struck by the way, as she did with her music, Joni had turned a company man's obligation into a gift.

CHAPTER 7

ALL THE KING'S MEN

Elvis Impersonators and
White Working-Class Masculinity

*I haven't figured out why Detroit has this attraction [to] Elvis. But this
is a blue-collar town with down to earth people, the kind Elvis liked.*
—Danny Vann, Elvis impersonator, 1993

something in their psyche insists on elvis
—Lucille Clifton, "them and us," 1993

AS THE PLANE TOUCHED THE TARMAC of McCarran Airport, a
nearby passenger, as if on cue, sang out: "Viva, Las Vegas!" As how
could he not, since Elvis Presley occupies as central a place in Vegas's
mythology as Vegas does in Elvis's. It was all part of the script, one
in which my own enquiring mind fit all too well. No room here for
academic-renegade posturing: my desire to attend the fifth annual
Elvis Presley International Impersonators Association convention
in July 1994 in the interest of pinning down the purpose of Elvis
impersonation only confirmed my status as interloping voyeuristic outsider, or as fan—even as it suggested my resemblance to the
culture-industry vampires (from talk shows to magazine segments
to camp cinema) who had made Elvis impersonators such a hot

commodity of late. Nonetheless, what I found largely contradicted the scripted scenarios and easy critiques of Elvis impersonation that circulated so smugly through both academe and pop life in the 1990s and indeed has ever since. The truly numberless performers of Presley give eerie and perhaps dubious body to the shade of Elvis; they inhabit and prolong the irradiating afterglow that is the lingering cultural presence of Elvis Presley. Yet an initial approach to the meaning of that habitation lies in the fact that the great majority of these impersonators are working-class white men who stress the Pelvis's route from rags to king of rock 'n' roll. Like baseball and the Statue of Liberty, the figure of Elvis guards the way into America.

Not, of course, to everyone's satisfaction. The lines of critique have been familiar enough. For cultural doomsayers, Elvis impersonators confirm the cretinizing powers of "mass" culture. In an America of simulation and deceit, a Joe Elvis or Elvis Little may seem another instance of the chronic ache of "hyperreality," as Umberto Eco called it, being one more fake in a land without qualities.[1] William McCranor Henderson's novel *Stark Raving Elvis* (1984), as its title implies, tells the story of an Elvis impersonator lost to madness because of his overinvestment in the fiber-optically circulated image of Elvis.[2] However, for black pop groups like Public Enemy or Living Colour, fakery in this case means (at best) a performer who got more from black culture than he gave to it. For too many, Elvis has been mistakenly coronated. Per PE:

> Elvis was a hero to most
> But he never meant shit to me
> Straight up racist that sucker was
> Simple and plain
> Motherfuck him *and* John Wayne![3]

Living Colour's spectacular "Elvis Is Dead" aims for a similar effect while, in accord with the peculiarly meiotic logic to which dead Elvis has given rise, keeping his image in circulation.[4] Still another, though more adoring, critique of Elvis's apotheosis emerges in camp appropriations of him. Marjorie Garber has written of Elvis impersonators' "unmarked transvestism," and strong whiffs of camp sensibility hover around such phenomena as the film *Honeymoon in Vegas* (1992), with its skydiving Elvises, or Elvis impersonator / parodist El

Vez, the Mexican Elvis, who is rather more marked in the transvestite sources of his travesty.[5]

I am not specifically concerned here with any one of these critiques, but taken together they define the territory I want to occupy. The phenomenon of Elvis impersonation is still worth looking at for what it reveals about the racial and class unconscious of white working-class masculinity, certainly in the 1990s when I interviewed a broad cohort of Elvis performers and impersonators as well as their fans and most likely in the present as well.[6] The influence of the culture industry on the formation of the white Imaginary, the "white-Negro" resonance of Elvis's image, and the cross-dressing aura of his impersonation all bear importantly on this unconscious, and all have a place in my account. In some respects, however, these emphases have bequeathed us terms of dismissal rather than of analysis. If I rely on such emphases only for the purpose of broad orientation, it is because I want, by way of the Elvis impersonator, to know how working-class white men live their whiteness. Elvis impersonation in essence constitutes a series of popular appropriations of Elvis, a figure himself constituted out of black-mirror appropriations crossing racial lines he refused to respect, and attests to the kinds of meanings that since his death in 1977 have been constructed in his name. As the impersonators themselves by and large take this mode of performance seriously, it seems to me to deserve not supercilious irony or mere censure but an attempt at critical investigation.

The discourse around and my own conversations with these performers yielded the information on which I draw. My undertaking was made easier by the consolidation of the aforementioned Elvis Presley International Impersonators Association, a "clearing house for information regarding activities of Elvis performers *worldwide*," and by the publication of *I Am Elvis: A Guide to Elvis Impersonators* (1991).[7] The EPIIA convention, which for a time brought together a multitude of performers and codified its parent organization's cultural politics, was a fascinating affair—somewhat of a cross between a Moose Lodge gathering's hearty camaraderie and an academic conference's meeting of stars, minds, "experts," rivals, and paraphernalia hawkers. The *Guide* is an apparently sober document recording the biographies and vital statistics—birthdate, height and weight, astrological sign, and agent's phone number—of sixty-five performers of varying resemblance to the King. There are heavily bearded Elvises, four-year-old Elvises, and Elvis duos; Italian Elvises, Greek Elvises, Jewish Elvises, a Lady Elvis, even a Black Elvis. (Impersonator impresario Ed Franklin boasts, "We've had every type of Elvis there is in the world.") As ethnographic study has hosted some of the richest work in cultural studies, what follows owes as well to the methodological and practical explorations by writers such as Phil Cohen, Paul Willis, Janice Radway, Donna Gaines, and others.[8] My broadest—and most fiercely held—assumption is summed up in Paul Willis's remark that cultural forms, however idiosyncratic or marginal, "may not say what they know, nor know what they say, but they mean what they do," and in so doing legitimate the attention we give them.[9] Such forms are part of larger, shared patterns of life, and the logic of their practice extends to broader relations of feeling and practice. And there is a point to them. Impersonating Elvis may seem a tad bizarre, but it has a human rationale that deserves articulation. I do not mean that such performance is mystified and inarticulate without the help of the heroic cultural inquirer. Nothing could be further from the truth. It might be more exact to say that mine is an effort of translation, submitting the gestures of the impersonators to another set of codes or social area of language. I only follow what the impersonators themselves intimate about their work. As onetime EPIIA president and impersonator Rick Marino (a veritably Bill Clintonian figure of political smoothness, intergenerational bonding, and show-biz smarts) told me of the impersonators' (literal) investments in Elvis: "When you're growing up, sometimes, you know, if you're a man, you need somebody to look at, to get a guidance or some kind of direction for the type of man you want to be. . . . A lot of the guys, you know, maybe their dad didn't quite do it for 'em and so they look to Elvis and in a kind of an offbeat way, maybe, he kind of like, you know, made 'em feel good."[10]

Just how Elvis makes them feel good will, I hope, become clear—cultural forms mean what they do. First a few words about this form's historical and cultural contexts are in order. For one thing, working-class men's traditional gender self-definition, despite glimmers of its recuperation in Hollywood and elsewhere, has for some time been under siege amid what Barbara Ehrenreich calls the "androgynous drift" of the last several decades.[11] That self-definition, a well-known persona of hard-bitten manliness, has since the onset of the Industrial Revolution been a gendered response to class oppression.[12] Substituting physical resourcefulness and strength for power in the workplace, valorizing and in some subjective sense choosing a life of manual labor that only oppresses them, working-class men have developed a compensatory way of being in the world. In *Learning to Labour,* Paul Willis describes the formation of this dynamic in the context of the contemporary school, where working-class kids' refusal of middle-class culture and its overinvestment in mental labor entails a corollary celebration of truancy and manual work—the result of which is to slot them, for good, into working-class jobs. Willis demonstrates the extent to which this refusal—often expressed in the most imaginative if unruly ways—is extremely clear-headed in its suspicion that the credentials the school offers are bogus and that the work it promises for even the most "behaved" working-class student will be boring and utterly meaningless. This affirmation of manly mastery, to be sure, also depends on a commonsense sexism that is extremely oppressive to women in the workplace as well as the home, and which certainly qualifies its clarity. And it often depends as well on an extreme ambivalence toward working-class black men, whose class proximity and racial difference make them useful Others for white group solidarity but whose masculinist self-definition (and cultural difference) also earn the fascination and respect of white working-class males. We can expect to see these important differentiations again shortly.

This white working-class self-conception perhaps had its heyday in the 1960s, when the subjective sense of physical power was, for once, matched by the so-called embourgeoisement of American workers. The extent to which this embourgeoisement occurred remains a matter of debate, and it was in any case to erode rather precipitously (with the auto and related industries) in subsequent decades.[13] Changes in the ideologies of manhood, including the 1960s counterculture's embrace of androgyny, the encroaching obsolescence of anticommunist machismo, and the looming attractiveness of the "sensitive man," were undergirded by a massive shift in political economy.[14] Simply put, this was a shift from Fordism to post-Fordism, from an industrial regime of mass assembly-line production to a halting and low-wage service economy in which, moreover, the sexual division of labor was blurred. Economy and identity came together in working-class men's felt inability to *provide*—a masculine ideal the social script increasingly disdained anyway.[15] As the service sector fully emerged, so too did "office" styles of manhood in which class prejudices were physically encoded. This is not to lament the passing of older modes of working-class masculine self-styling, or to claim that many of the worst effects of that older conception of masculinity no longer exist, much less to suggest that those effects do not extend even now to middle-class men. If anything, male physical violence and abuse, for instance, have redoubled in hysterical fashion in the face of troubled self-definition.

The resulting situation of "embattled" masculinity dovetailed with another context—that of "identity politics." Whether in the guise of affirmative action and "quotas" or pluralizing syllabi and multicultural identities, this development seemed to put the squeeze on even a reconstructed category of straight-white-male. For many working-class white men, however wrongly, "preferential" treatment for victims of historical injustice has seemed a great betrayal of the American worker, facilitating an already-insistent migration of jobs to foreign locales and bodies. In this context the rhetoric of multiculturalism and diversity hover with great belittling force. Too often studies of the whiteness of the white working class put forward bleak views of working-class tastes and attitudes and help gird an intellectual community for whom the working-class white male is the most backward and least regenerable portion of the population today.[16] For this reason the perils of an unapologetically academic undertaking like this one ought to be plainly and frankly acknowledged. Given the standard run of attempts on the part of the academy to represent working-class culture, there is plenty of room to worry about the ideological effects of rendering working-class interests and desires for (mostly) other academics. My own sense is that left intellectuals, though inevitably caught up in economies of prestige and therefore subject to various class disidentifications, are not necessarily doomed from the start when they try to investigate working-class life. Surely there are massive dangers involved in their attempts to do so, ones that stem directly from their social location in the academy both as producers of a certain kind of class-based knowledge and as credentializers willy-nilly committed to the partial reproduction of social hierarchy. Just as surely are attempts by erstwhile working-class people to live and identify themselves as working class within the academy up against the most hideous pressures to declass and dis-identify themselves. But those disidentifications do not completely corrupt imaginative acts of working-class cultural reconstruction. The air may be fouled with commonsense definitions of working people as inbred, bloated, bigoted fools, but these definitions exist on precisely the plane one occupies with different readings in order to combat them. This plane may be worlds away from working-class culture proper, but that does not invalidate its capacity for clarity or militancy—though it does entail a necessary intellectual vigilance on the part of the cultural critic. Confronted with the uncertainty and instability of audience response to writing like mine—the im-possibility of guaranteeing that discourse will be received as it was intended to be—there is always the potential for political disaster, but the hazard seems worth courting in the interest of the little good such work might do, and—who knows?—wayward responses of sa-dism and embarrassment could themselves be more edifying than we imagine. At the very least they open to view class feelings that usually remain masked by genteel academic or, conversely, "pro-gressive" decorum.

I will argue that the purpose of Elvis impersonation is to provide "magical" resolutions of these social pressures confronting white working-class masculinity.[17] Buffeted by an era of post-white-male politics, based on an economy of labor that is well-nigh ob-solete in post-Fordist times—in every respect a relic of the postwar working class's better days—blue-collar machismo is produced and reclaimed in the Elvis impersonator but in appropriately damaged and partial form. The fate of working-class masculinity in a postwar era of embourgeoisement followed by scarcity seems subtly en-coded in the arcana and trajectory of Elvis's career, in which most of the impersonators are wholly versed: his meteoric rise in the mid-1950s, the long (if banal) holiday of often (but not always) silly movies in the 1960s, the shattering 1968 comeback, the late con-cert tours before the sad decline to death in 1977. While some of the impersonators perform a whole range of Presley music, the raw 1950s Elvis and the kitschy 1970s Elvis are the favorites, ac-cording to the two principal myths that give "imaginary" form to

Fig. 7. Elvis and Brian, 1994, photo by the author

white working-class masculinity. These myths are less discrete than their historical sources might suggest, sometimes overlapping in a given performer and sometimes not. In any case I take Diana Fuss's point that the identity they help construct owes to the processes of mirroring, mimicry, and identification I am studying here.[18] If the outward signs of working-class affiliation are less and less "given" or inevitable because of the confusing disarticulation of laboring identities in our time—if they now derive much more from the realm of culture than that of work—the two chief Elvis performance styles exist as a place where working-classness may be adopted, confirmed, or secured, even if unconsciously. The first of these, the younger Elvis, is a fantasy of working-class "blackness," and invokes a long American tradition of cultural impersonation. The second, the Vegas Elvis, is a fantasy of "whiteness," which is to say class in displaced form. Both fantasies are rooted in styles of masculine embodiment that owe in turn to the dynamic at the heart of Elvis impersonation—a constant shuttling between looking like a fan and feeling like a king.

The Man Who Would Be King

The art of impersonation is built on a contradiction. Appreciation, deference, spectatorship, and emulation compete with inhabitation, aggression, usurpation, and vampirism. In Elvis impersonation as in other kinds of impersonation, there is an unsteady but continual oscillation between these stances. Elvis impersonators' remarks about their idol reflect a remarkably schizophrenic movement from prostration to megalomania and back again. Bert Hathaway, like a great many of these performers, calls Elvis "the greatest person that has ever walked the face of the earth" (*Guide* 62); Ron Dye remarks with casual seriousness that Elvis was "sent by God for a purpose—to help during troubled times" (*Guide* 43); and several impersonators credit Elvis and his music with helping them through severe personal traumas. Yet even as they recognize the uniqueness and special power of Elvis Presley, these performers yearn in often unconscious ways to unseat the master. Former construction worker and logger Clayton Benke-Smith claims that he is able to wear custom-made jumpsuits made from patterns bequeathed by Elvis's seamstress to their maker, B&K Enterprises, which are "Elvis' *exact* size" (*Guide* 13). Elvis impersonators typically indulge this sort of fortuitousness with trinitarian fervor. On an August 1992 segment of the CBS magazine program *48 Hours* devoted to Elvis impersonators, former car salesman Dennis Wise spoke of impersonating Elvis as "my calling for the last fifteen years. . . . You can't teach somebody to be Elvis—you either have it or you don't." And the impersonator Michael alleges that during one of his re-creations of Elvis's 1973 *Aloha From Hawaii* TV special, a woman gave him a red lei at *precisely the same moment* Elvis received one in the original show (*Guide* 84). These near-oedipal fantasies of replacing the father appear again in Henderson's *Stark Raving Elvis* ("He was the King. . . . *Beat that, Elvis!*" [67]) and in the several performers, like Dennis Wise himself, who have undergone plastic surgery in their quest for authenticity. Yet impersonators are equally happy to make baldly regicidal connections: "The crowds went crazy. They thought I was the real thing," says trucker Ray Kajkowski. On *48 Hours* Dennis Wise remarked, "When people come up to me and say, 'Man, I shut my eyes and I swore it was Elvis up there'—that's when you know you've *got* it." For electronics worker Mike Moat, the "ultimate compliment" would be to have "Elvis fans think of me when they hear Elvis songs"—a peculiar enough inversion of the usual relation of mimic to star to suggest a revealing confusion of motives (*Guide* 91).

This confusion in Elvis's most loyal fans might be understood as a mixing-up of two kinds of looking at Elvis. Laura Mulvey famously codified these (in regard to the movies) as fetishistic scopophilia and voyeurism. The first stems from the pleasure of using someone as an object of sexual stimulation through sight, and is a function of the sexual instincts; the second comes from identification with the projected image, and is a function of ego libido.[19] While in film these looks are essentially spread across differently gendered actors—the woman there to be looked at in a sexual way and the man taking on the male spectator's identification as his perfect or ideal ego—the body of Elvis bears both looks in the arena of Elvis impersonation. Sometimes, as we have seen, he is the fetishized object of impersonators' fascination; at others he is the ideal ego they seek to inhabit or even replace. To be Elvis or to have him—that is the (unacknowledged) question. The issue, though, isn't nearly so clear-cut as this since, as Diana Fuss argues (contra Freud and Lacan), "the desire to be *like* can itself be motivated and sustained by the desire to *possess:* being can be the most radical form of having."[20] As impersonator James Wallace says:

> JW: It's like, I'm James first and Elvis second, and when I'm on the stage, you know, I can be the Elvis side of me, and when I'm offstage I'm James, definitely. It gives me an opportunity to be a fan in the front row, like I said, in the sense that the excitement is in the air for me, similar to what he was able to enjoy himself. . . .
>
> EL: What's it feel like to be Elvis?
>
> JW: Sometimes it feels real powerful and exhilarating and other times it's, uh, kind of scary in the similarities that I have when you visually look at me. Some people have taken it to the extreme of thinking, like, it's the ghost, or the brother, or, you know, things like that.

The oscillation between—or conflating of—Elvis as a source of identification and as a source of contemplation accounts for the impersonators' schizophrenic responses to their idol. Here, though, the two kinds of looking are acted out, white masculinity performed, putting the impersonator at much greater risk than the average cinematic spectator.

For while the ideal ego of a larger-than-life Elvis might seem an attractive counter to the life of forklift and shopfloor, the fact is that it may also implicate the performer in something to which he is never adequate—a confirmation, in psychoanalytic terms, of castration.[21] There may, in other words, be elements of masochism built into the imaginary projection of the ego that Elvis impersonation seems to hold out for its practitioners. So much is suggested by the impersonators' repeated assertions that, as Bill Cochran puts it, "Nobody can ever be another Elvis so to copy him exactly would be virtually impossible" (*Guide* 28). Such disavowals not only confess failure, they let impersonators off the hook, and perhaps account for the number of performers who claim not really to impersonate Elvis so much as recall his aura. "I don't impersonate Elvis, I put on a show," says Rick Marino; telephone worker Danny Vann concedes, "I know I'm not Elvis, nobody can replace him. . . . I don't consider myself an impersonator—I consider myself an interpreter" (*Guide* 113); Donn Jett prefers to think of himself as an impressionist rather than an impersonator, perhaps a distinction without a difference (*Guide* 67). The inherent inability to live up to Elvis's image presents a great problem for this mode of performance, and produces the peculiar situation in which self-apotheosizing results in simultaneous self-damage. Elvis's image is in this sense a kind of fetish which, as Christian Metz writes, enables a phallic self-inflation but also exposes the insufficiency that requires it: "The fetish signifies the penis as absent, it is its negative signifier; supplementing it, it puts a 'fullness' in place of a lack, but in doing so it also affirms that lack."[22] Perhaps this is another reason why landscaper James Wallace finds inhabiting Elvis "kind of scary," a word several impersonators use to describe the experience of being placed on Elvis's pedestal by awestruck fans. In any case, those impersonators who feel this pressure most strongly displace feelings of inadequacy into Elvis-like humility. "They didn't come to see me," says Bob Erickson of his most memorable performance; "they came to see an Elvis show" (*Guide* 52). The irony of all this is that imaginary self-assertion has in practice become a kind of fan-like deference.

Similar reversals attend the other kind of looking at Elvis embodied in his impersonation. Dennis Wise's remark that "I loved [Elvis] with all my heart" and have "dedicated my life to him" suggests (mostly unconsciously) an erotic agenda underlying the fascinated spectatorship of Elvis that returns with potentially disrupting force.[23] Impersonators' enthusiastic accounts of their makeup and apparel ("When I feel like a red night," said Wise on *48 Hours,* "I wear my red one here") perhaps suggest nothing more than the variety of purposes that lie behind transvestism—or as Australian ambulance supervisor Ken Welsh, who personally spent 140 hours embossing his jumpsuit with jewelry, asks defensively, "Who said men can't sew?" (*Guide* 120). But the widespread embarrassment and innuendo surrounding Elvis impersonation points more directly to the homoerotic implications built into such acts. "He's a fag, you know," says a cowboy of Byron Bluford, the impersonator in *Stark Raving Elvis* (36); or as EPIIA head Ron Bessette says of the men who could finally "sing like Elvis, walk like Elvis, be Elvis" once they hooked up with his organization: "A lot of these guys have been in the closet for so long."[24] Often contemplation of the figure of Elvis threatens to become fascination with Elvis's literal figure, as in Clayton Benke-Smith's boast that he and Elvis wear the exact same size of jumpsuit.[25] This must account for former Ford worker and impersonator Marc Roberts's steady disavowal of such intentions: "I loved the guy, but, you know, it's not like a . . . sort of like a homosexual type deal, it's more like how you would love your brother, or a family member, something like that." One feels a bodily fascination with Presley everywhere in conversations with impersonators, but it is true that it comes to the surface in the most displaced ways. These often take the form of curiously adjusted matrimonial scenarios, as in Port Arthur, Texas, entertainer Sammy Stone Atchison's remark that his ultimate fantasy would consist of being recognized as the only good Elvis impersonator, or "the *King's best man in music*" (*Guide* 11). The role of court counselor puts one close enough to the King's person; but how much more so fantasies of taking his place in the marriage bed: ad agent Craig MacIntosh's wife on occasion dresses up as Elvis's onetime wife, Priscilla, while Darrin Race fantasizes about marrying whoever might be found to impersonate Ann-Margret in the role she played in *Viva Las Vegas!* I hope I may be forgiven if this proliferation of impersonations, recalling the Elvis impersonator's own, strike me as displacements of homoerotic attention to Elvis himself.[26] All of this is submerged in the act of performance, but it also typically disguises itself as the concern we have seen with sartorial display, where any too-specific homoerotic charge is buried in a sublimated admiration for Elvis spectacle, the lure of the image. The irony of such spectacle, and of the other displacements, is plainly that the admiring spectatorial contemplation of Elvis becomes a mode of one-upping self-assertion.

Such contradictions and cross-cuttings of feeling and desire in the art of Elvis impersonation make it a highly unstable form, where intended gestures and effects constantly threaten to turn into their opposites. Even before one enters onto the terrain of race and class, the predicament of masculine performativity has unsettled the whole affair. This instability traverses the structures of feeling that so insistently connect Elvis impersonation with the unconscious of working-class white men, to which we must now begin to turn.

The White Negro

Perhaps one of the most curious things about the cult of Elvis is that no fan club or subcultural stylistic affectation will suffice; the body of Elvis must be inhabited. Behind this seemingly bizarre demand lies a history of imitation in which Elvis figures quite centrally. Himself an alleged imposter, the historical referent of Norman Mailer's 1957 "The White Negro," Elvis inherited a blackface tradition that lives a disguised, vestigial life in his imitators.[27] Nobody who thinks with their ears can dismiss Elvis as merely a case of racial rip-off, but the legacy of blackface does lie behind both Elvis and the need for his impersonation. If only as a performative signifier of racial difference through which everyday cross-racial interest was at once facilitated and denied, blackface designates the complex cultural mix that inspired Elvis Presley's music. Given what Robert Cantwell calls the "deep Afro-American hues" of country music's Grand Ole Opry, there was a certain logic, however questionable, behind Opry performers' occasional practice, in the 1930s and after, of playing in blackface. If Elvis's early country songs recalled this practice (Opry star Bill Monroe wrote Presley's hit "Blue Moon of Kentucky"), his early blues songs especially wore a blackface hue. Recall Presley guitarist Scotty Moore's whoop (in a kind of blackvoice falsetto) after a sensual Elvis performance of "Blue Moon" in an early recording session: "*Damn,* nigger!"[28] Presley's not-quite and yet not-white absorption of black style was inevitably indebted to a musical tradition of racial impersonation.[29] Mimicking him, Elvis impersonators impersonate the impersonator in a hall of mirrors, a repetition that nearly buries this racial history even as it suggests a preoccupation with precisely the blackface aura of Elvis (as do, more literally, impersonators' renditions of Dan Emmett's 1859 blackface standard, "Dixie," in the context of Presley's "American Trilogy"). In any case, this double mimicry everywhere implies that Elvis's "otherness" is a partial motive for his impersonators.

Chicago impersonator John Paul Rossi puts a familiar spin on this idea:

EL: You have this really interesting remark [in the *I Am Elvis* guide], "Like Elvis, I think I am a black man wrapped in white skin." Can you say more about that? Because I think people do have this sense that he was kind of a racial crossover figure.

JPR: Ultimately, yeah, I think he was, pretty much—rhythmically, you know, and timing-wise—it's just that rhythm thing of his, right. And like a James Brown, too, he had a lot of that James Brown shtick in there too, and the way he went about singing.

EL: So you really see his music and his whole mode of performing to be indebted to black sounds.

JPR: Definitely, sure, but for that he would have never made it. . . .

EL: Do you get your moves from—do you listen to black records, or watch black performance?

JPR: Yeah, I've bought now, in a row, about six blues CDs, in the last month or so! I'm pretty much indebted to that early blues sound from the '30s, '40s, '50s—Muddy Waters's stuff, Howlin' Wolf, yeah.

Surely Rossi's remark about being a "black man wrapped in white skin" resorts to the dubious and essentialist racial signifiers whose gradual withering away allowed Elvis Presley not to wear black-face. As John Szwed has it, the fact that white-Negro performers like Presley can communicate "blackness" without blackface illustrates the at least partial detachment of culture from color and the increasing interpenetration of black and white styles.[30] However, rhetorical figures like Rossi's ought not be dismissed too grandly, for they rightly register the degree to which "racial" cultures still exist in the face of Elvis's transgressions, and gesture toward some of the more urgent questions raised by Elvis impersonation. Reversing the metaphor of blackface and positing a fundamental "blackness" about Presley, Rossi's words indicate that part of the drama of his impersonation is indeed a racial crossing over. There is no way to partake of an embodied, not to say hidden, "blackness" ("wrapped in white skin") without becoming that body. The problem is how to *represent* this crossing into "blackness" without blackface, and it is here that Elvis impersonation comes to the rescue. It is as though such performance were a sort of second-order blackface, in which, blackface having for the most part overtly disappeared, the figure of Elvis himself is now the apparently still necessary signifier of white ventures into black culture—a signifier to be adopted bodily if one is to have success in achieving the intimacy with "blackness" that is crucial to the adequate reproduction of Presley's show. Eric "Elvis" Domino says that rather than duplicate Elvis's technique, he calls on moves inspired by James Brown, Michael Jackson, Jackie Wilson, and Prince: "In order to do it, you have to *feel* it inside" (*Guide* 39). To feel it inside without betraying it outside is to become Elvis Presley; "blackness" is both an indispensable and invisible part of Elvis impersonation. Blackface minstrelsy has here given way to its iconic, nearly vaporous, suggestion.

The scandal of the black Elvis impersonator makes this fact perfectly clear. His aura of transgression indicates, first, that the image of Elvis is founded on a usually unspoken racial crossing and a phantom or specular evocation of "blackness." Consider a remark from the entry in *I Am Elvis* on house painter Clearance Giddens, a black Elvis: "Fans . . . don't seem to mind that Clearance doesn't look the part because he certainly *sounds* like Elvis" (*Guide* 58). And no wonder, since he's the "source" of Elvis's "act," or at least its goal. While we will see that black meanings do get effaced in the cult of Elvis, it is important to note the sort of racial rapprochements that may also occur in its midst. One *Geraldo* show of August 1992, for example, devoted itself to Elvis impersonators (with, incidentally, Geraldo Rivera himself in impersonator garb and at key moments—usually while talking to black audience-members—in blackvoice). Black Elvis Giddens (who does sound astonishingly like Presley) was a focus of both controversy and extreme fascination, garnering almost as many questions as all of the white impersonators combined. With Geraldo offering little but gawking unease, Giddens both acknowledged the irony of his own position and sought to turn it to the account of interracial solidarity—a desire reciprocated by both the mostly white audience and the white impersonators (and confirmed by the white impersonators I interviewed).

Following Geraldo's smirking query regarding the typical reception of Giddens's act came this exchange:

CG: When I started out, it was unreal, you know . . .

GR: What does "unreal" mean?

CG: Well, they kept saying, "What is a black Elvis?" you know, and uh, then they got to see the show [and] they say, "OK, we can deal with it, it's happenin'."

To this perhaps overly sunny assessment of white racial feeling, Giddens added that his audience at first "was an all-white crowd—now, over the years, it's a mixed crowd now—it's lookin' good!" This upbeat perspective was soon interrupted by the sort of charged moment Geraldo has become notorious for manufacturing. A black audience member stood up and attacked Giddens for betraying his race by mimicking a white entertainer, and a revealing set of exchanges occurred:

BLACK MAN: I'd like to say to the guy in red [Giddens] . . . I think that it's very disrespectful for you to be as a black man, you're supposed to represent us, running around tryin' to be somebody you could never be.

WHITE WOMAN [SHOUTING]:   He's got my vote, he's very good and I like him, as a black Elvis I like him because Elvis dealt a lot with black people, and he's very good!

.   .   .

GIDDENS: What folks gotta understand is music don't have a color to it, you know . . . [applause]

.   .   .

WHITE MAN: Elvis used to listen to gospel music and he's also in effect part black because he did listen to gospel and his musical background is from the black heritage.

.   .   .

WHITE IMPERSONATOR RUSS HOWE: . . . What he's doing is beautiful. [shakes Giddens's hand, to loud applause]

Handshake and applause both, be it noted, were (at least in intention) unpatronizing. No doubt this occurrence came off with an air of rebuke toward black impatience with the figure of Elvis; it also displayed a remarkable ease with the literal return of Presley to his "roots." So does the EPIIA's showcasing of C. J. Charlton, an excellent Cherokee / African American performer and a ringer for James Brown whose prominent place on the 1994 Las Vegas program advertised a certain, if exceptional, commitment to interracial appropriations of Elvis. For their part, black impersonators seem to see Elvis performance as a route of assimilation without an abandonment of cultural complexity; Charlton told me he thought Elvis's meaning could be summed up in one word—"U.S.A."—giving it an inclusive spin that probably exceeds that of most white impersonators.[31]

For the black Elvis's scandal also says that the only legitimate crossing over is from white to black—that for a black man to become Elvis is an implicit humiliation or exposure or ironizing of Presley, a telling form of sacrilege. In comments such as the one I just quoted from the *I Am Elvis* guide, the oscillation between black Elvises' resemblance and nonresemblance to Presley points up an anxiety about the adequacy of Elvis's own impersonation of black cultural practices—indeed an anxiety about his needing (or taking) them in the first place—and an implicit desire to keep him securely this side of the racial divide. This is perhaps the meaning of the necessary hiddenness of "blackness" in Elvis and especially his impersonators; more than simply laying claim to a sort of omniracial cultural power, subsuming the "blackness" on which you depend may just be self-protection—a defense against accusations of theft or inadequacy. Though it seems peculiar for impersonators to access black practices by mimicking a white man, it really is safer that way. In this sense the Elvis impersonator recalls Jack Nicholson's Joker of the film *Batman* (1989), who, as Andrew Ross observes, evokes a threatening racial subtext (his movements underwritten by the Prince soundtrack, he speaks in a sort of rap-rhyming and schemes to spike commercial beauty products with skin-altering substances) that is, however, "wholly occluded."[32] Like the Joker, Elvis and even more so his impersonators are in *whiteface.* The effect of this is, in the end, to bypass the rich play of cultural sources behind Presley's music. Getting a feel for Elvis's black "inside" through his white "outside" ends with the erasure of black culture and the whole dynamic of black mirroring that initially gave rise to Elvis. Thus the real achievement of Elvis impersonators is to both glorify *and* repress the white working-class fascination with "blackness." In the largest sense, impersonating Elvis is a way of living the proximity of one's working-class whiteness to black culture while aggressively forgetting that proximity.

Impersonator Danny Vann emphasizes just this spatial dimension of the matter in his remarks on Elvis's estate, Graceland: "To me, Elvis didn't hold to no race. I mean in fact, if you look where Graceland is, it is now and has always been in the ghetto of Memphis. He was surrounded by more black people than he was white." This imagines Elvis, properly I think, in a geography of racial-cultural adjacency even as it leaves Elvis lording over—and obscuring, at least in white fans' eyes—the scene of which he became the musical representative. This is a situation, in other words, of extraordinary ambivalence, in which black working-class masculinity both aids and threatens white working-class male self-definition. The popularity of

Elvis and his impersonators suggests that the assumption of white working-class codes of masculinity in the United States is partly negotiated through an imaginary black interlocutor but that the latter must remain only dimly acknowledged. Moreover, if white male fantasies of black men partially structure white "manliness," the consequences of this affair are quite complex. As Philip Cohen has observed, the threat of "blackness" may call forth vehement disavowals, but the subterranean accents of desire for and envy of black men and their imagined physical adeptness and grace may always return, a return that implies a recognition that black and white both inhabit the same proletarian public realm.[33] The relation of these lived outcomes to racist violence on one hand and organized radicalism on the other is itself complex and variable, though the pinched class context I have outlined surely tilts these complicated and ambivalent feelings in a less than liberatory direction. Yet the very form of Elvis impersonation suggests the great mistake of ignoring its racial complexity, and that of working-class white men generally. Certain classic studies of working-class racial attitudes and racial politics, it seems to me, unnecessarily close down the logical possibility of radicalism located in white working-class racial ambivalence. David Roediger's brilliant study of the racism of the nineteenth-century working class, *The Wages of Whiteness*, for example, ends up circumscribing the chances for cross-racial solidarity in the name of tough-mindedness and honesty. Certainly the book is a necessary corrective to the Old Left slogan "Black and white, unite and fight." But with such a straitened view of working-class racial politics, one is hard pressed to explain even the most fleeting instant of interracial solidarity or cross-racial interest, let alone exploit such instances for truly resistant uses.[34] If Elvis impersonation is any indication, white racial ambivalence is the unwitting host of certain generous impulses as well as of an inability to acknowledge the fascination with racial difference on which they are partly based. Such performance may indeed be saying that constrictions of material circumstance have exiled white workingmen's complexity of racial feeling from everyday life into fantasy about the figure of Elvis Presley.

To the extent that black cultural resonances are suppressed even in Elvis impersonation, the masculine problematic I discussed earlier reveals just how this occurs. In approximating Elvis's assumed "blackness," approaching his "otherness," the impersonators, I would suspect, fear coming up short. The threat of inadequacy in the identification with an Elvis ego-ideal is perhaps traceable less to the figure of Elvis in this case than to the black cultural components upon which his image absolutely depends, and which lie behind the substitution of Elvis for the black interlocutor—James Brown, say. (This substitution may speak to moments on the street of white male working-class racial hostility born of "castration anxiety.") Imaginary self-projection may quickly deflate when it is held up to the black "source," particularly when this is overlaid with white male fantasies of black men's sexual potency, and so perhaps requires black invisibility—and fetish-Elvis's replacement of this (b)lack—to be fulfilled. It may be that the longing to replace one's performative ideal, whether Elvis or his black alter-ego, is already a displacement (if not a component) of one's desire for it; we have seen how easily the spectatorial admiration on which Elvis impersonation depends can flip over into homoerotic interest—the presence of which may well indicate another reason for the disavowal of black maleness in this mode of performance. (One need only think here of the self-conscious banter concerning same-sex desire between Mel Gibson and Danny Glover in those demotic favorites, *Lethal Weapon, Lethal Weapon 2,* and *Lethal Weapon 3,* the banter both raising and dissolving the specter of interracial male desire.) But certainly the conventional displacement of homosex into male identification is in turn liable to cast into doubt one's ability to outdo the "original."[35] Therefore many Elvis impersonators circumvent "blackness" altogether in their performances, eclipsing an imagined set of attributes to which they are in fact powerfully attracted and indebted. Their solution to the felt embattlement of white masculinity is an assumption of the figure of Elvis, which to a great extent buries his "blackness" and at the same time appropriates its power.

What white impersonators are up against was demonstrated on the *Geraldo* episode that featured the impersonators en bloc. After they had all had a chance to perform during the course of the show, the audience was asked (by way of applause) to pick the best impersonator—or as Geraldo put it, the "most authentic Elvis." The winner: Clearance Giddens, the black Elvis. Proving that the attractiveness of "blackness" lies hidden in the skin of Elvis and his impersonators, this upset also revealed the reason for its constant, anxious suppression—a haunting sense of inadequacy expressing in distorted dreamwork form the diminished options of white working people.

Class Act

Loftier ideals surround "late Elvis," and give an extra twist to the term. A few impersonators credit themselves with sparking rumors of an Elvisian afterlife—"Elvis Alive and Well in Kalamazoo"—but more than a few have been touched by his posthumous presence. Janice K, the Lady Elvis, experienced an Elvis visitation that left a nearby tree "scorched and singed" (*Guide* 71). Mystical testimony abounds among Elvis impersonators. "In the beginning there was the word and the word was Elvis," says Clayton Benke-Smith (*Guide* 12). Sammy Stone Atchison remarks that "Elvis was the most charismatic person ever on earth except for Jesus" (*Guide* 10). Full-time impersonator Dave Carlson describes his audiences as "lonely people who are looking for someone to save them—and that's what Elvis was all about." Impersonators and their audiences aren't crackpots and hallucinators; rather they prove the force of V. S. Naipaul's view of Elvis in *A Turn in the South* (1989) as a sort of beatified redneck, with Graceland a version of the New Jerusalem.[36] The last shall be first, says this saint of the people.

   It is indeed the class profile of the carpenter from Galilee that inspires the impersonators. Sammy Stone Atchison, the man who compares Elvis's charisma to that of Jesus, also provides him a more secular gloss:

EL: [Elvis] is a pretty large figure, at this point, in the annals of American culture—what do you think he stands for, what does this figure mean in the larger sense, as a kind of myth, almost?

SSA: It's like what I've been hearing recently on some of these programs on Elvis that pretty well have described it. It was the American Dream—that if this man that had nothin' could go to that plateau in his life in America, well, then

other people could and that's what set all that off in the
'50s and it's still happening. They think about how he
persisted and he made it and he had nothin' as far as any
finances, and so they figure well, there's a chance for all of
us. It was a rags-to-riches story and that doesn't happen
very much and it's just something they saw happenin' and
could happen.

. . .

Elvis is a symbol of what America stands for, the choice
to start from the bottom and rise to the top—and remain
there. (*Guide* 10)

On the surface, at least, Elvis seems to embody an age-old tale about
the romance of rising in America. If the clinching phrase here strikes
one as a little odd—neither Jesus nor Elvis remained safely at the
top—its very overstatement is interesting. This is Elvis being willed
into the American Dream, or vice versa, the effort coming through
in the insistence that one *can* remain at the top even though one
chooses to start at the bottom . . . *what?* How is it that Elvis's success
gave people like him the idea that "there's a chance for all of us" if
this rags-to-riches story "doesn't happen very much"? The cracks in
Atchison's mightily overdetermined and heartfelt reading of Elvis
indicate that another chief reason for his impersonation is to provide an imaginary triumph over the working-class circumstances for
which he continues to stand.

Full-time impersonator E. P. King sums this up well: "What
I think of is a country boy that didn't have nothin', that started
out with nothin', and just made it and made himself the greatest
thing since popcorn, you know what I mean? I mean, anyone that
didn't have nothin', that lived in a *shack,* to go to the heights that
Elvis did—you've gotta give a man credit for that, you know." Impersonator Danny Vann's remarks suggest that this class revenge–
fantasy, apparently a significant aspect of Elvis's image among the
impersonators, depends by definition on Elvis's inwardness with
working-class life:

In my opinion, Elvis represented, to the people that grew
up with him and to the people today, a person who could

feel what they felt. He was a character that was bigger than life, that was able to get up there and *feel* his songs. If you listen to the way he sang the songs, he *lived* those songs he sang, and he reached out and touched people through those songs. He sang about life—you know, "Love Me Tender," "Don't Be Cruel," "I'm All Shook Up," "Burning Love"—you know, that's what country-western has been throughout all the years, too, is singing about life, but they always pick on the negative side; Elvis looked on the beautiful side.

Here is a version of what T. S. Eliot (of all people), in his obituary of working-class music-hall singer Marie Lloyd, called the "collaboration" between artist and audience "which is necessary in all art and most obviously in dramatic art." Eliot's rather untypical remarks about Lloyd quite resemble Danny Vann's about Elvis and his audience (which includes his impersonators, and *their* audiences): "It was, I think, this capacity for expressing the soul of the people that made Marie Lloyd unique, and that made her audiences, even when they joined in the chorus, not so much hilarious as happy. . . . It was her understanding of the people and sympathy with them, and the people's recognition of the fact that she embodied the virtues which they genuinely most respected in private life, that raised her to the position she occupied at her death."[37] Or, as young-Elvis impersonator Ray Guillemette puts it, "To me, you could see that he sang and he lived and he existed for those people that put him where he was." Elvis called (and still calls) forth working-class allegiances from audiences who, in Danny Vann's terms, know about "life." Elvis was, Vann's remarks intimate, one of "us"; he felt what "we" felt, was bigger than life but still *lived* it. And in the living came a victory over toil and limit (country-western's "negative side of life") that provides an imaginary victory ("the beautiful side") to this day for his impersonators and their followers. It is important to note that this imaginary victory does not deny or finesse but rather confirms and celebrates a particular kind of working-class cultural sensibility, a sensibility, moreover, that is less some immediate expression of any clearly defined U.S. working-class world than an achieved product of Elvis impersonators and their audiences.

Turning to the historical significance of this sensibility, Vann adumbrates what we might call the Cadillac connection. Vann's remarks not only stress the centrality of Elvis's class triumph to Elvis impersonation, they powerfully link a number of seemingly unrelated historical elements—Presley's popularity in the North, the auto industry, working-class structures of feeling, and the peculiar density of Elvis sightings and Elvis impersonators in Michigan, particularly the Detroit area:

DV: For those who grew up with him, [Elvis] was the kid next door, you know, rags-to-riches type thing, everyone can relate to that as well. We're a compassionate society, and when we see somebody who had it rough who made it big, our heart goes out to him, you know, and we're behind him. . . . *I* felt moved by what he sang; otherwise I don't think I could keep singing the same songs myself for twenty-five years and still enjoy them. . . . And I feel there are times when I'll do a song like "My Way," or something like that, that I even get choked up, even singing it, let alone, you know, what it does to the crowd. It's just that the whole atmosphere, the audience—having the opportunity to get up there and move an audience to their feet is just an unparalleled thrill, you know. So I really feel grateful for the opportunity.

EL: . . . You say there are more than three dozen Elvis impersonators in the [Detroit] area—this is really interesting to me. . . .

DV: A lot of auto workers migrated from the South. There's a lot of country folk here. They have a suburb of Detroit called Taylor, Michigan, and its nickname is "Taylortucky," there are so many people from Kintuck there, you know. I've done several shows there, and of course I have to do "Kentucky Rain," and it brings the house down! Detroit's a melting-pot city.[38]

A central fact of twentieth-century American social history is, I believe, encoded in the odd practice of Elvis impersonation. If, as so many have suggested, the decline of the auto industry is part and parcel of the constriction of working-class life in recent decades (the central episode in the erosion of working-class embourgeoisement and the masculine "pride of place" that accompanied it), it would be hard to overstate the significance of the Motor City's embrace of Elvis—mythologizer, owner, and bestower of pink Cadillacs. Apparently condensed in the figure of Elvis are a whole range of social facts and facts of feeling. To reclaim and embody Elvis is to recall the moment in U.S. history when auto workers drove an American prosperity and an empowered masculinity that they believed would shortly be their own. (A friend of mine who had worked all his life in State of Illinois warehouses and shopfloors used to tell me over and over that when he retired he was going to buy himself a Cadillac.) The figure for this power and success is Elvis himself, whom Danny Vann notes "had it rough [and] made it big" and whose example provides a similar kind of "opportunity" for Vann the impersonator and implicitly his audiences. The connection of "Kintuck" with the Detroit auto industry makes available a host of affective alliances and lends this triumphant mode of performance its air of working-class solidarity.[39] Vann's own intense emotion as he sings that ode to manly autonomy, "My Way," gives us a sense of its singular power as a working-class cri de coeur in addition to its singular kitschiness as a bleat of overstated individualism; and it's this class resonance Vann invokes when he says that "our heart goes out to" the poor-boy-made-good who could represent a "melting-pot" constituency so victoriously.

Much is made of the royal excesses that crowned Elvis's rise to the top—not only the Cadillacs but also the sideburns, the polyester, the sheer physical outwardness—by impersonators of the later, Vegas Elvis. These entertainers display the propensity of working-class men to resist their class subjection in and through the body, enacting rituals of self-assertion and imaginary beneficence. Simple pleasures become exorbitant emblems. We have already seen the great investment in costume; one of the impersonators on *Geraldo*, Mike Memphis, claimed that his jeweled cape alone cost eleven hundred dollars. Dave Carlson performs as part of his act an "Elvis in a Dream" sequence in which, as he explains it, "the guy who looks like the M.C. of the show, he says he fell asleep watching an old Elvis movie and he dreamed that Elvis was performing the show—then all of a sudden the *2001* music starts and the lights go down and smoke comes up and I appear out of that—it's like a dream." To a man, the impersonators capitalize on the theatrics of excess. The striving for enlarged and fantastical embodiment behind the accoutrements of Elvis spectacle calls to mind Georg Simmel's analysis of "adornment." "The radiations of adornment, the sensuous attention it provokes, supply the personality with . . . an enlargement or intensification of its sphere: the personality, so to speak, *is* more when it is adorned." Thus, according to Simmel, is *having* transformed into *being*.[40] In Elvis impersonation one acquires not only the majestic treasures of Elvis's person but, in a sense, Elvis's person too. This in turn *makes* more, as Simmel would have it, of the person of the impersonator. Onstage, aided by late Elvis's karate kicks, sweaty scarves, and myriad superfluous physical feats, the impersonators undergo an achieved, sometimes prosthetic, self-enlargement. As Ray Kajkowski says of his first Elvis performance:

> They had a '50s dance at the bowling alley, and they had an Elvis impersonator contest there—I didn't look anything like Elvis. . . . They only had one other contestant in it and the prize was fifty dollars, and I'd drank a couple three beers, I guess, and decided I was able to do it. . . . I got up there, and I don't remember what song I did, it was kind of a fast-moving song, you know I was wiggling the microphone and carrying on. And I watched this other guy . . . he just stood there with a guitar, I think he sang "That's Alright, Mama" or something, but you know, he didn't move or nothin', he just stood there and sang. So I says "No, Elvis *moved,*" you know, 'cause I watch those TV specials. So that's what I did. At the end of the song I dropped down on one knee, and there was this table of about eight gals old enough to appreciate Elvis, I dropped down on one knee and kissed this gal's hand. For two, two and a half minutes of stupidity I made fifty dollars! I decided if I could do that I might as well go into doing it. . . . That was in October of '87 and in January of '88 I did my first show. So it just started growing from that. Now I've got two limousines, and I take bodyguards, and all that.

From his sense that Elvis *moved* to his hiring of limos and body-guards, Kajkowski here calls on precisely the physical bigness that translates into personal power: out of the bowling alley and into the showroom.[41]

Ron George says he sought such self-enlargement in concert performances as opposed to small clubs or dance halls:

> When I started doing this, I was doing, like, the cabaret thing in Nevada, and all of them are not like night-clubs. . . . They're showrooms, and they hold anywhere from three hundred to five hundred people, but they're still basically a showroom, you don't go dancing or any-thing, you go in, sit down, and you're entertained. So it's an entertainment concert, is what it is. Where if you took it into a small place—one time I was talked into doing one in a nightclub . . . people dancing, and that. And I just hated it, because that wasn't what he was about; he was about—like I said, it was a big, it was a spectacle. I mean, it might sound funny, the first time I ever saw him was when he came out in 1969, Oakland Coliseum in California, and I would say that—and I saw him six times afterwards—sitting in the audience with the people that are around you, and watching everybody in that place, 20,000 people, I would not be surprised that if Jesus walked out onstage that he would get any more attention than Elvis did. It was that amazing—it was like you didn't believe that was a real person actually coming out and doing that. . . . Nobody even comes close—*except* for Neil Diamond.

If the modern sports arena was the only venue capable of featuring Elvis's enormity, the impersonator's showroom seems necessary to help call that enormity back. No surprise, then, that imperson-ator Marc Roberts's favorite performance memory is a pregame gig in Cleveland Stadium for 45–50,000 baseball fans that was covered by three major networks, CNN, ESPN, and the Sports Channel. The important point about all of these instances of performative self-aggrandizement is that their rootedness in the spectacle of the body is no mistake, more a cause than an effect of the vogue of Elvis impersonation. It is an extension of a working-class male dynamic of social puissance through physical assertion.

And this emphasis on the body is, I would insist, a cultural handling of class opposition—not the mindless flash or entertaining distraction that most are quick to assume working-class audiences want. That very assumption was treated with great disdain by the impersonators with whom I spoke. "A lot of the media . . . [ask] really dumb questions," Dave Carlson told me. "They would say, 'So, you guys all sittin' around eating cheeseburgers?,' stuff like that. And I'd say, 'If you're gonna talk to me like that I won't even talk to you, if you're gonna ask something serious, I'll be glad [to talk].' "[42] This from the man who does the immaculately tasteful "Elvis in a Dream" act! It may well be in direct antagonism to the popular view of late Elvis and his impersonators that Elvis performers embrace the overblown, stress the kitsch, wear it like a badge of honor. What reads to many as "bad taste" may just be a refusal to conform to middle-class dictates on such matters, and when impersonators are called on their excessive behaviors, they retort with a pointed fuck-you. If class is indeed a "relational" category, as E. P. Thompson taught us generations ago, then the working-class habits and tastes to which Elvis impersonators give one form arise at least partly in response to—against—middle-class expectations and observations.[43] In Elvis impersonation, I would argue, the middle-class (academic no less than corporate media) gaze is forcefully returned, and many of the impersonators seem to be aware of the fact. John Paul Rossi admits that he occasionally visits the supermarket dressed as Elvis:

EL: Lots of jokes are always made about Elvis impersonators, and my sense is that people like you are a lot more serious about it than these jokes suggest. Do you ever treat it as a joke? Or are you treated like a joke by some people? Do you get wisecracks or anything?

JPR: Some of the times when I'm seen, like, in a supermarket, 'cause sometimes I wear my hair long with the sideburns, people will look at me kind of cross-eyedly, you know. "Why do you look like that?" "Well," I tell 'em, "I do the Elvis thing, you know." And they'll kind of start laughing.

That's really about the only time when I'm looked upon as a negative. . . .

EL: It's interesting to me, though, that you go out to the grocery store looking like that. I mean, that's cool. Why do you do that—it's just, you feel like it, or it's after a performance, or it's before a performance, or what?

JPR: I guess it's kind of like a psych-out thing. I do it a lot before a performance. I'll let my hair out and the sideburns, and all that there. Just to see if I can get any attention, too— sometimes I like to be the center of attention.

Dick Hebdige once read punk fashion as a violent working-class negation of the middle-class look;[44] I read the investment in Elvis as a more "traditionalist" version of this resistant sense of stylistic difference. As impersonator Joe Paige says of his seventh-grade mimicry of Elvis: "It was the age of Elton John and Led Zeppelin, and liking Elvis was a little different."[45] Impersonator Ron George stresses (again) the physical, "manly" dimension of this class feeling. "Of all the guys that were in the business, [Elvis] was the rough-and-tumble asskicker. . . . All of the others, the Ricky Nelsons, and Fabian, and Pat Boone, and all—they were all kind of, you know, the little sissy kind of guys; Elvis was a street kid, kick-ass. All the guys could relate to that."[46]

The finale of impersonator Tony Grova's version of Presley's "American Trilogy" at the 1994 EPIIA convention makes plain the working-class traditionalism of Elvis impersonators' cultural politics. At once embarrassing and stirring, Grova's emphatic bended-knee, back-turned presentation of an eagle-embossed sequined cape announced a twin devotion to American nationalism (the eagle in flight) and to the sequin implicit in this form's aggressive stylistic heroics. The performance of determined class self-respect as "American Trilogy's" masculine, kitschy, and frankly nationalist theatricality, however, ought to be marked as a working-class statement of the firmest sort. If the impersonators suggest this persona equally rejects the liberated sexual ethos of Elton John *and* the middle-class reactionary persona of Pat Boone, this is because there is here a popular investment in reclaiming American nationalism from its perceived usurpers—however similar their politics may seem on the face of it—and dissenting from their unearned, complacent jingoism. Tony Grova's "American Trilogy" communicated something close to a spellbinding working-class rendition of "America the Beautiful" I once heard—a confounding spectacle, it would seem, of some of American nationalism's main victims celebrating (with feeling) the sentiments used to exploit their labor at home and their bodies in wars abroad. Not so confounding, in fact. The vehemence of this crowd's collective shout, like certain Elvis impersonators' overblown finales, momentarily took back the nation and gave it to some of the people on whose backs it had been built.

The fantasies of Elvisian excess, then, mean anything but upward mobility; imperial selfhood, rather, not class envy but self-validation. I read Sammy Stone Atchison's fantasia of mobility, which I have quoted, as a trope of triumph rather than a longing to enter a higher class. Even in Atchison's idea that you can choose to start at the bottom, there is a muted identification with people *down here* rather than *up there*. Henderson's *Stark Raving Elvis* makes the case: "Here was a man who made pure style out of being white trash. He was dazzling. He didn't apologize for anything. He turned it into gold. With Elvis as your guide, there was no need to hide your bush-hog status in front of rich kids—you strutted it right in their faces. . . . Being Elvis was being *somebody*" (12). The flip side of this self-conscious class will is a collective ethos affirming a commitment to working-class mutuality and solidarity. For example, the EPIIA conventions significantly refuse to mount impersonator competitions; the collective, celebratory "showcase" is the chosen form. Moreover, a few performers do only charity work, and nearly all of them consider such work an important part of their schedules.[47] Impersonator Rick Ardisano from Illinois prizes Elvis's image as a "humanitarian, you know, giving things to people no matter what race, creed, or color, you know, it didn't matter to him. . . . They were a human being like everybody else, he treated everybody the same—and that's what I like about him"; Pittsburgh impersonator Dave Atkins says the figure of Elvis stands for "helping people . . . and that's what I enjoy doing"; Bobby Erickson dreams of doing a "show for charity that would generate millions of dollars for many needy children" (*Guide* 52). This impulse appears in other impersonators as a desire to bestow on friends the sudden extraordinary gifts of which Elvis was capable.[48] Louie Michael Bunch Jr. says he "would love to be able to go into a dealership and order a fleet of cars for my friends and family" (*Guide* 22). Talking to the impersonators, one gets the idea that Elvis went wrong not because of his famed indulgences but because, in the end, the signs of collectivity—the exorbitantly outfitted party spaces, the handsome gifts—substituted for the social relations they were meant to cement. Thus EPIIA president Rick Marino lovingly recalled to me the camaraderie that attended waiting all day in line for Elvis tickets and then, three months later, seeing the show. And Ray Kajkowski stresses Elvis's "tender-hearted, easy-going" side:

> You see [Elvis] played up a lot as a bad temper, and all that. Well, I think he probably had a little temper; I do too, you know. But, you know, I care about somebody standing there with a sign that says "I'll work for food," too, you know, I care about those people. I think some of my feelings are on the same lines, as far as I care about people. I certainly'll never be anything like he was, you know, as far as a big name or nothing. . . . But I think, you know, because of the type of person—he cared for people and their needs, their real needs, not just givin' 'em money and saying, "Here, here you go."

Real needs, not just money: the bottom line is human connection. This is a rather striking emphasis in a mode of performance known for its glitter and monomania.

It is nevertheless significant that, as far as I was able to make out, this elemental collective urge is manifested only in ideologies of charity. No overtly political persona of a distinctly working-class kind obstructs the purity of the Elvis impersonator's emphasis on style (in this, as in so many other ways, the impersonators are true to Presley himself). The summer of 1994 when I visited Vegas for this work, the 40,000-member Culinary Workers Local 226, affiliate of the Hotel and Restaurant Employees International, happened to be engaged in pitched rhetorical and often sidewalk combat with the 5,005-room megaresort MGM Grand Hotel and Theme Park, which had refused to sign a union contract for its 8,000 union-eligible workers. This struggle, involving protest gatherings (to the blared music of Elvis's fellow "traditionalist" Bruce Springsteen) and routine picketing (one picketer confidently assured me a union victory), emblematized Las Vegas's status as the "last great union town in America" and MGM Grand's place in that town as a possible "River Rouge of gambling."[49] Not one of the impersonators I spoke to at the convention had even heard of the struggle. Post-Fordism in a nutshell, I thought; the CIO is dead, and with it any sense of national political solidarity to accompany the impersonators' working-class nationalist cultural politics. But this was overhasty: such cultural politics, in precisely post-Fordist fashion, are a key place where erstwhile political solidarities are outlined and affirmed, the historical template through which class is now often defined. This is why Bill Clinton won partially on what we might call an Elvis slate (an impersonator gigged at Clinton's inaugural ball), and why his abandonment of that slate in his politically transparent "middle-class bill of rights" was so terminally disappointing.[50]

Elvis impersonators work their cultural solidarities to create something beyond the hype: a *promesse de bonheur* that embodies the group good time of a liberated Saturday night.[51] Recall T. S. Eliot's words about Marie Lloyd making her audiences "not so much hilarious as happy." This collective principle of hope shows up in the utopian strain in many impersonators' remarks. Over and over the performers told me that they helped recall for Elvis's fans a better, happier time—what we have seen Danny Vann call the "beautiful side" of life. Rick Marino put it to me like this: "Seems like everybody thinks about when they were young when they think about Elvis. It takes a lot of people back to an earlier time in their life, where we didn't have all the problems we have today.... Things just seemed to be, you know, going to a Dog 'n' Suds and using the phone, and—it just seemed to be more fun. I don't think that people today have fun and I think that Elvis is a real large symbol of that." Ron George, who concurs nearly verbatim with this view, concludes: "And the people, of course, that look at it, the media, they want to make fun of it because they don't understand it." The elements of escapism in these remarks are balanced by the sense that Elvis's fans understand something that the media and other outsiders don't—that "cunning and high spirits," as Walter Benjamin wrote, best equip one to meet the world.[52] Impersonator Dave Carlson remarks that Elvis "made us happy, made us feel good, and that obviously is the goal of every entertainer, that's what we're hired for, is to make people happy." Jordanian American impersonator Nazar Sayegh told me that his purpose in performance is to "try to give back as much as possible the euphoria that this man had left behind." No trivial affair, this: for all wish-fulfillment, as Ernst Bloch wrote, even fairy tales and pulp fiction, may be "castle in the air par excellence, but one in good air and . . . the castle in the air is right." Speaking of the pulp fiction hero, who bears an unmistakable resemblance to Elvis Presley, Bloch writes:

> [He] does not wait, as in the magazine story, for happiness to fall into his lap, he does not bend down to pick it up either like a bag thrown to him. Rather [he] remains related to the poor thickskin of the folk-tale, the bold boy who sets corpses on fire, who takes the devil for a ride. . . . The romanticism of the robber thus shows a different face, one which has appealed to poor folk for centuries, and colportage [pulp fiction] knows all about it. . . . Here there is immature, but honest substitute for revolution.[53]

It bears keeping in mind that this is the best moment of the working-class wish-fulfillment visible in Elvis impersonation. For its collective esprit does depend on male physical prowess and includes women only insofar as they become fans, admirers, and passive gazers—hands for the impersonators to kiss. Impersonator Bert Hathaway's wife, Linda, makes a virtue of this particular "necessity": "It is exciting seeing the women go after [Bert] like that" (*Guide* 62). Throughout my analysis we are firmly in the realm of male aggrandizement and self-definition, the mundane, bruising privileges of patriarchy, which is only partially redeemed by its class ethos. In Lillian Rubin's *Worlds of Pain* there is ample documentation of working-class women's struggle to be something more than mere dependencies, subordinate to the male "provider" (who, as often as not, is not the sole provider). As one young repairman remarked of his wife, "She doesn't want there to be a king in this household" (176). King onstage, then, if not within the family. Impersonator Ron George concedes point-blank that Elvis was "a sexist," and most impersonators play to predominantly female working-class audiences whose particular investment in Elvis impersonators deserves some comment.

What I found in talking to female fans of the impersonators was a volatile mixture of apparent devotion, frankly spectatorial desire, and a healthy dose of ironic distance. Las Vegas fan Ruth Madeiras and California fan Jana Stanford conveyed the respectful ruling tone of female audience-members in averring that their role was (in Madeiras's words) "keeping him alive" and (in Stanford's words) supporting the men who "keep the legend alive." But I caught other accents as well. Stanford is herself a sometime impersonator, and thus struck me as a more self-conscious member of the audience than might have appeared to be the case: she was an implicit rival as well as admirer, perhaps taking full stock of the performers beneath her official fealty to them; and she knew from their vantage point what they needed from an audience, perhaps performing that role as on other occasions she performs its opposite number. It is hard to believe, watching the seemingly spontaneous combustion of female adoration for the Elvis performer (quite a spectacle in its own right, as women line up to kiss the performer and receive a sweated scarf), that some such self-consciousness is entirely absent from the public erotic indulgence that is at any rate given free rein by many female fans. Nor is outright irony banished from the audience though it be repressed onstage. I spoke with two women attending the EPIIA convention together who were perfectly capable of laughing it up about the flying Elvises in *Honeymoon in Vegas* even as they made fine and serious distinctions among the performers they liked at the convention. They too had seen *Geraldo*'s impersonators show, and made merciless fun of his masculine pretensions: "Maybe people should impersonate Geraldo." The culture of impersonation itself seemed the brunt of some buried amusement here, a hunch that was confirmed by a remark that followed. Geraldo, said one of the women, is "probably an Elvis wannabe and he's just jealous." As Geraldo goes, so go the impersonators—none of the King's men immune to the feminist deflations that may occur in the demanding and audacious audience that Elvis performers try to regard as one more prop. We underestimate the female fans of Elvis's performing male fans if we miss their complex ensemble of motives and impulses, including not only selfless celebration but also self-conscious theatrics, not only love but unspoken identification, frank sexual objectification, and severe ironic humor.

The needy ambience of Elvis performing—its requiring fawning women spectators who at any moment may ridicule or dump you—suggests the sense of inadequacy that haunts it; a built-in hidden injury returns to dampen the working-class transcendence of Elvis shows. As Byron Bluford, *Stark Raving Elvis*'s working-class impersonator protagonist, complains: "There's no way to rest, you never go far enough." This is what beats him in the end: "Colonel Parker [Elvis's manager] didn't need him, didn't need a new Elvis. There would be no heir to the King, no such thing, none of them would take his place, nobody. . . . Kneel down and eat your fantasy, boy! And who the hell were we even talking about now? Byron. Byron. Byron. Who the hell was that now?" (181, 203–204). The literally masochistic configuration of this scene, in which the performer's inability to replace or reproduce Elvis becomes prostration before the master and then an emptying of the self, is the fabulist version of the everyday high-wire act that Elvis impersonators perform. This drama of inferiority is obviously played out in both gender and class terms; the masculine anxiety that requires Elvis performers' self-verifying self-projection overdetermines its proletarian struggle for self-validation. The "secondary identification" (to borrow from Freud) with Elvis through which self-projection occurs seems something like a theatricalized oedipal introjection of him—necessary to the achievement of identity but never securely accomplished. Byron Bluford's dazed repetition of his own name to himself, a name that seems to verge on the meaningless and so requires repetition, is the perfect picture of this dilemma.[54] More impersonators than fictional Byron Bluford have betrayed this problem to us, safe to say; but I would stress that it suffuses the class drama of Elvis impersonation as a sort of performative requirement rather than a group psychological profile: because it sums up something about the achieved working-classness of the disparate impersonators and their audiences rather than expresses in any given or direct way their immediate social or psychological circumstances. By the same token, this deep sense of inadequacy is not *simply* a hazard or by-product of impersonating Elvis Presley. I would argue that amid this feeling of being unable

192 || Black Mirror

to fully capture or represent Elvis is a subjective recognition of oppression. The structure of Elvis impersonation perfectly grasps structures of masculine working-class feeling because the failures and embarrassments that shadow it are homologous with working-class "injured dignity," as Richard Sennett and Jonathan Cobb call it. Sennett and Cobb's notion of the "hidden injuries of class," while it underestimates the clarity about class possessed by the popular classes, aptly describes one moment of working-class subjectivity wherever it lives—that resort to self-blame in a context of American individualism which "reminds" white workingmen that the class position they have inherited and which they resist in so many ways is ultimately their own fault (79, 95–96, 151–188, 256).

This is not to parrot the conventional wisdom about working-class people lacking in self-esteem because they have "failed," a pitying and condescending view that carries with it more than a whiff of blame. It is, rather, to note the working-class resonance of a performance in which the "star" strives to be *somebody*—Elvis—that, in the end, he can't be. Elvis impersonating results in an apt scene of abjection: it surely is every man for himself, sawing the air and getting nowhere but doing it with style. Impersonator James Wallace's moving and insightful remarks on Elvis's decline, so unlike the glibly cynical renderings of both academe and TV, illustrate, I think, a sense of the injury Elvis seems to represent and that the impersonators, for class reasons, appear to want to claim:

> And as for his later years and his downfall, you know, as a lot of people tend to call it, I don't know—I mean, if he wasn't Elvis Presley out there in the world he'd be another person who had some bad things hit him in his life and he wasn't able to handle it and he had a downfall trying to handle it, you know. If any other person had their mother fall away from him, and that was the closest thing to his heart, and then his replacement was Priscilla and she left him, and he had a lot of problems with his physical stature because of the hours he was living and the life he was leading, it'd be quite depressing and hard to keep. . . . If it was you or I we wouldn't hear about it, but it's him and he's a public figure where the world sees it in a negative light. . . .

He was very insecure about doing anything that he was doing, 'cause he didn't think he had the magnetism he did. But when he got out there, he almost kind of was giddy about it 'cause he'd just laugh like, "Why they acting like that?," you know, "What am I doing?" One guy said to him, I don't remember who it was, "Just get out there and do it again, boy, you're doing great." . . .

You can look at a man and you can degrade a man, but he's the one who's gonna have to be makin' the decision on his own self, and he did whatever decisions he had to make.

It is the tragic view of Elvis that links him with "you or I" in Wallace's remarks—just another person "who had some bad things hit him." The blind-sided vulnerability of that phrase is as surely a language of class as the sense of insecurity Wallace attributes to Elvis and by implication to his impersonators is its performative analogue. And yet responsibility for one's own fate is here laid at the doorstep of workingmen everywhere—not only a (perhaps contradictory) assertion of one's own agency and humanity in the face of overwhelming odds but an echo of shame about that fate which is best depicted in the impossibility of impersonating Elvis Presley.

Elvis, then, as metaphor: a retro fantasy in spectral garb; an imaginary resolution of a historical predicament that working-class white men can neither fully face nor forget. No doubt Elvis functions in working-class life as a sort of cultural herald, something to rally round and reclaim. What else were all the tabloid stories, all the impersonations in so many VFWs and Moose Lodges, but a momentary reclamation of something "they" are imagined to have taken from "us"? Impersonating Elvis is in this sense a sustained and intense moment of performative working-class self-creation or production. We have seen the ambivalences and compromises of that production, the embattled racial and gender postures, the haunting sense of insufficiency, themselves telling and somewhat depressing summations of working-class feeling. While reports of Elvis Presley's death, as the tabloids still sometimes remind us, may be greatly exaggerated, the "king" is, in the ways I have sketched, surely ailing. And yet in the realm of the spirit, Elvis, for better and worse, lives on.

CHAPTER 8

JUST LIKE JACK FROST'S BLUES

Masking and Melancholia in
Bob Dylan's *"Love and Theft"*

WHEN GRAVITY FAILS AND NEGATIVITY don't pull you through, put on a mask. America is a land of masking jokers, Ralph Ellison said, trying to find some kind of way outta here.[1] Latitude is what you want, to beat the fixity of location and identity. Bob Dylan is the Nobel laureate of this maneuver, starting with the mask he called, at a 1964 Halloween show, "my Bob Dylan mask." When Dylan turned to "Jack Frost" to produce his 2001 album *"Love and Theft,"* he generated one more mask to handle the cultural mash he advanced, where, as he put it in an interview, the original influences are represented but not anymore in their original form, like barley into whiskey. This often involves trafficking in someone else's stuff, the mixed erotic economy of racial celebration and exploitation that drove blackface minstrelsy and has driven much of the pop music since. Authenticity is a ludicrous, even pernicious, category, but that doesn't mean the dilemmas of cultural appropriation are easy to ford. If Dylan's version of this mash is a little sour, it's because it's so fully aged. Dylan could only have made this record at sixty, not just because it showcases a ripped and ragged voice but also because of its incredible range, literary, musical, and philosophical. In addition to its reflections on the musical relations of race and artistic

Fig. 8. Barack Obama presents Bob Dylan with the Presidential Medal of Freedom, 2012, NASA/Bill Ingalls

borrowing more generally—its theory of culture—Dylan's *"Love and Theft"* advances as well an intricately related musical theory of affective life in late middle age. (A potentially life-threatening heart infection in 1997 had Dylan thinking he might be seeing Elvis soon, as he later joked, but he lived to tell.) The album is one of the most self-conscious examples I know of black mirroring, and it provides a sort of template for this book, which is why it tickles me that Barack Obama was able to award Dylan the Medal of Freedom in 2012. If once Dylan used "ideas as . . . maps," on *"Love and Theft"* he's older than that now, feeling his way, pledging his time, lyin' in winter, mapping his country.[2]

No word before or after the record's release on why Dylan chose its title, the only one of his many album titles to date to be placed in quotation marks. The liner notes by Larry "Ratso" Sloman to one of Dylan's official bootleg series releases, *Tell Tale Signs,* finally admit that the title came "from an academic book about 19th century blackface minstrel shows."[3] I suspect Dylan liked my title for its general resonance, in which stolen hearts and emotional misdemeanors stalk the sweetness of love, as they usually do in Dylan's songs. More particularly, though, he knows full well the cross-cultural indebtedness of music in the Americas, his included, and alludes to it in the songs as well as the title, itself stolen, of *Love and Theft.*" Dylan is certainly no stranger to blackface; as he remarked in a 2001 interview, "*Desolation Row*? That's a minstrel song through and through. I saw some ragtag minstrel show in blackface at the carnivals when I was growing up, and it had an effect on me, just as much as seeing the lady with four legs."[4] That carnival atmosphere suffuses Dylan's 2003 film *Masked and Anonymous,* which at a key moment features a muse-like Ed Harris in full darky regalia. "High Water (For Charley Patton)," with its banjo, tambourine, and other clattering percussion, is the *"Love and Theft"* song that sounds the most like nineteenth-century minstrel-show music, which is interesting not only since it's influenced by and dedicated to Delta bluesman Patton (cf. Patton's "High Water Everywhere" and "High Water Everywhere, Part Two"[5]) but also because it is a song of high seriousness, as though ultimate truths are rooted in cultural plunder. "Some of these bootleggers / They make pretty good stuff / Plenty of places to hide things here / If you want to hide them bad enough," Dylan affirms on the record's "Sugar Baby." Moonshiners, sure, but pirated recordings, too, one of Dylan's most enduring legacies, and pirated sources as well, which floated many of those recordings. On *"Love and Theft"* alone the range and number of these is astonishing: they include, at the very least, Lewis Carroll, Tennessee Williams, the myth of Icarus, Robert Johnson, Johnny Cash, Elmore James, a Parchman farm prison song, the work song "Rosie," Elvis, *The Great Gatsby,* Blind Willie McTell, W. C. Fields, *West Side Story,* Stephen Foster, *Romeo and Juliet,* Charley Patton, Joe Turner, *Jane Eyre,* Clarence Ashley, Dock Boggs, *Night of the Hunter,* "Ode to a Nightingale," John Donne, P. T. Barnum's Chang and Eng, *Othello,* "The Three Little Pigs," knock-knock jokes, Howlin' Wolf, *Don Pasquale,* the Bible, and "Darktown Strutters' Ball," as if Dylan is daring us to accuse him of theft—which people subsequently did (again) when it was discovered that he had lifted quite a bit of the song "Floater" from a Japanese gangster memoir, Junichi Saga's *Confessions of a Yakuza* (1991), or that the very melody of "Sugar Baby" was boosted from a 1928 Gene Austin pop number called "Lonesome Road."[6] As Dylan once sang, Who's gonna throw that minstrel boy a coin?

No one's going to call Dylan simply a blackface artist, like Michelle Shocked a little too abjectly proclaimed herself to be on her 1992 album *Arkansas Traveler,* the cover of which was originally to feature her in blackface makeup (shades of Joni Mitchell).[7] No: cultural "miscegenation"—a stupid word, not only because of its racist origins but also because you probably can't adduce an instance of culture that isn't somehow mixed in kind—is on the contrary a spur to newness and uniqueness for Dylan. "If there's an original thought out there I could use it right now," Dylan jokes in "Brownsville Girl" (1986), that opus spun out of Wild West movies, border ballads, gospel music, Dust Bowl sagas, Sam Shepard plays, Alamo fables, and parables and paradoxes and a hundred other sources. Yet however much he's borrowed and stolen, and as we all know that's *a lot,* Dylan's music has always been full of original thoughts. What's fascinating with great artists is that it is usually tricky to specify where minstrelsy or obvious cultural appropriation stops and something different and fresh begins. Sometimes they coexist outright, in, say, Biz Markie or the Beastie Boys. It is far easier to spot lame bizzers like Michael Bolton or Robert Palmer (not that one, the other one) than it is to say how an obvious borrower like Dylan or Elvis nonetheless somehow makes the music his own. I have been amused if not edified by, say, Run C&W's country versions of R&B tunes; such efforts break down musical barriers but can't help also reinscribing them—C&W is already blacker than they reckon.[8] But while the ingrown persistence and cold corruptions of blackface still structure our feelings, at least we know better now how much American pop music jes' grew out of the gold-standard rush of minstrel-show writers like Stephen Foster and Dan Emmett—both of whom, by the way, Dylan has covered.

What interests me about *"Love and Theft"* is that it seems bent on demonstrating all this. I don't mean to turn a fabulous record into a dull dissertation, but it does cap in knowing ways the artistic process Dylan (re-)discovered in the 1990s on *Good as I Been to You* (1992), *World Gone Wrong* (1993), and *Time Out of Mind* (1997), albums full of blues, ballads, and other timeless tunes that constitute, as Dylan put it, a "physical plunge into Limitationville."[9] Its borrowings are voluminous and pointed, but unlike the covers on *Good as I Been to You* and *World Gone Wrong,* they are sublated into Dylan's own compositions, and unlike the "party's-over" vibe of *Time Out of Mind* (perhaps three of whose eleven songs aren't end-obsessed blues),[10] *"Love and Theft"* makes loss and unwholesome gain an occasion for cultural and autobiographical self-consciousness. ("I've never recorded an album with more autobiographical songs," Dylan remarked of the record. "This is the way I really feel about things. It's not me dragging around a bottle of absinthe and coming up with Baudelairian poems [which to my ears is how *Time Out of Mind* often sounds, an effect not helped by Daniel Lanois's overstylized production]. It's me using everything I know to be true.")[11] The album's governing terms, "love" and "theft," become multidimensional metaphors for heartbreak, crime, and time unredeemed as well as Dylan's career and musical choices—these latter ranging from rockabilly ("Tweedle Dee & Tweedle Dum"), jump blues ("Summer Days"), and soft-shoe shuffles ("Bye and Bye") to country swing ("Floater"), Tin Pan Alley pop ("Moonlight"), and roadhouse blues ("Honest with Me"). That is, if love-and-theft can be taken as the defining relationship not only of minstrel-show but probably all American music, Dylan knows that the terms of his title point in at least two directions. "Love" is that cross-cultural attraction among U.S. musical formations responsible for the heady mix Dylan has always tapped. This is the cultural democracy of mirrored musicking that for Ralph Ellison amounted to an American ideal and that presaged where it did not as yet parallel political democracy. Even in the case of blackface minstrel performers, we have seen Ellison remark, "these fellows had to go and listen, they had to open their ears to [black] speech even if their purpose was to make it comic."[12] "Theft," on the other hand, points to the exploitative conditions—from chattel slavery to the chitlin' circuit and beyond—that have often afforded the sharing of Anglo- and African American musical influences, inflections, forms, phrasings, verses, and titles. We might indeed play on the sense of "title" as ownership and note that Dylan doubly undermines his claim to the mixed-up musical territory on *"Love and Theft,"* no matter how striking or original it is in Dylan's hands: he wryly implies his thievery in the album's name, and with scare quotes calls attention to his thievery *of* the name.

But it's not as though the cultural relations of love and those of theft can be so sweetly separated. This is the United States, after all. "I'm gonna establish my rule through civil war," Dylan sings in "Bye and Bye"; high water's risin' night and day, especially in New Orleans, and if that challenge to survival isn't enough, "They got Charles Darwin trapped out there on Highway Five" (there's a Highway 5 in creationist Kansas, fittingly enough, not too far from the Kansas City that Big Joe Turner makes it to in "High Water").[13] It would be pretty to think that the terms of cross-cultural attraction are free and clear, but the society in which current rockers live is still (if in transmogrified ways) the society structured in dominance that gave rise to the musical loves of white minstrel men, to say nothing of the black music they loved. Just as there's probably no racially unmixed instance of American culture, so there's no mixed instance not marked in some way or other by inequalities of power. Love is shot through with theft, and theft with love. Think about "High Water." Where in the long musical history by which plantation slaves invigorated Anglo-Irish folk tunes with a post-African percussive sensibility only to be commercially represented on the U.S. theatrical stage by white men who gave rise to generations of "white" rural string music, eventually to be taken up in homage to black blues musician Charley Patton by somebody (self-) named Bob Dylan ("Hm, Bob Dylan, I wonder what it was before," Marshall Berman reports his mother musing when she first heard the name fifty years ago)[14] on an album called *"Love and Theft"*—where in all this can you even think of escaping the rigors and mortises of racialized cultural life in these United States?

Berman, in an essay called (what else?) "Love and Theft," puts Dylan in a line of performers that begins with Al Jolson in *The Jazz Singer* (1927): "When Jolson paints himself black, he performs multicultural America's first sacrament: he constitutes himself as both the mixer and the mix" (73). (The echo there of Yeats's "Among School Children" is appropriate given Yeats's affinity for masks.)[15] "'Bob Dylan,'" Berman adds, "sounds roughly as real—or real in the same way—as 'Jack Robin,'" Jakie Rabinowitz's anglicized stage name in *The Jazz Singer*. I think this train of thought is both just and misleading—misleading because one ought to be harder on the racial opportunism of *Jazz Singer*'s "mix" than Berman appears to be (think Michael Rogin's *Blackface, White Noise*)[16] and just to the extent that such racial opportunism can't but underlie Bobby Zimmerman's particular brand of blues-based musical innovation. Be a mixer, by all means—who can avoid it? But no one figure can, as Berman has it, "constitute" the universal mix—white people too often turn out to be the exemplary mixers, *become* white by being exemplary mixers. Given that you can't elude this dilemma when you're "following the southern star," as Dylan does in "Mississippi," the surprise is that you sometimes come through the looking glass and find that cultural theft leads to genius and cultural love is well-nigh impossible. Think of the moment in *Masked and Anonymous* when the benefit-concert promoters (John Goodman and Jessica Lange) are imploring Jack Fate (Dylan) to agree to perform "Jailhouse Rock." The absurdity of the request, I think we're meant to gather, comes in the fact that Elvis, however much he was a cultural cover artist, the white Negro and so on, was unique, untouchable, not to be covered, even by way of embrace. Jack Fate tries to walk out on the benefit concert, but not before these parting lines, in the key of growl: "You ever heard of cellulose? It's in the grass. Cows can digest it, but you can't—and neither can I." Elvis was *indigestible;* we're still chewing on him.

By the same token, I would guess that Dylan regards minstrelsy, say, whatever its ugliness, as responsible for some of the United States' best music as well as much of its worst—without the wishful fantasies of musical racelessness that sometimes mar Greil Marcus's invocations of the "old, weird America."[17] I argued earlier that the emancipatory depictions of Jim in *Adventures of Huckleberry Finn* (such as when Jim and Huck are reunited on the raft after their separation in a fog) are no less indebted to minstrelsy than the more stereotypical ones, which is to say there's no "transcending" or circumventing through sheer will the internally contradictory structures of blackface feeling. Stephen Foster's "Oh! Susanna" (1848), written in "black" dialect with some less than palatable suggestions about African American mental capacity, is nonetheless a fucking great song that exhibits a great deal of sympathetic identification with the black family separated by slavery depicted in it. Dylan hasn't covered it, to my knowledge, but he has recorded Foster's minstrel-inflected but nondialect "Hard Times" (1854), another great song that Dylan encyclopedist Michael Gray, for one, has convincingly argued is one of Dylan's greatest vocal performances.[18] Then there is "Dixie," the 1859 Dan Emmett blackface tune appropriated in short order as the national anthem of the Confederacy, which Dylan performed in Richmond and other cities well before he featured it as a set piece in *Masked and Anonymous*. What the hell? Maybe, as a scholar of old-time music, Dylan has read of the competing claims to the song's authorship—a whole book has been devoted to investigating its alleged African American Ohio source—and sought to reopen "Dixie" to cultural instability.[19] Maybe he knows the possible origins of the word "Dixie" in nineteenth-century showmen's terms for the black South.[20] Maybe, like Michelle Shocked, he wants to step up and face the racial facts of one of the traditions he inherited. As part of a film taken with the idea of music and myth, the myth of Dylan in particular, I think it is fair to suggest that in Dylan's eyes "Dixie" is among all other things a highly resonant song so corrupted by mythmaking that it's almost impossible to really hear—like many of Dylan's own songs, hence the defamiliarizing covers of them, in several different languages to boot, that crowd the film's soundtrack (the most fitting of which, for me, is Shirley Bassey's cover of the always-already gospel number "Gotta Serve Somebody"). After all, Dylan and band perform the song after the many references to Jack Fate's mythic, has-been status, and just after it the potted journalist Tom Friend (Jeff Bridges)—"a leech, a bleeder, some kind of two-faced monster, a spy," Bobby Cupid (Luke Wilson) calls him; "Lee, he probably woulda had him shot, Sherman woulda hung 'im"—demands that Jack Fate disclose the meaning of his (and others') mythic dimensions, from the tale of his dead twin brother (shades of Elvis) to Jimi Hendrix's persona to "Jack Fate's" absence from Woodstock. As the journalist puts it in a later scene, "Now what pipe of power you smokin' from? C'mon man, tell me, you're supposed to have all the answers." An impossible demand, and it's one of the movie's reasons for being to tell us so, to lay waste to the idea that the artist or his art is the sum of other people's myths about them. Just after the first "interview" with Jack Fate (it's more of a rant), we get a black girl's sweet a cappella rendition of "The Times They Are A-Changin' " for a poker-faced Dylan, and the shock of it is that in her mouth we hear the song anew. *Masked and Anonymous* asks us to hear the songs beyond the meanings that have encrusted them over time.[21] Stepping away from his role as legend or mythic author, a posticonic Dylan spends most of the movie listening to others.

Dylan's performance of "Dixie" in the film, despite one fumbled moment, gives the tune's proud strut an austere authority that peaks when Dylan, with phlegmy conviction, sings the word "die"—"to live and die in Dixie." It's not kitsch, and there's no wink; he's singing for keeps. The black faces in his carnival audience seem uniformly skeptical of the song, but a mock Abe Lincoln stands among them (Lincoln does appear to have been a fan of "Dixie"), and when the song is over, it earns warm applause. There may, in other words, be an affect there worth reclaiming—a roots feeling, for a particular locality, where present and past are linked through memory ("old times there are not forgotten"). Nor is the song's blackface underside ignored in the film at large: Jack Fate is rescued from a fight with the journalist when Bobby Cupid clobbers the latter with the guitar once owned by "Blind Lemon" (Jefferson, presumably, but no one ever says)—black music again the weapon that saves a white career—and just a little later blackface muse Oscar Vogel (Ed Harris) materializes. It is here that the dynamic of love and theft converges on a corollary theme, that of age, loss, and memory. "Hello, Jack. Do ya know me?" Vogel asks, Dylan's "Dirt Road Blues" (with its debt to Howlin' Wolf) playing in the background. "You look familiar," is Fate's response, a necessary one given all the foregoing. Announcing himself the former star of the show, like Jack Fate now, and one of Fate's father's favorite performers, Vogel proceeds to speak rather mysteriously of his responsibility for Fate's father's death. What is striking here is less Vogel's dematerializing and replacement by a black man who stares down at Fate—that we should by now know to expect—than the odd proximity of blackface and paternal death, as though there is some sort of link between them. If we go back to *"Love and Theft,"* I think we do see a connection between loss—lost love, lost relatives, lost time—and the blues format in which Dylan has chosen to represent that loss.

"Love and Theft" is preoccupied with loss and futility in direct proportion to its refusal to give up—"never say die," as Dylan

sings on "Po' Boy." This sets it apart (again) from *Time Out of Mind* and gives the record its overall sense of melancholic lift. Song by song, the singer's pathway stones are announced and recuperated by the general buoyancy of his wit and his music: "I got love for you and it's all in vain" ("Tweedle Dee"); "Stayed in Mississippi a day too long" ("Mississippi"); "I got my hammer ringin', pretty baby, but the nails ain't goin' down" ("Summer Days"); "I'm not even acquainted with my own desires" ("Bye and Bye"); "I tell myself something's comin'/But it never does" ("Lonesome Day Blues"); "I left all my dreams and hopes/Buried under tobacco leaves" ("Floater"); "'Don't reach out for me,' she said/'Can't you see I'm drownin' too?'" ("High Water"); "I'm stranded in the city that never sleeps" ("Honest With Me"); "Ridin' first class trains—making the rounds/Tryin' to keep from fallin' between the cars" ("Po' Boy"); "I'm on the fringes of the night, fighting back tears that I can't control" ("Cry a While"); "Your charms have broken many a heart and mine is surely one" ("Sugar Baby"). The oscillation between death drive and pleasure principle is not unique to *"Love and Theft"* but is a structuring principle of all blues; the music's repetitions don't aim to drown in sorrow but to exorcise it, allow the repressed to briefly return on its way out of the psyche. The *sound* of loss and trauma returning in order to be remade comes in the "dirty" tones, the falling pitches, the flatted E's and B's of the blues scale—and on *"Love and Theft"* in the voice of gravel that intones whole realms of aging and struggle.[22] Dylan does seem singularly intent here, though, on capturing a state Freud termed "melancholia": not the failed mourning of his 1917 essay "Mourning and Melancholia," even less a synonym for depression, but a middling state in which, as Freud summed it up in *The Ego and the Id,* the lost love object is retained as a (historical) component of the self. In these terms, the content of one's emotional life is nothing less than the transferential sum of abandoned or lost loves, a nexus of ghostly emotional attachments, "the sedimentation," as Judith Butler has put it, "of objects loved and lost, the archaelogical [*sic*] remainder, as it were, of unresolved grief."[23] Loss inevitably undergirds the self, on this view, and if that tends in a variety of ways to haunt us, it also connects us concretely and materially to the past, to history. It thus has an immensely productive aspect for thinkers and creative artists, which is why I'd argue that the key line on the whole of *"Love and Theft"* is "I wish my mother was still alive" ("Lonesome Day Blues").

Dylan's mother Beatty Zimmerman, it turns out, died in late January of 2000. To make too much of this fact would be as foolish as thinking it had nothing to do with the feel and spiritual vibe of the album Dylan wrote and recorded a little more than a year later. It is certainly one of the ways *"Love and Theft"* is an "autobiographical" record, to recall Dylan's remark. The line above seems to come out of nowhere, at the end of a disjointed verse in the middle of the internally dissociated "Lonesome Day Blues," as though live and direct from the unconscious. Closer inspection reveals the connections, which have the odd effect of making the song seem even more self-exposing. Singing against a heavy blues downbeat, the song's speaker sits thinking, his "mind a million miles away." It is on the whole a roving set of reflections on drastic loss. He left his long-time darlin' standing in the door; his pa died and left him, his brother got killed in the war; Samantha Brown lived in his house for four or five months but he didn't sleep with her eeeeven once. Then comes this:

> I'm forty miles from the mill—I'm droppin' it into over-drive (2x)
> > Settin' my dial on the radio
> > I wish my mother was still alive

In some deep current of feeling, mother and radio are bound up with each other: it's a genius couplet. Both are major modes of cultural and more specifically musical transmission ("overdrive" indeed). The mother is the prelinguistic source of all music, her heartbeat the first rhythm we hear, her hum among the first melodies; losing her in the process of individuation is our first loss, the first lost object to be introjected as part of the ego's melancholia and one template for our later relationships. The radio mimics the mother's subsequent status as ghosted, disembodied musical source (hand on dial), and its status as a technological anachronism in an age of streaming digital devices casts upon it a similarly vestigial and recursive shadow (that is to say, when you hear the radio, you remember the first times you ever heard the radio; the same goes, unconsciously, for the pull—or push—of your mother's voice). So it is no real surprise that the two references might come one after the other, or, as the syntax of the line suggests, that the radio itself might remind the singer of his mama. The phrase "love and theft" finds an especially poignant resonance in the context of Dylan's mother being stolen away; such is the power of her originary position, moreover, that she might even *be* the long-time darlin' the singer last left standing in the door. (As a Stanley Plumly sonnet once had it: "Freud says / every fuck is a foursome.")[24] In any case, Dylan singing about his mother opens rather effortlessly onto singing about music and by implication his career, and given that doing so has helped create a powerful song on a powerful album, we might say that loss is recuperated here by, and in the service of, a melancholic art.

Writing of German baroque theater, that form shot through with melancholia, Walter Benjamin once suggested that it compensated for its keenly felt sense of the "destructive effect of time, of inevitable transience" with an "enthusiasm for landscape," the alternative to temporality's decay being not timelessness but place and setting, "chronological movement . . . grasped and analysed in a spatial image."[25] "Lonesome Day Blues," like much of *"Love and Theft,"* issues in a landscape of loss or stasis pocked by washed-out roads, barren fields, enigmatic whispering winds, and rustling leaves. This is the psychic space of melancholia through which the album feels its way. (And incidentally, considering the way melancholia generates topographical fictions, from late Freud's map of the mind—ego, id, and superego—to Dylan's Mississippi, one might say that "Dixie land" too operates as a melancholic topographical repository.) As I take my last waltz through this tattered terrain, in many respects the terrain of *Black Mirror* at large, let me give you some parting glimpses of what I see.

While this place is age-old, it also strikes me as age-specific, namely, that moment in middle age at which the fragility of the body—your parents', your partner's, your own—wakes you up to the realities of life in Limitationville. "Time is pilin' up . . . / We're all boxed in," goes "Mississippi"; that's why "You can always come back, but you can't come back all the way." But one determines to go on, for love or money: "I'm drownin' in the poison, got no future, got no past / But my heart is not weary, it's light and it's free." You tell yourself that "old, young, age don't carry weight," but it's only because "It doesn't matter in the end" ("Floater"). "Time and love has branded me with its claws / Had to go to Florida, dodgin' them Georgia laws" ("Po' Boy"), you sing, and this hesitation between states (in every sense), the ambivalence of all the above lines, is a hallmark of melancholia. "Well I'm drivin' in the flats in a Cadillac car / The girls all say, 'You're a worn out star'" ("Summer Days"). There *is* a solution: "I'm gonna buy me a barrel of whiskey—I'll die before I turn senile" ("Cry a While").

But it's the memories that haunt you, things acquired, loved, and lost. "Some of these memories you can learn to live with and some of them you can't" ("Sugar Baby"). So many things cluster here: the people you once clung to, the wrongs you couldn't help ("So many things that we never will undo / I know you're sorry, I'm sorry too," Dylan sings in "Mississippi"), the very sources of your energy and your art. "These memories I got, they can strangle a man" ("Honest with Me"), not a good thing for a singer, but understandable if what you've got in your throat are traces of a thousand different songs from apartheid America. Race, memory, and music meet in musical melancholia, where you get by with materials you barely remember taking in the first place: you were too young, or they were too available, or both, and they work so well, speak so solidly to your condition. You reach back to your roots, you work through your masks, and you find yourself again in the land where the blues began.

CODA

RIFFING ON EDMUND BURKE'S INQUIRY into "the Sublime and Beautiful," Fred Moten produced the coinage "The Subprime and the Beautiful," which captures the material / symbolic dialectic of value that drives the traffic in blackness (though Moten is working in a different context than mine—the context that would run guerrilla operations on that dialectic).[1] The coinage is especially apt given the way Burke's evocation of the sublime turns on the sudden sight by a formerly blind person of "a negro woman" who strikes in him the "great horror" that opens onto the sublime. Black symbolic capital is made, however unevenly, to serve the reproduction of whiteness; black property the reproduction of white capital. The subprime debacle depended on both of these at once. Some voices (those of certain presidential contenders, even) taunt that breaking up the big banks would do nothing to "end racism"; critics such as Walter Michaels, conversely, argue that ending racism would do nothing to break up the big banks. In fact, the subprime crisis came about because so-called ghetto loans by Wells Fargo (a principal offender) and others were targeted at black homeowners who have traditionally avoided Wall Street and placed their equity in their homes (the figures hover at around two-thirds of such subprime loans made between 2000 and 2007). The pitch was to use one's home equity as an ATM. Refinance and flourish! Descending on redlined black neighborhoods, real estate hustlers pushed and quickly signed loans that were immediately sold to speculators, who packaged them for resale at huge profit to pension funds and other investors, making everyone a lot of money on the backs of black homeowners. And when it all collapsed, President Obama bailed out the banks. "Race," Matt Taibbi wrote in *Rolling Stone,* "was always at the very center of the crash story."[2] Representational ideologies of racial and "ghetto" formation fueled bank predation in black communities, generating white wealth out of black *refusal* to invest in Wall Street, a consequence based on quite race-specific redlining histories of residential segregation. Putatively antiracist pols, through a glass darkly, claimed the side of the racial angels while night-riding with the banks; putative class anglers, meanwhile, missed the ways their pitch might cover the racial waterfront. The material surplus behind the black mirror, as in Langston Hughes's embodiment of The Negro Problem on Park Avenue at eight, is never simply one thing or the other.

Something of this was conveyed, I think, in Michelle Obama's speech at the Democratic National Convention in July of 2016. "That is the story of this country," she said, "the story that has brought me to this stage tonight, the story of generations of people who felt the lash of bondage, the shame of servitude, the sting of segregation, but who kept on striving and hoping and doing what needed to be done so that today, I wake up every morning in a house that was built by slaves, and I watch my daughters, two beautiful, intelligent, black young women, playing with their dogs on the White House lawn." This is another, rather different tale of homeownership, temporary though it is, at an address whose reverse-redlining has been once and for all disrupted if not forever destroyed. The mirroring with which I began, which brought the Obamas to Pennsylvania Avenue, reclaimed the transgenerational equity lodged there that for so long redounded to white interests.[3] True to the mirror, this reclamation, as I have argued, was by definition fraught with the contradictions that define state power and state fantasy; premature black death and white capital both did not experience a sudden demise. But white fantasy's black mirror, to paraphrase Jacqueline Rose, activates or re-elaborates and therefore partly recognizes histories and transgenerational hauntings struggling against psychic odds to be heard.[4]

One last set of mirrors, then. At the 2015 Kennedy Center Honors show, one of whose honorees was songwriter Carole King, Aretha Franklin leaned in with a near-Benjaminian nod to the struggle that will continue. Launching into King and Gerry Goffin's "(You Make Me Feel Like) A Natural Woman," itself a white-authored black-mirror gospel anthem written for Franklin, Aretha reflected it on Barack Obama, who was sitting in the balcony. Aretha started with great authority at the piano, from which she delivered the first two verses about how "a mighty good man came along" to lift her out of depression and doubt and give her peace of mind. Singing all around the beat, adding new lyrical flourishes, she made it clear that this fine old song had itself been transformed by Obama's ascendency, the story proposed in the song as sung nearly fifty years earlier in 1967 unfinished—a future unwritten—until this moment. The new interpolated words went "*he* makes me feel, *he* makes me feel, *he* makes me feel": and she was looking straight up at President Obama. But there was, for me at least, an interesting wrinkle. "Now I'm no longer doubtful / Of what I'm living for," she sang, and the new urgency I heard in that line suggested that while Obama's rise fulfilled Aretha's life, she was claiming as well that her art helped make his rise possible: without her and her song helping pave the way, no Obama. It's a more than plausible suggestion if you take seriously the force of cultural mirrors. In any case, who could prove her wrong? Rising from the piano, now holding the mic and singing, Aretha got happy, going for the upper room while letting her long fur coat drop from around her to the floor. The natural woman owned the house. Aretha's presidential address summoned a deep emotional undercommons with no postracial illusions, a struggle for happiness in the democratic dark.

NOTES

1. Black Mirror

1. There were other examples, coming just before Obama's ascendancy, among them the variously raced characters played by Tracey Ullman in her Showtime mockumentary "State of the Union" (including a West Indian airport security guard called Chanel Monticello) and the revolting Shirley Q. Liquor stand-up act by comedian Chuck Knipp. Joshua Alston, "The Dark Side of 'Corking Up,' " *Newsweek* (14 March 2008); Neely Tucker, "Hollywood's About-Face on Blackface," *Washington Post* (16 March 2008), M8. I have profited very much from the renewed attention to this tradition to be found in Nicholas Sammond's excellent *Birth of an Industry: Blackface Minstrelsy and the Rise of American Animation* (Durham, NC: Duke UP, 2015); more generally, see Susan Gubar, *Racechanges: White Skin, Black Face in American Culture* (New York: Oxford UP, 1997); and John Strausbaugh, *Black Like You: Blackface, Whiteface, Insult and Imitation in American Popular Culture* (New York: Penguin, 2006).

2. Jacques Derrida, *Specters of Marx: The State of the Debt, the Work of Mourning, and the New International* (1993; New York: Routledge, 1994), 10; Ian Baucom, *Specters of the Atlantic: Finance Capital, Slavery, and the Philosophy of History* (Durham, NC: Duke UP, 2005), chap. 12.

3. Daniel Bell, *The Cultural Contradictions of Capitalism* (New York: Basic Books, 1976). Michael Rogin uses the terminology of surplus symbolic value in *Blackface, White Noise: Jewish Immigrants in the Hollywood Melting Pot* (Berkeley: U of California P, 1996).

4. Donald E. Pease, *The New American Exceptionalism* (Minneapolis: U of Minnesota P, 2009); see also Jacqueline Rose, *States of Fantasy* (Oxford: Clarendon, 1996): "In fact the word 'state' has a psychological meaning long before its modern-day sense of polity, or rather one which trails beneath the shifting public and political face of the word" (6); W. J. T. Mitchell, *Seeing Through Race* (Cambridge, MA: Harvard UP, 2012), 7–62.

5. Since this sort of thing tends to turn up everywhere you look, it is worth noting that Daniel Day-Lewis began his career in blackface. His first acting role, in a school production of *Cry, the Beloved Country,* was that of a little black boy. "I had to cover myself in black makeup, and what gave me the greatest pleasure was that I could never wash all of it off. Every night it sullied the sheets. For once I could be a *legally* disruptive influence." Oh, those nights—how fantasy does cling to cross-racial desire. Richard Corliss, "Dashing Daniel," *Time* (21 March 1994), 66–69, quote at 67.

   There is also, conversely, Suzan-Lori Parks's *The America Play* (1994), in which a black Abraham Lincoln impersonator charges customers a penny to play the role of John Wilkes Booth and take a shot at him.

6. West speaking on *Democracy Now!* (9 November 2012). An offended but somewhat clueless Touré, writing in *Time* magazine, termed West's charge "a verbal Molotov cocktail"; Touré, "Viewpoint: What's Behind Cornel West's Attacks on Obama," *Time* (15 November 2012).

7. I am obviously playing here and throughout on Jacques Lacan's account of the "mirror stage" (1949): Lacan, *Ecrits: A Selection,* trans. Alan Sheridan (New York: Norton, 1977), 1–7; see also Elizabeth Grosz, *Jacques Lacan: A Feminist Introduction* (New York: Routledge, 1990), 31–47. I continue to think Christian Metz's account of the mirror stage and its extension and complication in the cinema a fecund resource for thinking about the specular and spectatorial dynamics that organize my objects of study; Metz, *The Imaginary Signifier: Psychoanalysis and the Cinema,* trans. Celia Britton, Annwyl Williams, Ben Brewster, and Alfred Guzzetti (1977; Bloomington: U of Indiana P, 1982), 45–52; see also Jane M. Gaines, *Fire and Desire: Mixed-Race Movies in the Silent Era* (Chicago: U of Chicago P, 2001), 24–51 and passim.

   I acknowledge and indeed salute the rather different mobilization of the black mirror idea by artist Betye Saar for a 1973 exhibition of work by black women artists under that name—"We want YOU to look into OUR mirror"—a project nonetheless aimed at the unjust spectatorial relations I study in this book; see Betye Saar, "Black Mirror," *Womanspace Journal* 1.2 (1973): 22 and Rebecca K. Vandiver, "Off the Wall, Into the Archive: Black Feminist Curatorial Practices of the 1970s," *Archives of American Art Journal* 55.2 (2016): 26–45. And while my book had its title before I became aware of the television series *Black Mirror,* I acknowledge the merits of the series' focus on the technological screens, from TVs to smartphones, that structure the hive mind (I too focus on them as surrogate mirrors), adding only that race and racial fantasy still strike me as having the far greater force in structuring societies in dominance; the locus classicus is Stuart Hall, "Race, Articulation and Societies Structured in Dominance," in *Sociological Theories: Race and Colonialism* (Paris: UNESCO, 1980): 305–45.

The black mirror dynamic I describe is the inverse, in a curious way, of the paradox Kenneth Warren outlines in *What Was African American Literature?* There, black writers owe their very condition as writers to the state-sponsored white dominance against which they write; here, whiteness owes its existence to a phantasmatic black interlocutor generated out of a long-standing caste system broadly assumed to have been transcended; Warren, *What Was African American Literature?* (Cambridge, MA: Harvard UP, 2011).

The work in "whiteness studies" by Cheryl Harris, David Roediger, Elizabeth Esch, George Lipsitz, Grace Hale, Richard Dyer, Noel Ignatiev, Mike Hill, Matthew Frye Jacobson, and many others is now well enough known not to need extensive citation just here; one good engaging overview among many is Peter Kolchin, "Whiteness Studies: The New History of Race in America," *Journal of American History* 89.1 (2002): 154–73; some fresh perspectives appear in George Yancy, ed., *What White Looks Like: African-American Philosophers on the Whiteness Question* (New York: Routledge, 2004) and Nell Irvin Painter, *The History of White People* (New York: Norton, 2010); newer engagements with white racial formation are well treated in the forum edited by Cynthia A. Young and Min Hyoung Song, "Whiteness Redux or Redefined?," *American Quarterly* 66.4 (2014): 1071–1115.

8. David R. Roediger, *How Race Survived U.S. History: From Settlement and Slavery to the Obama Phenomenon* (New York: Verso, 2010); Thomas J. Sugrue, *Not Even Past: Barack Obama and the Burden of Race* (Princeton, NJ: Princeton UP, 2010); George Lipsitz, *How Racism Takes Place* (Philadelphia, PA: Temple UP, 2011); Touré, *Who's Afraid of Post-Blackness? What It Means to Be Black Now* (New York: Simon and Schuster, 2011); Michael P. Jeffries, *Paint the White House Black: Barack Obama and the Meaning of Race in America* (Stanford, CA: Stanford UP, 2013); Morton Keller, *Obama's Time: A History* (New York: Oxford UP, 2015); Michael Eric Dyson, *The Black Presidency: Barack Obama and the Politics of Race in America* (New York: Houghton Mifflin, 2016).

9. West also referred to Obama as a "global George Zimmerman" (the killer of Trayvon Martin) (*Democracy Now!*, 22 July 2013). It is widely assumed that West is merely piqued at not having been invited to the White House in return for having stumped extensively for Obama; when asked about this he denies it, usually following the denial with a mention of the sixty-four events he staged without White House recompense. So he finds a clever way to call Barack Obama the worst possible names, turning our first black president himself into Langston Hughes's Problem (West would apparently jump at the chance to be wined and dined on Pennsylvania Avenue at eight). You might recall the moment in West's memoir where he recounts his irrecusable marriage proposal to one of his future wives: "Elleni, marry me and become the First Lady of Black America." I suppose it's tough when someone steals your fantasy. Cornel West with David Ritz, *Brother West: Living and Loving Out Loud, A Memoir* (New York: Smiley-Books, 2009), 196. See also Benj DeMott, "Grassroots Nuances," in Perspectives

by Incongruity: *First of the Year* Vol. IV, ed. Benj DeMott (New Brunswick, NJ: Transaction, 2012), 36.

10. I am indebted here to the powerful chapter "Tricks of the Trade: Pop Art and the Rhetoric of Prostitution," in Jennifer Doyle's *Sex Objects: Art and the Dialectics of Desire* (Minneapolis: U of Minnesota P, 2006), 45–70, and more generally Toni Morrison, *Playing in the Dark: Whiteness and the Literary Imagination* (Cambridge, MA: Harvard UP, 1992); Greg Tate, "Nigs R Us, or How Blackfolk Became Fetish Objects," in *Everything but the Burden: What White People Are Taking from Black Culture*, ed. Greg Tate (New York: Broadway, 2003), 1–14; Cherise Smith, *Enacting Others: Politics of Identity in Eleanor Antin, Nikki S. Lee, Adrian Piper, and Anna Deavere Smith* (Durham, NC: Duke UP, 2011).

11. John Howard Griffin, *Black Like Me* (New York: New American Library, 1961), 15–16.

12. Carol Vogel, "The Inside Story on Outsiderness: Glenn Ligon's Gritty Conceptualism Makes Art Out of Others' Words," *New York Times* (27 February 2011), Arts 21; see also Peter Erickson, "Black Like Me: Reconfiguring Blackface in the Art of Glenn Ligon and Fred Wilson," *Nka: Journal of Contemporary African Art* 25 (2009): 30–47.

13. Judith Butler, *Bodies That Matter: On the Discursive Limits of "Sex"* (New York: Routledge, 1993); Joan Riviere, "Womanliness as a Masquerade," *International Journal of Psychoanalysis* 10 (1929): 303–13.

14. Raymond Williams, *Marxism and Literature* (Oxford: Oxford UP, 1977), 128–35.

15. Lacan, *Ecrits*, 4.

16. For representative work, see Walter Benn Michaels, *Our America: Nativism, Modernism, and Pluralism* (Durham, NC: Duke UP, 1995); Michaels, *The Shape of the Signifier: 1967 to the End of History* (Princeton, NJ: Princeton UP, 2004); Michaels, *The Trouble with Diversity: How We Learned to Love Identity and Ignore Inequality* (New York: Metropolitan, 2006); and Michaels, "Why Identity Politics Distracts Us from Economic Inequalities," *Chronicle of Higher Education Review* (15 December 2006), B10–12 (and my rejoinder in the same issue, "A Wrongheaded Focus on Class," B13); Adolph Reed Jr., "The Liberal Technocrat," *The Nation* (6 February 1988), 167–70; Reed, "The Real Divide," *The Progressive* (November 2005), 27–32; Warren, *What Was African American Literature?*; Warren, "A Reply to My Critics," *PMLA* 128.2 (2013): 403–8; Warren, "Sociology and *The Wire*," *Critical Inquiry* 38.1 (2011): 200–7; Karen E. Fields and Barbara J. Fields, *Racecraft: The Soul of Inequality in American Life* (New York: Verso, 2012); David Harvey, *Justice, Nature, and the Geography of Difference* (Oxford: Blackwell, 1996), 338, 341–42.

17. Sammy Davis Jr. and Jane and Burt Boyar, *Yes I Can: The Story of Sammy Davis Jr.* (1965; New York: Farrar, Straus and Giroux, 1990), 30.

18. In his second autobiography, *Why Me?*, Sammy Davis reports being picketed in Washington, D.C., in 1960 on the eve of his marriage to white actress May

Britt by "neo-Nazi storm troopers" shouting "GO BACK TO THE CONGO, YOU KOSHER COON." Crystal's Davis is precisely "kosher cooning." Sammy Davis Jr. and Jane and Burt Boyar, *Why Me?* (New York: Farrar, Straus and Giroux, 1989), 116.

19. According to Davis, Jackson was forgiving on this score. Soon after shilling for Nixon, Davis did a fund-raiser for Jackson's PUSH (People United to Serve Humanity) organization in Chicago, personally donating $25,000; when a portion of the crowd booed Davis, Jackson defended him from the stage. For Davis's account of the Nixon and Jackson episodes, see Davis, Boyar, and Boyar, *Why Me?*, 270–83.

20. Just one of the many reasons for Adolph Reed Jr.'s brilliant takedown of that film, "*Django Unchained,* or, *The Help,*" nonsite.org (February 2013).

21. Barack Obama, *Dreams from My Father: A Story of Race and Inheritance* (1995; New York: Three Rivers, 2004), 123–24.

22. Donald E. Pease, "Black Orpheus, Barack Obama's Governmentality," *Altre Modernita: Rivista di studi letterari e culturali* (2011): 1–28; in "Barack Hussein Obama, or, The Name of the Father," *S&F Online* 7.2 (2009), Tavia Nyong'o brilliantly reads this episode against the grain of Obama's installation of the paternal line at the expense of his mother, thus adducing another axis of contradiction here, one that Obama seems rather less aware of. See also W. T. Lhamon Jr., "Turning Around Jim Crow," in *Burnt Cork: Traditions and Legacies of Blackface Minstrelsy,* ed. Stephen Johnson (Amherst: U of Massachusetts P, 2012), 18–50.

23. Donald E. Pease, "The Global Homeland State: Bush's Biopolitical Settlement," *boundary 2* 30.3 (2003): 1–18; and Pease, "Between the Homeland and Abu Ghraib: Dwelling in Bush's Biopolitical Settlement," in *Exceptional State: Contemporary U.S. Culture and the New Imperialism,* ed. Ashley Dawson and Malini Johar Schueller (Durham, NC: Duke UP, 2007), 60–87.

24. Weber, *From Max Weber: Essays in Sociology,* ed. H. H. Gerth and C. Wright Mills (New York: Oxford UP, 1946), 123.

25. Richard Engel and Robert Windrem, *NBC* (5 June 2013); see also just one of many examples, Peter Baker, "Obama Apologizes after Drone Kills American and Italian Held by Qaeda," *New York Times* (24 April 2015), 1, A10–11; the *Times* cites one expert who reported that "an average of separate counts of American drone strikes by three organizations, the New America Foundation, the Bureau of Investigative Journalism and The Long War Journal, finds that 522 strikes have killed 3,852 people, 476 of them civilians. But those counts, based on news accounts and some on-the-ground interviews, are considered very rough estimates" (A11). Good studies include Medea Benjamin, *Drone Warfare: Killing by Remote Control* (New York: Verso, 2013); and Mark Mazzetti, *The Way of the Knife: The CIA, a Secret Army, and a War at the Ends of the Earth* (New York: Penguin, 2013).

26. Thrush, *Politico* (6 June 2013); see also Robin D. G. Kelley, "Empire State of Mind," *Counterpunch* (16 August 2013).

27. In Davis, according to Early, the hardworking, upwardly mobile aspirations of Horatio Alger's Ragged Dick meet a Faustian search for sensation, pleasure, and luxury no matter the cost; the visible sign and end result of both is money. See Early's superb introduction to *The Sammy Davis, Jr. Reader,* ed. Gerald Early (New York: Farrar, Straus and Giroux, 2001), 3, 11. Davis himself suggests as much in his own account of recording an ode to wish-fulfilling fantasy ("The Candy Man"), one he found thoroughly revolting, for purely mercenary, commercial reasons; see Davis, Boyar, and Boyar, *Why Me?,* 252–54, 268–70.

28. Ernst Bloch, *The Principle of Hope,* vol. 1, trans. Neville Plaice, Stephen Plaice, and Paul Knight (1959; Cambridge, MA: MIT P, 1986).

29. Rose, *States of Fantasy,* 3.

30. Bryan Wagner, *Disturbing the Peace: Black Culture and the Police Power after Slavery* (Cambridge, MA: Harvard UP, 2009).

31. Felicia R. Lee, "Famous Black Lives through DNA's Prism," *New York Times* (5 February 2008), B1.

32. Henry Louis Gates Jr., *Finding Oprah's Roots: Finding Your Own* (New York: Crown, 2007), 164.

33. Lee, "Famous Black Lives," B1. Such material interest took a hard turn in summer 2015 when a WikiLeaks hack of Sony Pictures Entertainment emails disclosed that one featured guest, actor Ben Affleck, had lobbied Gates not to include mention of a slave-owning ancestor. After some hand-wringing, Gates caved and chose not to include it, later insisting that other of Affleck's forebears, an occult enthusiast and a Revolutionary War veteran, were more interesting. PBS briefly suspended the show for the rather revealing malfeasance; genealogy is, at bottom, story. John Koblin, "A PBS Show, a Hacking at Sony, and a Loss of Face," *New York Times* (26 June 2015), B3.

For more on the fate of Gates's ideas since his pathbreaking work in the 1980s, see my "Criticism in the Vineyard: Twenty Years after '*Race,' Writing, and Difference,*" *PMLA* 123.5 (2008): 1522–27. All along, I argue, Gates has wanted black indigeneity, but somehow without essence; black tradition, but without the political crudity of negritude: what Kenneth Warren once termed a depoliticized "plum of black unity," a sort of *Jet*-magazine politics of noncontroversial racial success, or at best a strategy of formalist critical elaboration and literary canon-making as dodges for an explicit cultural ideology. See Warren, "Delimiting America: The Legacy of Du Bois," *American Literary History* 1.1 (1989), 187, as well as Adolph Reed Jr., *W. E. B. Du Bois and American Political Thought: Fabianism and the Color Line* (New York: Oxford UP, 1997), 138–62.

Some years ago, bemused by a Penn State student's conclusion that a DNA test administered by her professor showed that she was "58 percent European and 42 percent African," Patricia J. Williams noted the way the vagaries of ancestral geographical origins (plenty of white people in Africa) and shifting historical definitions of race (the Irish didn't become white until fairly recently) can get boiled down into dangerous new fictions. "There is," Williams rightly observed, "a remarkable persistence in re-inscribing race onto the narrative of biological inheritance." With eerie prescience, Williams suggested that "our linguistically embedded notions of race seem to be on the verge of transposing themselves yet again into a context where genetic percentages act as the ciphers for culture and status, as well as economic and political attributes," perhaps one unfortunate by-product of the work Gates is doing now. Patricia J. Williams, "Genetically Speaking," *The Nation* (20 June 2005): 10. The reinscription of race onto the radical complications of biological inheritance and the reading off of strivings and status from genetics are exactly what Kwame Anthony Appiah warned against in "The Uncompleted Argument: Du Bois and the Illusion of Race," itself included in Gates's *"Race," Writing, and Difference* (Chicago: U of Chicago P, 1986)!

34. Jay-Z, "Open Letter," now the bonus track on the vinyl issue of his album *Magna Carta Holy Grail* (2013); but see also Kelley, "Empire State of Mind." Like Kelley, I would not let Jay, or Obama, off so easily. When images of Jay and Bey enjoying themselves got back to the States, and I frankly think it was the spectacle of black enjoyment that truly bothered white people, the Obama administration caught hell for its supposed laxity—Obama joked, "I got 99 problems and Jay-Z is one"—whereupon Press Secretary Jay Carney passed the buck and directed all inquiries to the Treasury Department (interesting), the body charged with okaying trips to Cuba. Jay-Z correctly caught the class and racial stakes afoot—"Boy from the hood but got White House clearance." Reminding one of Martin Delany's *Blake,* Jay-Z elasticizes the reach of the nation-state and recapitulates an Atlantic cartography (in *Blake* it's Cuba-Africa-U.S.-Canada-U.S.-Cuba-Africa-Cuba; in "Open Letter" it's Havana-Atlanta-Brooklyn-Houston-China and updated by way of electronic broadcasting gizmos) in a quintessentially Atlantic musical form, Bronx and Brooklyn out of Jamaica and other parts Caribbean. "I done turned Havana to Atlanta / Guyabera shirts and bandanas / Every time you think they got me I switch the planner / Bulletproof this, radio scanners." *Blake*'s diaspora sensibility, with its embedded responses to Harriet Beecher Stowe and Stephen Foster, finds its analogue in Jay's responses to the calls of politicians, gusanos, cops, haters, and above all Barack Obama: "Obama said 'Chill, you gonna get me impeached' / But you don't need this shit anyway, chill with me on the beach."

The exhilarating whiff of the Situationists that trails off that line—under the state's paving stones, the beach!—is followed by some thoughts on the perplexities of communism's uneven criminalization—"I'm in Cuba, I love Cubans / This communist talk is so confusing / When it's from China, the very mic that I'm using." States police until (and if you're Jay even after) capital outdoes them—something like this seems to be the drift here. Which may offer helpful context for the fact that a month after this pop venture into Marx and Coca-Cola (as Jean-Luc Godard once termed it), it was announced that former New York Black Panther Assata Shakur (charged among other things with robbing banks in the early 1970s) had been named to the United States' Most Wanted Terrorist list with a $2 million bounty on her head. As if in recompense for the Jay and Bey affair, the Obama administration in May 2013 criminalized, *as a terrorist,* a grandmother in her sixties living quietly in Cuba for the last thirty years after escaping from a U.S. prison in 1979 in the wake of a conviction by a kangaroo court (attorney William Kunstler's word) for crimes including the killing of a New Jersey police officer. I wish I could tell you that Jay-Z was on record then or now in response to Assata or to the Obama administration's racially objectionable attention to national security in this case. His "Open Letter," to the contrary, is derailed by neoliberal self-regard. "Hear the freedom in my speech / Got an onion from Universal, read it and weep / Would've brought the Nets to Brooklyn for free / Except I made millions off it, you fuckin' dweeb / I still own the building, I'm still keeping my seat." It's the new Fordism—designer Tom Ford, I mean, to whom Jay raps an ode on *Magna Carta.* Boasting about owning Basquiats and Warhols rather than what they mean to him, Jay takes his eyes off the prize. Wars of position waged in the realm of representation, he should well know, require every ounce of our rigorous *political* attention. The Barclays Center, the House That Jay Built, is named for the British banking firm with, as their own website attests, "over 300 years of history and expertise in banking." Its long and direct links to the slave trade helped create the black Atlantic formation that gave rise to Jay-Z's very art, but that doesn't mean it deserves a big wet kiss. On this evidence it seems Jay-Z has yet to learn the lesson of his own open letter: work all the way through those cruel attachments that will always let you down.

35. Paul Gilroy, *The Black Atlantic: Modernity and Double Consciousness* (Cambridge, MA: Harvard UP, 1993), 57, 37, 202.

36. Bertolt Brecht, *Brecht on Theater: The Development of an Aesthetic,* trans. and ed. John Willett (New York: Hill and Wang, 1964), 6.

37. Pease, *New American Exceptionalism,* 207, 210.

38. Perspectives in line with mine include Jody Rosen, "Mrs. Carter Holy Grail," *New York Magazine* (6–13 January 2014), 78–80; Hilton Als, "Beywatch," *New Yorker* (30 May 2016), 66–69; Greil Marcus, *The History of Rock 'N' Roll in Ten Songs* (New Haven, CT: Yale UP, 2014), 77–84.

39. Jacques Derrida, *Dissemination,* trans. Barbara Johnson (1972; Chicago: U of Chicago P, 1981); Rodolphe Gasche, *The Tain of the Mirror: Derrida and the Philosophy of Reflection* (Cambridge, MA: Harvard UP, 1986). Fred Moten, *In the Break: The Aesthetics of the Black Radical Tradition* (Minneapolis: U of Minnesota P, 2003), 171–231, has been an important interlocutor for the pages that follow.

40. Rogin, *Blackface, White Noise,* 14, 270. My thanks to David Anthony for reminding me of the "Dandy Jim from Carolina" sheet music.

41. Wagner, *Disturbing the Peace,* 194–212. See also Saidiya V. Hartman, *Scenes of Subjection: Terror, Slavery, and Self-Making in Nineteenth-Century America* (New York: Oxford UP, 1997), 17–78; Eva Cherniavsky, "Introduction," in *Incorporations: Race, Nation, and the Body Politics of Capital* (Minneapolis: U of Minnesota P, 2006);

Lindon Barrett, *Blackness and Value: Seeing Double* (Cambridge: Cambridge UP, 1999), 11–93; Tavia Nyong'o, *The Amalgamation Waltz: Race, Performance, and the Ruses of Memory* (Minneapolis: U of Minnesota P, 2009), chap. 3. W. T. Lhamon's extensive work on the history of minstrelsy has immeasurably deepened our understanding of it, though I have elsewhere registered certain dissenting opinions: Lhamon, *Raising Cain: Blackface Performance from Jim Crow to Hip Hop* (Cambridge, MA: Harvard UP, 1998); Lhamon, *Jump Jim Crow: Lost Plays, Lyrics, and Street Prose of the First Atlantic Popular Culture* (Cambridge, MA: Harvard UP, 2003); and Lhamon, *Jim Crow, American: Selected Songs and Plays* (Cambridge, MA: Harvard UP, 2009); see also Johnson, ed., *Burnt Cork*. See also Daphne A. Brooks, *Bodies in Dissent: Spectacular Performances of Race and Freedom, 1850–1910* (Durham, NC: Duke UP, 2006) and Jayna Brown, *Babylon Girls: Black Women Performers and the Shaping of the Modern* (Durham, NC: Duke UP, 2008) have taken such study in entirely new and utterly salutary directions.

42. Jean Baudrillard, *For a Critique of the Political Economy of the Sign,* trans. Charles Levin (St. Louis, MO: Telos, 1981); Tate, ed., *Everything but the Burden.*

43. Ellison's most succinct statement of his long-standing position, "What America Would Be Like Without Blacks," from which this quotation comes, was originally published in *Time* magazine in 1970; it was later included in his *Going to the Territory* (New York: Random House, 1986), 108.

44. Michael O'Malley, *Face Value: The Entwined Histories of Money and Race in America* (Chicago: U of Chicago P, 2012), 81.

45. Eric Lott, *Love and Theft: Blackface Minstrelsy and the American Working Class* (1993; New York: Oxford UP, 2013), chaps. 2, 5, and 6.

46. Blackface is offered up, if too briefly, as a "metaphor for the commodity . . . the sign of what people paid to see . . . the image consumed . . . a trademark" in Susan Willis (writing about Michael Jackson), *A Primer for Daily Life* (New York: Routledge, 1991), 125.

47. Karl Marx, *Capital: A Critique of Political Economy,* vol. 1, trans. Ben Fowkes (1867; New York: Vintage, 1977), 164–65.

48. Which is to say that I disagree with the reading of the film put forward in Judith Halberstam, *Skin Shows: Gothic Horror and the Technology of Monsters* (Durham, NC: Duke UP, 1995), 4–5, which argues that despite the film's self-conscious exploration of racial construction, it nonetheless reproduces the racist myth of the black rapist; my view is closer to that of Aviva Breifel and Sianne Ngai, "'How Much Did You Pay for This Place?' Fear, Entitlement, and Urban Space in Bernard Rose's *Candyman,*" *Camera Obscura* 37 (1997): 71–91.

49. Clive Barker, *In the Flesh* (New York: Simon and Schuster, 1986), 89–147.

50. I have profited from two studies of phantasmagoria's *longue durée:* Terry Castle, "Phantasmagoria: Spectral Technology and the Metaphorics of Modern Reverie,"

Critical Inquiry 15.1 (1988): 26–61; and Marina Warner, *Phantasmagoria: Spirit Visions, Metaphors, and Media into the Twenty-First Century* (New York: Oxford UP, 2006).

51. Henri Lefebvre, *The Production of Space,* trans. Donald Nicholson-Smith (1974; Malden, MA: Blackwell, 1991); Patricia Yaeger, "Introduction: Narrating Space," in Yaeger, ed., *The Geography of Identity* (Ann Arbor: U of Michigan P, 1996), 4–6.

52. There is also, quite frankly, the fact that in the unavoidable mediation of the film by the Hollywood star system, Philip Glass was at the time the movie's only marquee name. Responsible for the film's ambience, pointedly featured throughout the narrative at moments of spatial transition along Chicago's streets from middle-class enclaves to the inner city, *Candyman*'s star is never seen onscreen. Truly spectral, the not-seen everywhere-evidenced Glass is used in the film as a figure for some process of urban direction or planning that yet cannot be shown or seen within its frame: a perfect realization of Marx's theorizing of the commodity's "hieroglyphic" nature. Appearing when it does, Glass's music, its cultural capital, its power to confer on *Candyman* a legitimacy always in short supply in the precincts of horror, offers us the clearest presentation of the occulted racial-capitalist decision-making encrypted in the spatial arrangements the film depicts (and therefore in the film itself). To fight this power, *Candyman* suggests, you first have to find it, that is, find a way to *narrate* its manifold and enigmatic operations and consequences. I am inspired in these reflections by Fredric Jameson's classic essay, "Class and Allegory in Contemporary Mass Culture: *Dog Day Afternoon* as a Political Film," *College English* 38.8 (1977): 843–59, later reprinted in Jameson, *Signatures of the Visible* (New York: Routledge, 1992), 47–74.

53. It is the great achievement of Avery Gordon's *Ghostly Matters: Haunting and the Sociological Imagination* (Minneapolis: U of Minnesota P, 1997) to explore the way phantoms, specters, and ghosts, in a great variety of texts and historical contexts, help conjure hauntological connections and political openings—all those occluded or otherwise unseen forces that we have seen Marx refer to as "supra-sensible or social." Joseph R. Roach's words are from his foundational *Cities of the Dead: Circum-Atlantic Performance* (New York: Columbia UP, 1996). See also Anne McClintock, "Imperial Ghosting and National Tragedy: Revenants from Hiroshima and Indian Country in the War on Terror," *PMLA* 129.4 (2014): 819–29. An extended genealogy for an African American "monster" such as Candyman is detailed in Elizabeth Young's subtle, complex, and deeply read romp through the last two centuries of transatlantic literary and cultural history, *Black Frankenstein: The Making of an American Metaphor* (New York: NYU P, 2008).

I should mention here that *Candyman* almost inevitably, indeed hauntologically, yielded two sequels, *Candyman: Farewell to the Flesh* (1995) and *Candyman: Day of the Dead* (1999), the first set in New Orleans and the second in Los Angeles, with different directors and casts (save for the fittingly eternal Tony Todd as the titular ghost); despite intermittent flashes of interest in each, there is a considerable falling off in intensity with respect to both the dynamics of white racial fantasy and the contours of urban investigation.

54. Arnold R. Hirsch, *Making the Second Ghetto: Race and Housing in Chicago, 1940–1960* (1983; Chicago: U of Chicago P, 1998). By far the most important studies for my thinking about Chicago city space (indeed city space generally) and cultural depictions of it are Carlo Rotella, *October Cities: The Redevelopment of Urban Literature* (Berkeley: U of California P, 1998); and Rotella, *Good With Their Hands: Boxers, Bluesmen, and Other Characters from the Rust Belt* (Berkeley: U of California P, 2002). There is no studying Chicago without St. Clair Drake and Horace R. Cayton Jr., *Black Metropolis: A Study of Negro Life in a Northern City* (New York: Harcourt, Brace, 1945); Carl Smith, *Urban Disorder and the Shape of Belief: The Great Chicago Fire, the Haymarket Bomb, and the Model Town of Pullman* (Chicago: U of Chicago P, 1995); and Smith, *The Plan of Chicago: Daniel Burnham and the Remaking of the American City* (Chicago: U of Chicago P, 2006).

55. Hirsch, *Making the Second Ghetto;* Davarian L. Baldwin, *Chicago's New Negroes: Modernity, the Great Migration, and Black Urban Life* (Chapel Hill: U of North Carolina P, 2007); Gregory D. Squires, Larry Bennett, Kathleen McCourt, and Philip Nyden, *Chicago: Race, Class, and the Response to Urban Decline* (Philadelphia: Temple UP, 1987); Larry Bennett and Adolph Reed Jr., "The New Face of Urban Renewal: The Near North Redevelopment Initiative and the Cabrini-Green Neighborhood," in *Without Justice for All: The New Liberalism and Our Retreat from Racial Equality,* ed. Adolph Reed Jr. (Boulder, CO: Westview, 1999), 175–211; George Lipsitz, *The Possessive Investment in Whiteness: How White People Profit from Identity Politics* (Philadelphia: Temple UP, 1998); Douglas S. Massey and Nancy A. Denton, *American Apartheid: Segregation and the Making of the Underclass* (Cambridge, MA: Harvard UP, 1993); Mitchell Duneier, *Ghetto: The Invention of a Place, the History of an Idea* (New York: Farrar, Straus and Giroux, 2016).

The legend of Candyman that circulates through the film's academic community—a sorry lot indeed, as the film has it, but no less tale-telling for that—records that he was born the son of a slave who upon emancipation after the Civil War grew very wealthy by inventing a device crucial to the mass-production of shoes (not incidentally Carrie Meeber's first Chicago employment in Theodore Dreiser's *Sister Carrie*). Rich, young Candyman the son goes to the best schools and lives among polite society, becoming a portrait painter of the rich. A white landowner commissions him to paint his daughter—which begins a love affair that results in the daughter's pregnancy, whereupon the landowner pays some hooligans to chase Candyman down, saw off his right hand, and smear honey on his "prone, naked body" which is stung to death by bees from a nearby apiary. The body is burned and its ashes scattered over the site where Cabrini-Green stands. This little embedded allegory of landed versus rising-industrial wealth speaks directly to the making of the second ghetto in the postwar period. We know, for example, that Chicago's Land Clearance Commission, in collaboration with white enterprise, effectively scuttled the first (prewar) ghetto's black capital base through a kind of classic expropriation of a low-caste society from the soil. This capital (and social) base—black-owned beauty parlors, funeral homes, grocery stores, small manufactories, hat blockers, dry cleaners, bars, eateries—was not to be recovered with the coming of postindustrial society (in Daniel Bell's reifying phrase) but was merely absorbed into the general municipal economy or scattered across a rearticulated landscape of power in "urban renewal." More generally the Candyman legend foregrounds land itself, à la Marx's analysis of ground rent in *Capital Vol. I,* as the commodity prior to and determining of all future Chicago spatial production.

56. Heidi J. Nast, "Mapping the 'Unconscious': Racism and the Oedipal Family," *Annals of the Association of American Geographers* 90.2 (2000): 215–55.

57. Alice Walker, "Advancing Luna—And Ida B. Wells," in *You Can't Keep a Good Woman Down* (New York: Harcourt Brace Jovanovich, 1981), 85–104; Jacquelyn Dowd Hall, " 'The Mind That Burns in Each Body': Women, Rape, and Racial Violence," in *Powers of Desire: The Politics of Sexuality,* ed. Ann Snitow, Christine Stansell, and Sharon Thompson (New York: Monthly Review, 1983), 328–49; Robyn Wiegman, *American Anatomies: Theorizing Race and Gender* (Durham, NC: Duke UP, 1995), 81–114; Sandra Gunning, *Race, Rape, and Lynching: The Red Record of American Literature, 1890–1912* (New York: Oxford UP, 1996); Martha Hodes, *White Women, Black Men: Illicit Sex in the Nineteenth-Century South* (New Haven, CT: Yale UP, 1997), 176–208; Dora Apel, *Imagery of Lynching: Black Men, White Women, and the Mob* (New Brunswick, NJ: Rutgers UP, 2004); Shawn Michelle Smith, *Photography on the Color Line: W. E. B. Du Bois, Race, and Visual Culture* (Durham, NC: Duke UP, 2004), 113–46; Jacqueline Goldsby, *A Spectacular Secret: Lynching in American Life and Literature* (Chicago: U of Chicago P, 2006); Amy Louise Wood, *Lynching and Spectacle: Witnessing Racial Violence in America, 1890–1940* (Chapel Hill: U of North Carolina P, 2009), 19–44, 71–112, 179–222; Sandy Alexandre, *The Properties of Violence: Claims to Ownership in Representations of Lynching* (Jackson: U Press of Mississippi, 2012), 3–54. All of this crucial work follows in the footsteps of Wells-Barnett's pamphlets scorning white southern black-rapist mythology as a cover story for legal and extralegal violence, economic and residential segregation, and social and political repression.

58. Derrida, *Specters of Marx,* 170, xviii; Michael Sprinker, ed., *Ghostly Demarcations: A Symposium on Jacques Derrida's* Specters of Marx (London: Verso, 1999); P. J. Brendese, "Remembering Democratic Time: Specters of Mexico's Past and Democracy's Future," *Polity* 41.4 (2009): 436–64.

2. Our Blackface America

1. Mark Twain, *Mark Twain's Letters,* ed. Edgar Marquess Branch et al., vol. 1, 1853–1866 (Berkeley: U of California P, 1988), 4.

2. Mark Twain, *Autobiography of Mark Twain*, ed. Benjamin Griffin and Harriet Elinor Smith, vol. 2 (Berkeley: U of California P, 2013), 294. Henceforth cited parenthetically in the text as AU.

3. Susan Gillman, *Dark Twins: Imposture and Identity in Mark Twain's America* (Chicago: U of Chicago P, 1989).

4. The term is Jonathan Arac's in *Huckleberry Finn as Idol and Target: The Functions of Criticism in Our Time* (Madison: U of Wisconsin P, 1997). See also the delightfully stirring remarks on class, Twain, and his early geographical location in David R. Roediger, *Colored White: Transcending the Racial Past* (Berkeley: U of California P, 2002), 44–54.

5. See, for instance, David Reynolds, *Beneath the American Renaissance: The Subversive Imagination in the Age of Emerson and Melville* (New York: Knopf, 1988); and Reynolds, *Walt Whitman's America: A Cultural Biography* (New York: Knopf, 1995).

6. Samuel Langhorne Clemens, *Adventures of Huckleberry Finn* (1884; New York: Norton, 1977), 27.

7. Nice compendiums of minstrel songs and skits include Sam Dennison, *Scandalize My Name: Black Imagery in American Popular Music* (New York: Garland, 1982); and W. T. Lhamon Jr., *Jump Jim Crow: Lost Plays, Lyrics, and Street Prose of the First Atlantic Popular Culture* (Cambridge, MA: Harvard UP, 2003).

8. David R. Roediger, *The Wages of Whiteness: Race and the Making of the American Working Class* (London: Verso, 1991).

9. John B. Jentz, "The Anti-Slavery Constituency in Jacksonian New York City," *Civil War History* 27.2 (1981): 101–22; Williston Lofton, "Abolition and Labor," *Journal of Negro History* 33.3 (1948): 249–83; Joseph G. Rayback, "The American Workingman and the Antislavery Crusade," *Journal of Economic History* 3.2 (1943): 152–63; Eric Foner, "Abolitionism and the Labor Movement in Ante-Bellum America," in *Politics and Ideology in the Age of the Civil War* (New York: Oxford UP, 1980), 57–76; Herbert Shapiro, "Labor and Antislavery: Reflections on the Literature," *Nature, Society, and Thought* 24 (1989): 471–90.

10. Interview with Ralph Ellison, quoted in Shelley Fisher Fishkin, *Was Huck Black? Mark Twain and African American Voices* (New York: Oxford UP, 1993), 90. Perhaps the strongest cases for working-class minstrel-show interracial solidarity are Dale Cockrell, *Demons of Disorder: Early Blackface Minstrels and Their World* (New York: Cambridge UP, 1997); and W. T. Lhamon, *Raising Cain: Blackface Performance from Jim Crow to Hip Hop* (Cambridge, MA: Harvard UP, 1998).

11. Ralph Ellison, *Shadow and Act* (1964; New York: Vintage, 1972), 50.

12. "Lubly Fan," in S. Foster Damon, comp., *Series of Old American Songs* (Providence, RI: Brown University Library, 1936), no. 39.

13. For examples of each tendency, see Lawrence Levine, *Black Culture and Black Consciousness: Afro-American Folk Thought from Slavery to Freedom* (New York: Oxford UP, 1977), 190–366.

14. Anthony J. Berret, "*Huckleberry Finn* and the Minstrel Show," *American Studies* 27.2 (1986): 37–49.

15. Paul Fatout, *Mark Twain on the Lecture Circuit* (Carbondale: Southern Illinois UP, 1960), 204–31.

16. Fredrick Woodard and Donnarae MacCann, "*Huckleberry Finn* and the Traditions of Blackface Minstrelsy," *Interracial Books for Children Bulletin* 15.1, 2 (1984): 5.

17. Guy Cardwell, *Twins of Genius* (East Lansing: Michigan State College Press, 1953), 105; Steven Mailloux, *Rhetorical Power* (Ithaca, NY: Cornell UP, 1989), 57–99; Forrest G. Robinson, *In Bad Faith: The Dynamics of Deception in Mark Twain's America* (Cambridge, MA: Harvard UP, 1986), 111–211.

18. George M. Fredrickson, *The Black Image in the White Mind: The Debate on Afro-American Character and Destiny, 1817–1914* (New York: Harper & Row, 1971), 101–2.

19. Woodard and MacCann, "*Huckleberry Finn* and the Traditions of Blackface Minstrelsy"; Woodard and MacCann, "Minstrel Shackles and Nineteenth-Century 'Liberality' in *Huckleberry Finn*," in *Satire or Evasion? Black Perspectives on Huckleberry Finn*, ed. James S. Leonard, Thomas A. Tenney, and Thadious M. Davis (Durham, NC: Duke UP, 1991), 141–53; Bernard Bell, "Twain's 'Nigger' Jim: The Tragic Face Behind the Minstrel Mask," *Mark Twain Journal* 23.1 (1985): 10–17.

20. David L. Smith, "Huck, Jim, and American Racial Discourse," in *Satire or Evasion?*, ed. Leonard et al., 103–20; James M. Cox, "A Hard Book to Take," in *One Hundred Years of "Huckleberry Finn,"* ed. Robert Sattelmeyer and J. Donald Crowley (Columbia: U of Missouri P, 1985), 386–403.

21. Fishkin, *Was Huck Black?*, 83–84.

22. Gladys-Marie Fry, *Night Riders in Black Folk History* (1975; Athens: U of Georgia P, 1991), 9–10.

23. Richard Jackson, ed., *Stephen Foster Song Book* (New York: Dover, 1974), 101–2, 89–91.

24. Leslie Fiedler, "Come Back to the Raft Ag'in, Huck Honey!," in *The Collected Essays of Leslie Fiedler* (New York: Stein & Day, 1971), Vol. 1, 142–51; the best antihomophobic unpacking of Fiedler's argument is Christopher Looby, "'Innocent Homosexuality': The Fiedler Thesis in Retrospect," in *Adventures of Huckleberry Finn: A Case Study in Critical Controversy*, ed. Gerald Graff and James Phelan (Boston: Bedford, 1995), 535–50.

25. Homi K. Bhabha, "The Other Question: The Stereotype and Colonial Discourse," *Screen* 24.6 (1983): 18–36.

26. Antonio Gramsci, *Selections from Cultural Writings,* ed. David Forgacs and Geoffrey Nowell-Smith, trans. William Boelhower (London: Lawrence & Wishart, 1985), 207, 209–11.

27. On immanent criticism, see Theodor Adorno, "Cultural Criticism and Society," in *Prisms,* trans. Samuel and Sherry Weber (Cambridge, MA: MIT P, 1967), 32.

28. Justin Kaplan, *Mr. Clemens and Mark Twain* (New York: Simon & Schuster, 1966), 270.

29. Ibid., 174.

30. Mark Twain and William Dean Howells, *Mark Twain–Howells Letters: The Correspondence of Samuel L. Clemens and William Dean Howells, 1872–1910,* ed. Henry Nash Smith and William Gibson (Cambridge, MA: Harvard UP, 1960), Vol. 1, 10–11.

31. Mark Twain, *Mark Twain's Letters to His Publishers, 1867–1894,* ed. Hamlin Hill (Berkeley: U of California P, 1967), 152–53.

32. See Fishkin, *Was Huck Black?,* passim.

33. Samuel Langhorne Clemens, *Pudd'nhead Wilson and Those Extraordinary Twins,* ed. Sidney E. Berger (1894; New York: Norton, 1980), 8–9.

34. In thinking about *Pudd'nhead Wilson,* I am indebted to several essays collected in *Mark Twain's "Pudd'nhead Wilson": Race, Conflict, and Culture,* ed. Susan Gillman and Forrest G. Robinson (Durham, NC: Duke UP, 1990): James M. Cox, "*Pudd'nhead Wilson* Revisited," 1–21; Forrest G. Robinson, "The Sense of Disorder in *Pudd'nhead Wilson,*" 22–45; Eric J. Sundquist, "Mark Twain and Homer Plessy," 46–72; Michael Rogin, "Francis Galton and Mark Twain: The Natal Autograph in *Pudd'nhead Wilson,*" 73–85; and Myra Jehlen, "The Ties That Bind: Race and Sex in *Pudd'nhead Wilson,*" 105–20; see also Sandra Gunning, *Race, Rape, and Lynching: The Red Record of American Literature, 1890–1912* (New York: Oxford UP, 1996), 48–76; and Henry B. Wonham, "'I Want a Real Coon': Mark Twain and Late-Nineteenth-Century Ethnic Caricature," *American Literature* 72.1 (2000): 117–52.

35. On the predicament of abjection, which produces unstable and permeable borders of the self in its separation from the mother and a consequent, repetitive search for stability and borderedness, see Julia Kristeva, *Powers of Horror: An Essay on Abjection,* trans. Leon S. Roudiez (1980; New York: Columbia UP, 1982), 1–13.

36. For a discussion of this excised passage, see Fishkin, *Was Huck Black?,* 122–23.

37. Hershel Parker, *Flawed Texts and Verbal Icons: Literary Authority in American Fiction* (Evanston, IL: Northwestern UP, 1984), 123–25.

38. Wesley Brown, *Darktown Strutters* (Amherst: U of Massachusetts P, 1994).

39. Karl Marx, "A Criticism of American Affairs," from *Die Presse* (9 August 1862), in Saul K. Padover, ed., *On America and the Civil War: The Karl Marx Library,* vol. 2 (New York: McGraw-Hill, 1972), 211–12.

3. The Mirror Has Two Faces

1. Richard Corliss and Jeffrey Ressner, "Peter Pan Grows Up: But Can He Still Fly?," *Time* 149.20 (19 May 1997): 75.

2. Anonymous [Joe Klein], *Primary Colors: A Novel of Politics* (New York: Random House, 1996), 3. As noted by "computer humanist" Donald Foster—Foster analyzed *Primary Colors* and became the first to determine Klein to be the author—Klein leaves this clue to the book's authorship in its first paragraph; Foster, "Primary Culprit: Who Is Anonymous?" *New York Magazine* 29 (1996): 50–57.

3. Michael Rogin, *Blackface, White Noise: Jewish Immigrants in the Hollywood Melting Pot* (Berkeley: U of California P, 1996).

4. Paul Buhle and Edward Portnoy, "Al Jolson in Black and White," *Tikkun* 11.6 (1996): 67–70.

5. Neal Gabler, *An Empire of Their Own: How the Jews Invented Hollywood* (New York: Crown, 1988).

6. For a far more complex version of this position, see Charles Musser, "Why Did Negroes Love Al Jolson and *The Jazz Singer*? Melodrama, Blackface, and Cosmopolitan Theatrical Culture," *Film History* 23 (2011): 196–222. Further turns in the post-Rogin debate include Susan Gubar, *Racechanges: White Skin, Black Face in American Culture* (New York: Oxford UP, 1997), 66–78; Jeffrey Melnick, *A Right to Sing the Blues: African Americans, Jews, and American Popular Song* (Cambridge, MA: Harvard UP, 1999); Linda Williams, *Playing the Race Card: Melodramas of Black and White from Uncle Tom to O.J. Simpson* (Princeton, NJ: Princeton UP, 2001), 136–58; and Arthur Knight, *Disintegrating the Musical: Black Performance and American Musical Film* (Durham, NC: Duke UP, 2002), 29–33, 54–56. One of my favorite discussions of appropriation and (non)attribution in and around such Hollywood texts as *The Jazz Singer* remains Carol J. Clover, "Dancin' in the Rain," *Critical Inquiry* 21.4 (1995): 722–47.

7. Stephen Steinberg, *The Ethnic Myth: Race, Ethnicity, and Class in America* (1981; Boston: Beacon, 2001); Adolph L. Reed Jr., *The Jesse Jackson Phenomenon: The Crisis of Purpose in Afro-American Politics* (New Haven, CT: Yale UP, 1986), 88–98; David R. Roediger, *Colored White: Transcending the Racial Past* (Berkeley: U of California P, 2002); Roediger, *Working toward Whiteness: How America's Immigrants Became White* (New York: Basic, 2005); Micaela di Leonardo, *The Varieties of Ethnic Experience: Kinship, Class, and Gender among California Italian-Americans* (Ithaca, NY: Cornell UP, 1984), 47–151; di Leonardo, *Exotics at Home: Anthropologies, Others, American Modernity* (Chicago: U of Chicago P, 1998), 79–144; Matthew Frye Jacobson, *Whiteness of a Different Color: European Immigrants and the Alchemy of Race* (Cambridge, MA: Harvard UP, 1998); Jacobson, *Roots Too: White Ethnic Revival in Post-Civil Rights America* (Cambridge, MA: Harvard UP, 2006); Paul Berman, "The Other and the Almost the Same," *New Yorker* (28 February 1994), 61–71. The surpassing richness of Eric J. Sundquist,

Strangers in the Land: Blacks, Jews, Post-Holocaust America (Cambridge, MA: Harvard UP, 2005), lies precisely in its voluminous demonstrations of cross-racial engagement and embrace shot through with all manner of fracture and fissure.

8. Werner Sollors, *Beyond Ethnicity: Consent and Descent in American Culture* (New York: Oxford UP, 1986), 20–26; Reynolds J. Scott-Childress, "Race, Nation, and the Rhetoric of Color: Locating Japan and China, 1870–1907," in *Race and the Production of Modern American Nationalism,* ed. Reynolds J. Scott-Childress (New York: Garland, 1999), 6; Gwendolyn Mink, *Old Labor and New Immigrants in American Political Development: Union, Party, and State, 1875–1920* (Ithaca, NY: Cornell UP, 1986); Roediger, *Working toward Whiteness,* 31–32, 57–130; Jacobson, *Whiteness of a Different Color,* 12, 91–135, 274–80. Thus do works such as Jonathan Freedman's otherwise quite splendid *The Temple of Culture: Assimilation and Anti-Semitism in Literary Anglo-America* (Oxford: Oxford UP, 2000) downplay the antinomy on which I am insisting; positing the Jew as the ur-unassimilable person in the West who thus allows Anglo-American culture to assume coherence, it overlooks the ways Jews as eventual whites rise on the backs of African Americans (Freedman's celebratory nod late in the book to black jazz artist Don Byron's playing of klezmer music does not suffice to ford the contradictions [221–23]). Freedman's brilliant "What's Love Got to Do with It? Love and Theft in the 21st Century," *Los Angeles Review of Books* (1 November 2015), is a superbly dialectical account of cross-racial pop mirroring across the last fifty or so years.

9. Michael Denning, *Mechanic Accents: Dime Novels and Working Class Culture in America* (London: Verso, 1987), 81.

10. Sigmund Freud, "The Antithetical Meaning of Primal Words" (1910), in *The Standard Edition of the Complete Psychological Works of Sigmund Freud,* trans. James Strachey (London: Hogarth, 1957), 11:155–58.

11. Lawrence Levine, *Black Culture and Black Consciousness: Afro-American Folk Thought from Slavery to Freedom* (New York: Oxford UP, 1977), 5–80, 155–89; Albert J. Raboteau, *Slave Religion: The "Invisible Institution" in the Antebellum South* (New York: Oxford UP, 1978); Melnick, *Right to Sing the Blues,* 165–96; Paul Gilroy, *The Black Atlantic: Modernity and Double-Consciousness* (Cambridge, MA: Harvard UP, 1993), 205–12; Sundquist, *Strangers in the Land,* chap. 2.

12. For *Show Boat*—Edna Ferber novel (1926), Kern and Hammerstein–composed Ziegfeld Broadway show (1927), and films (not one but three, 1929, 1936, 1951)—see Richard Dyer, *Heavenly Bodies: Film Stars and Society* (New York: St. Martin's, 1986), chap. 2; Lauren Berlant, *The Female Complaint: The Unfinished Business of Sentimentality in American Culture* (Durham, NC: Duke UP, 2008), 69–106; and Williams, *Playing the Race Card,* 158–86. Based on racist southern sketches by white author Roark Bradford and the (Pulitzer Prize–winning) play built out of them by Broadway writer Marc Connelly, the film *Green Pastures* is far less remarked on, but

see Donald Bogle, *Toms, Coons, Mulattoes, Mammies, and Bucks: An Interpretive History of Blacks in American Films* (1973; New York: Continuum, 1994), 67–69; Thomas Cripps, *Slow Fade to Black: The Negro in American Film, 1900–1942* (New York: Oxford UP, 1977), 258–62; Cripps, introduction and annotations to *The Green Pastures,* ed. Thomas Cripps (Madison: U of Wisconsin P, 1979); Curtis J. Evans, *The Burden of Black Religion* (New York: Oxford UP, 2008), chap. 6; Paula J. Massood, *Black City Cinema: African American Urban Experiences in Film* (Philadelphia, PA: Temple UP, 2003), 22–30; and Cedric J. Robinson, *Forgeries of Memory and Meaning: Blacks and the Regimes of Race in American Theater and Film before World War II* (Chapel Hill: U of North Carolina P, 2007), 358–60.

13. Knight, *Disintegrating the Musical,* 67–70.

14. See Cripps, *Green Pastures,* 34–35.

15. Two important studies that put the black spiritual at the nexus of intense cultural contestations somewhat prior to their Hollywood appropriation are Jon Cruz, *Culture on the Margins: The Black Spiritual and the Rise of American Cultural Interpretation* (Princeton, NJ: Princeton UP, 1999); and Ronald Radano, *Lying Up a Nation: Race and Black Music* (Chicago: U of Chicago P, 2003), 164–229. See Freedman, "What's Love Got to Do with It?," for an excellent reading of Isaac Hayes's Black Moses persona.

16. Susan Gubar, "Racial Camp in *The Producers* and *Bamboozled,*" *Film Quarterly* 60.2 (2006 / 2007): 26–37.

17. Scott Saul, *Becoming Richard Pryor* (New York: HarperCollins, 2014), 384–92.

18. Ibid., 389.

19. On *Bamboozled,* see Stanley Crouch et al., "Minding the Messenger: A Symposium on *Bamboozled,*" *Black Renaissance / Renaissance Noire* 3.3 (2001): 9–32; the symposium in *Cineaste* 26.2 (2001): 10–17 featuring Greg Tate, Armond White, Michael Rogin, Saul Landau, and others; Tavia Nyong'o, "Racial Kitsch and Black Performance," *Yale Journal of Criticism* 15.2 (2002): 371–91; Gregory Laski, "Falling Back into History: The Uncanny Trauma of Blackface Minstrelsy in Spike Lee's *Bamboozled,*" *Callaloo* 33.4 (2010): 1093–1115; Gubar, "Racial Camp," 31–34; Massood, *Black City Cinema,* 207–9; and Knight, *Disintegrating the Musical,* 235–48. The defense of blacks in blackface in the chapter on *Bamboozled* in Yuval Taylor and Jake Austen, *Darkest America: Black Minstrelsy from Slavery to Hip-Hop* (New York: Norton, 2012), chap. 10, rings even more hollow than the rest of the book.

20. Stefano Harney and Fred Moten, *The Undercommons: Fugitive Planning and Black Study* (Brooklyn, NY: Minor Compositions, 2013).

21. Joel Dinerstein, "The Soul Roots of Bruce Springsteen's American Dream," *American Music* 25.4 (2007): 441–76.

22. A point Jack Hamilton has made with respect to 1960s and 1970s rock quite broadly in *Just around Midnight: Rock and Roll and the Racial Imagination* (Cambridge, MA: Harvard UP, 2016).

23. Carl Wilson's fine *Slate* review of Springsteen's memoir *Born to Run* also susses this dynamic (27 September 2016). But see also Samuele F. S. Pardini, *In the Name of the Mother: Italian Americans, African Americans, and Modernity from Booker T. Washington to Bruce Springsteen* (Hanover, NH: Dartmouth College P, 2017), 231–39.

24. Bruce Springsteen, "Girls in Their Summer Clothes," *Magic* (Columbia, 2007).

25. Bob Dylan, *Modern Times* (Columbia, 2006); Jonathan Lethem, "The Genius and Modern Times of Bob Dylan," *Rolling Stone* (7 September 2006).

26. Howard Sounes, *Down the Highway: The Life of Bob Dylan* (New York: Grove, 2001), 370.

27. Daphne A. Brooks, "'This Voice Which Is Not One': Amy Winehouse Sings the Ballad of Sonic Blue(s)face Culture," *Women and Performance* 20.1 (2010): 37–60.

28. Frank Sinatra with Count Basie and the Orchestra, *Sinatra at the Sands* (Reprise/Warner, 1966). Fine accounts (among several) of Sinatra's career (that do not, however, dwell on the *Sands* album) include Will Friedwald, *Sinatra! The Song Is You: A Singer's Art* (New York: Scribner, 1995); Pete Hamill, *Why Sinatra Matters* (New York: Little, Brown, 1998); and James Kaplan, *Frank: The Voice* (New York: Doubleday, 2010). I have also profited from Pardini, *In the Name of the Mother,* 218–31.

29. Margo Jefferson, "Seducified by a Minstrel Show," *New York Times* (22 May 1994), sec. 2, 1, 40.

30. Krin Gabbard, *Hotter than That: The Trumpet, Jazz, and American Culture* (New York: Farrar, Straus and Giroux, 2015).

31. Evelyn Nien-Ming Ch'ien, *Weird English* (Cambridge, MA: Harvard UP, 2005).

32. Gary Giddins, *Visions of Jazz: The First Century* (New York: Oxford UP, 1998), 226; Giddins's brief remarks on the *Sands* album at 221.

33. Thomas J. Ferraro, "Urbane Villager," in *Frank Sinatra: History, Identity, and Italian American Culture,* ed. Stanislao G. Pugliese (New York: Palgrave, 2004), 135–46; see also Ferraro, *Feeling Italian: The Art of Ethnicity in America* (New York: NYU P, 2005), 90–106.

34. For a telling, and excellent, exception, see David R. Roediger, *Working toward Whiteness: How America's Immigrants Became White* (New York: Basic, 2006), 235–44.

35. Ferraro, "Urbane Villager," 144–45.

36. John Gennari, "Mammissimo: Dolly and Frankie Sinatra and the Italian American Mother / Son Thing," in Pugliese, *Frank Sinatra,* 127–34.

37. Neal Gabler, *Barbra Streisand: Redefining Beauty, Femininity, and Power* (New Haven, CT: Yale UP, 2016), 76–77, 80.

38. Ibid., 204.

39. Armond White, *The Resistance: Ten Years of Pop Culture That Shook the World* (New York: Overlook, 1995), 356.

40. Robert Christgau, *Any Old Way You Choose It: Rock and Other Pop Music, 1967–73* (New York: Penguin, 1973), 169.

41. Sianne Ngai, *Ugly Feelings* (Cambridge, MA: Harvard UP, 2005), 6.

42. Phyllis Grosskurth, *Melanie Klein: Her World and Her Work* (New York: Knopf, 1986), 414.

43. Fredric Jameson, "Pleasure: A Political Issue," in *The Ideologies of Theory: Essays, 1971–1986,* vol. 2, *The Syntax of History* (Minneapolis: U of Minnesota P, 1988), 69.

44. *V* 61 (2009); Kandia Crazy Horse, "Digital Venuses: UK Pop Starlets Vie for America's Heart of Darkness," *San Francisco Bay Guardian* (9 May 2007); Brooks, "'This Voice Which Is Not One.'" See also J. Jack Halberstam, *Gaga Feminism: Sex, Gender, and the End of Normal* (Boston: Beacon, 2012), 63–64.

45. Ken Emerson, *Always Magic in the Air: The Bomp and Brilliance of the Brill Building Era* (New York: Viking, 2005), 11.

46. Steely Dan, *The Royal Scam* (ABC Records, 1976); Greg Tate and Vernon Reid, "Steely Dan: Understood as the Redemption of the White Negro," in *Everything but the Burden: What White People Are Taking from Black Culture,* ed. Greg Tate (New York: Broadway Books, 2003), 110–12. See also Brian Sweet, *Steely Dan: Reelin' in the Years* (1994; London: Omnibus, 2000); and Donald Fagen, *Eminent Hipsters* (New York: Penguin, 2013), esp. the chapter "The Devil and Ike Turner," 66–71. These pages on Steely Dan are dedicated to Duncan Faherty.

47. bell hooks, "Eating the Other: Desire and Resistance," in *Black Looks: Race and Representation* (Boston, MA: South End, 1992), 21–39.

4. House of Mirrors

1. Toni Morrison, *Playing in the Dark: Whiteness and the Literary Imagination* (Cambridge, MA: Harvard UP, 1992); Kenneth W. Warren, *Black and White Strangers: Race and American Literary Realism* (Chicago: U of Chicago P, 1993), 10–11; William Boelhower, *Through a Glass Darkly: Ethnic Semiosis in American Literature* (Venice: Edizioni Helvetia, 1984), 109; but see also James A. Snead, *White Screens, Black Images: Hollywood from the Dark Side,* ed. Colin MacCabe and Cornel West (New York: Routledge, 1994); Linda Williams, *Playing the Race Card: Melodramas*

of Black and White from Uncle Tom to O. J. Simpson (Princeton, NJ: Princeton UP, 2001); Krin Gabbard, *Black Magic: White Hollywood and African American Culture* (New Brunswick, NJ: Rutgers UP, 2004); and more specifically, Kelly Oliver and Benigno Trigo, *Noir Anxiety* (Minneapolis: U of Minnesota P, 2003); Eva Cherniavsky, *Incorporations. Race, Nation, and the Body Politics of Capital* (Minneapolis: U of Minnesota P, 2006), chap. 5; Michael Boyce Gillespie, *Film Blackness: American Cinema and the Idea of Black Film* (Durham, NC: Duke UP, 2016), chap. 3. A rather typical crypto-racial critical remark on noir comes from Foster Hirsch, *The Dark Side of the Screen: Film Noir* (San Diego, CA: A. S. Barnes, 1981): "In the flickering images of a movie screen, *film noir* seizes and penetrates a universal heart of darkness" (209).

2. Nino Frank, "Un Nouveau Genre 'Policier': L'Adventure Criminelle," *L'Ecran Francais* 61 (1946): 8–9, 14; Jean-Pierre Chartrier, "Les Americains Aussi Font des Films Noirs," *Revue Du Cinema* 2 (1946): 66–70; Raymonde Borde and Etienne Chaumeton, *Panorama du Film Noir Americain* (Paris: Editions de Minuit, 1955).

3. Charles Higham and Joel Greenberg, *Hollywood in the Forties* (Cranbury, NJ: A. S. Barnes, 1968), 19–36; Barbara Deming, *Running Away from Myself: A Dream Portrait of America Drawn from the Films of the Forties* (New York: Grossman, 1969); Paul Schrader, "Notes on Film Noir," *Film Comment* 8.1 (1972): 8–13; Janey Place and Lowell Peterson, "Some Visual Motifs of Film Noir," *Film Comment* 10.1 (1974): 30–35.

4. Mike Davis, *City of Quartz: Excavating the Future in Los Angeles* (New York: Vintage, 1990), 41; see also Paul A. Cantor, "Film Noir and the Frankfurt School: America as Wasteland in Edgar Ulmer's *Detour*," in *The Philosophy of Film Noir*, ed. Mark T. Conrad (Lexington: U Press of Kentucky, 2006), 139–61.

5. E. Ann Kaplan, ed., *Women in Film Noir* (London: BFI, 1978); see also Frank Krutnik, *In a Lonely Street: Film Noir, Genre, Masculinity* (New York: Routledge, 1991).

6. Joan Copjec, ed., *Shades of Noir: A Reader* (London: Verso, 1993).

7. Manthia Diawara, "*Noir* by *Noirs:* Toward a New Realism in Black Cinema," in Copjec, *Shades of Noir,* 261–63. Dean MacCannell's "Democracy's Turn: On Homeless *Noir*" in the Copjec collection (279–97) intermittently broaches the problem of noir's racial troping, but its primary interests lie elsewhere. Copjec's introduction faults certain historicized accounts of noir for referencing "external sources" (World War II, crime, the threat of working women, etc.) rather than locating the films' "generative principle"—"the genre's 'absent cause' . . . a principle that does not appear in the field of its effects" (xi–xii)—a fault the present study might seem to repeat. It is worth noting, however, as I will argue, that noir's racial reliances, while present in the field of its effects, are far more motivating in the films than is suggested by their apparent paucity, marginality, or, as in the case of Copjec's "The Phenomenal Nonphenomenal: Private Space in *Film Noir*" (*Shades of Noir,* 167–97), willed absence: the latter, in the course of a fascinating reading, symptomatically renders Walter Neff's office building in *Double Indemnity* (1944)

"vacant" and "uninhabited" (189) when in fact it is humming, not with white business people, to be sure, but with the black custodial workers whose presence, as I will show, bears significantly on Neff's predicament.

8. Peter Stallybrass and Allon White, *The Politics and Poetics of Transgression* (London: Methuen, 1986), 20.

9. Although this chapter was drafted well before the appearance of the splendid study by Jonathan Auerbach, *Dark Borders: Film Noir and American Citizenship* (Durham, NC: Duke UP, 2011), I have profited immensely from its reading of *Double Indemnity* as well as noir more generally. For useful critical remarks on the film, see also Richard Schickel, *Double Indemnity* (London: British Film Institute, 1992).

10. Barry Salt, *Film Style and Technology: History and Analysis* (London: Starword, 1983), 287–308; Place and Peterson, "Some Visual Motifs of Film Noir"; James Naremore, *More Than Night: Film Noir in Its Contexts* (Berkeley: U of California P, 1998).

11. Stephen Heath, "The Cinematic Apparatus: Technology as Historical and Cultural Form," in *The Cinematic Apparatus,* ed. Teresa de Lauretis and Stephen Heath (London: Macmillan, 1980), 7.

12. Richard Dyer, "The Colour of Virtue: Lillian Gish, Whiteness, and Femininity," in *Women and Film: A Sight and Sound Reader,* ed. Pam Cook and Philip Dodd (Philadelphia: Temple UP, 1993), 2; Dyer, *White* (London and New York: Routledge, 1997), 82–144.

13. Julia Kristeva, *Powers of Horror: An Essay on Abjection,* trans. Leon S. Roudiez (1980; New York: Columbia UP, 1982), 7–10.

14. Slavoj Žižek, *Tarrying with the Negative: Kant, Hegel, and the Critique of Ideology* (Durham, NC: Duke UP, 1993), 200–16.

15. Jacqueline Jones, *Labor of Love, Labor of Sorrow: Black Women, Work, and the Family from Slavery to the Present* (New York: Basic, 1985), 233–34, 236; August Meier and Elliot Rudwick, *From Plantation to Ghetto* (1966; rev. ed. New York: Hill and Wang, 1970), 242–44, 246–48; St. Clair Drake and Horace R. Cayton Jr., *Black Metropolis: A Study of Negro Life in a Northern City* (New York: Harcourt, Brace, 1945), 89–91; Fred Stanton, ed., *Fighting Racism in World War II* (New York: Monad, 1980), 75–79, 157–58; Chester Himes, "Now Is the Time! Here Is the Place!" (1942), in *Black on Black:* Baby Sister *and Selected Writings* (Garden City, NY: Doubleday, 1973), 213–19; Thomas Cripps, *Slow Fade to Black: The Negro in American Film, 1900–1942* (New York: Oxford UP, 1977), 374–83; Davis, *City of Quartz,* 43; Chester Himes, *The Quality of Hurt: The Autobiography of Chester Himes,* vol. 1 (Garden City, NY: Doubleday, 1972), 75.

16. Drake and Cayton, *Black Metropolis,* 91–94; Stanton, *Fighting Racism in World War II,* 258–75, 281–86, 342–44; Kenneth B. Clark and James Barker, "The Zoot

Effect in Personality: A Race Riot Participant," *Journal of Abnormal Psychology* 40.2 (1945): 143–48; Ralph Ellison, Unsigned Editorial, *Negro Quarterly* 1.4 (1943), 301–2; Chester Himes, "Zoot Riots Are Race Riots" (1943), in *Black on Black,* 220–25; George Breitman, "'Zoot Suit Riots' in Los Angeles," in Stanton, *Fighting Racism in World War II,* 254–55; Robin D. G. Kelley, *Race Rebels: Culture, Politics, and the Black Working Class* (New York: Free Press, 1994), 161–81; Eric Lott, "Double V, Double-Time: Bebop's Politics of Style," *Callaloo* 11.3 (1988): 597–605; Stuart Cosgrove, "The Zoot-Suit and Style Warfare," *History Workshop Journal* 18 (1984): 77–91; Kathy Peiss, *Zoot Suit: The Enigmatic Career of an Extreme Style* (Philadelphia: U of Pennsylvania P, 2011); Mauricio Mazón, *The Zoot-Suit Riots: The Psychology of Symbolic Annihilation* (Austin: U of Texas P, 1984), 15–53 and passim (quotation at 22); John Tagg and Marcos Sanchez-Tranquilino, "The Pachuco's: Flayed Hide: Mobility, Identity, and *Buenas Garras,*" in Tagg, *Grounds of Dispute: Art History, Cultural Politics and the Discursive Field* (Minneapolis: U of Minnesota P, 1992), 183–202; Eduardo Obregón Pagán, *Murder at the Sleepy Lagoon: Zoot Suits, Race, and Riot in Wartime L.A.* (Chapel Hill: U of North Carolina P, 2003); Mark A. Weitz, *The Sleepy Lagoon Murder Case: Race Discrimination and Mexican-American Rights* (Lawrence: U Press of Kansas, 2010); Dana Polan, *Power and Paranoia: History, Narrative, and the American Cinema, 1940–1950* (New York: Columbia UP, 1986), 1–3, 122–24.

17. Gary Gerstle and Steve Fraser, introduction to *The Rise and Fall of the New Deal Order, 1930–1980,* ed. Fraser and Gerstle (Princeton, NJ: Princeton UP, 1989), xix; Ira Katznelson, "Was the Great Society a Lost Opportunity?," in Fraser and Gerstle, *Rise and Fall,* 187.

18. Beth Tompkins Bates, *Pullman Porters and the Rise of Protest Politics in Black America, 1925–45* (Chapel Hill: U of North Carolina P, 2001); Larry Tye, *Rising from the Rails: Pullman Porters and the Making of the Black Middle Class* (New York: Henry Holt, 2004); Robert L. Allen, *Brotherhood of Sleeping Car Porters: C. L. Dellums and the Fight for Fair Treatment and Civil Rights* (New York: Routledge, 2014).

19. This connection is made again in Richard Fleischer's *The Narrow Margin* (1952), in which a black waiter's confusion explicitly figures the confusion of identities at the heart of the plot.

20. Michael Rogin, *Blackface, White Noise: Jewish Immigrants in the Hollywood Melting Pot* (Berkeley: U of California P, 1996), 220.

21. Alain Silver and Elizabeth Ward, eds., *Film Noir: An Encyclopedic Reference to the American Style* (rev. ed. Woodstock, NY: Overlook, 1992), 144.

22. Elaine Tyler May, "Cold War—Warm Hearth: Politics and the Family in Postwar America," in Fraser and Gerstle, *Rise and Fall,* 153–81; May, *Homeward Bound: American Families in the Cold War Era* (New York: Basic, 1988); Sheri Chinen Biesen, *Blackout: World War II and the Origins of Film Noir* (Baltimore, MD: Johns Hopkins UP, 2005).

23. In the novel from which *Murder, My Sweet* was adapted, Raymond Chandler's *Farewell, My Lovely* (1940), there exists an elaborated narrative of ethnic succession and racial troping—the visit by Marlowe and Malloy to Florians reveals the club to have become a "dinge joint," i.e., a black bar. This not only suggests the changes at work in L.A. during Malloy's previous eight years in jail (while affording the characters—and perhaps the author—the opportunity to evince some casual racism), it twins the fortunes of the book's underworld characters and black people, emphasizing Velma Valento's dark aspect as well as the functional accuracy of Florians' broken neon sign.

24. Pam Cook, "Duplicity in *Mildred Pierce,*" in Kaplan, *Women in Film Noir,* 68–82.

25. Larry Ceplair and Steven Englund, *The Inquisition in Hollywood: Politics in the Film Community, 1930–1960* (Berkeley: U of California P, 1983), 454, 195–97, 245–46, 49–50; the Losey quotation appears in Thom Andersen, "Red Hollywood," in *Literature and the Visual Arts in Contemporary Society,* ed. Suzanne Ferguson and Barbara Groseclose (Columbus: Ohio State UP, 1985), 187; Holly Allen and Michael Denning, "The Cartoonists' Front," *South Atlantic Quarterly* 92.1 (1993): 111–15.

26. Edward W. Said, *Reflections on Exile and Other Essays* (Cambridge, MA: Harvard UP, 2000), 159.

27. Donald E. Pease, "Borderline Justice / States of Emergency: Orson Welles' *Touch of Evil,*" *CR: The New Centennial Review* 1.1 (2001): 75–105.

5. White Like Me

1. John Howard Griffin, *Black Like Me* (New York: New American Library, 1961), front cover, 14. For more on Griffin's adventure, see Jeff H. Campbell, *John Howard Griffin* (Austin: Steck-Vaughn, 1970); Bradford Daniel, "Why They Can't Wait: An Interview with a White Negro," *Progressive* 28 (1964): 15–19; Ernest Sharpe Jr., "The Man Who Changed His Skin," *American Heritage* 40.1 (1989): 44–55; Bruce Watson, "Black Like Me, 50 Years Later," *Smithsonian Magazine* (October 2011); and especially Robert Bonazzi, *Man in the Mirror: John Howard Griffin and the Story of* Black Like Me (Maryknoll, NY: Orbis Books, 1997). Early reports on Griffin's trip appeared in *Sepia* 12.4–9 (April–September, 1960).

2. As quoted in Watson, "Black Like Me, 50 Years Later."

3. Rachel Doležal with Storms Reback, *In Full Color: Finding My Place in a Black and White World* (Dallas, TX: BenBella Books, 2017). Notable articles on the controversy that ensued include Cherise Smith, "Charleston, Doležal, and the 'Possessive Investment in Whiteness,'" *New Black Man in Exile* post (5 July 2015); and Jelani Cobb, "Black Like Her," *New Yorker* (15 July 2015). See also Baz Dreisinger, *Near Black: White-to-Black Passing in American Culture* (Amherst: U of Massachusetts P, 2008); and Alisha Gaines, *Black for a Day: White Fantasies of Race and Empathy* (Chapel Hill: U of North Carolina P, 2017).

4. These occur with calendrical regularity, as, for example, in actress Julianne Hough's 2013 Halloween blackface turn as Crazy Eyes from TV's *Orange Is the New Black*.

5. John F. Szwed, "Race and the Embodiment of Culture," *Ethnicity* 2.1 (1975): 27.

6. Richard Dyer, *White* (New York: Routledge, 1997); Alexander Saxton, *The Rise and Fall of the White Republic: Class Politics and Mass Culture in Nineteenth-Century America* (London: Verso, 1990); Tania Modleski, *Feminism Without Women: Culture and Criticism in a "Postfeminist" Age* (New York: Routledge, 1991), 115–34; David R. Roediger, *The Wages of Whiteness: Race and the Making of the American Working Class* (London: Verso, 1991); Toni Morrison, *Playing in the Dark: Whiteness and the Literary Imagination* (Cambridge, MA: Harvard UP, 1992); Vron Ware, *Beyond the Pale: White Women, Racism, and History* (London: Verso, 1992); Michael Rogin, *Blackface, White Noise: Jewish Immigrants in the Hollywood Melting Pot* (Berkeley: U of California P, 1996).

7. For two fine related analyses that situate this moment's literary racial liberalism in the context of the Cold War, see Kate Baldwin, "Black Like Who? Cross-Testing the 'Real' Lines of John Howard Griffin's *Black Like Me*," *Cultural Critique* 40 (1998): 103–43; and Jodi Melamed, *Represent and Destroy: Rationalizing Violence in the New Racial Capitalism* (Minneapolis: U of Minnesota P, 2011), chap. 1.

8. "Interview with Ben Cotton," *New York Mirror* (3 July 1897).

9. See the important account of French bohemia by Arnold Hauser, *The Social History of Art,* trans. Stanley Godman (New York: Vintage, 1951), Vol. 4, 189–93; see also Richard Miller, *Bohemia: The Protoculture Then and Now* (Chicago: Nelson-Hall, 1977), 27–78; Christine Stansell, *American Moderns: Bohemian New York and the Creation of a New Century* (Princeton, NJ: Princeton UP, 2009).

10. Hans Nathan, *Dan Emmett and the Rise of Early Negro Minstrelsy* (1962; Norman: U of Oklahoma P, 1977), 107, 110.

11. Morrison Foster, *My Brother Stephen* (1896; Indianapolis: Foster Hall, 1932), 83. William Austin disputes and complexifies this claim in *"Susanna," "Jeanie," and "The Old Folks at Home": The Music of Stephen Foster from His Time to Ours* (1975; Urbana: U of Illinois P, 1989), 238–39.

12. Mezz Mezzrow and Bernard Wolfe, *Really the Blues* (1946; New York: Citadel Underground, 1990); Gayle Wald, *Crossing the Line: Racial Passing in Twentieth-Century U.S. Literature and Culture* (Durham, NC: Duke UP, 2000), chap. 2.

13. Johnny Otis, *Upside Your Head! Rhythm and Blues on Central Avenue* (Hanover, NH: Wesleyan UP, 1993); George Lipsitz, *Midnight at the Barrelhouse: The Johnny Otis Story* (Minneapolis: U of Minnesota P, 2010); Dreisinger, *Near Black*, chap. 4.

14. As told in, for starters, the Curtis Hanson film *8 Mile* (2002); see also Eminem, *Angry Blond* (New York: HarperEntertainment, 2000); Anthony Bozza, *Whatever You Say I Am: The Life and Times of Eminem* (New York: Three Rivers, 2003); Carl

Hancock Rux, "Eminem: The New White Negro," in *Everything but the Burden: What White People Are Taking from Black Culture*, ed. Greg Tate (New York: Broadway, 2003), 15–38.

15. Leslie Fiedler, *Waiting for the End* (1966; New York: Stein and Day, 1972), 134. For suggestive remarks on Fiedler's analyses of interracial male bonding in the U.S. novel, see Donald E. Pease, "Leslie Fiedler, the Rosenberg Trial, and the Formulation of an American Canon," *boundary 2* 17.2 (1990): 155–98, esp. 172–77, 180–87; and Christopher Looby, " 'Innocent Homosexuality': The Fiedler Thesis in Retrospect," in *Adventures of Huckleberry Finn: A Case Study in Critical Controversy*, ed. Gerald Graff and James Phelan (Boston: Bedford, 1995), 535–50. See also Looby, " 'As Thoroughly Black as the Most Faithful Philanthropist Could Desire': Erotics of Race in Higginson's *Army Life in a Black Regiment*," in *Race and the Subject of Masculinities*, ed. Harry Stecopoulos and Michael Uebel (Durham, NC: Duke UP, 1997), 71–115.

16. Peter Stallybrass and Allon White, *The Politics and Poetics of Transgression* (London: Methuen, 1986), 5, 193–94; Anne Anlin Cheng, *The Melancholy of Race: Psychoanalysis, Assimilation, and Hidden Grief* (New York: Oxford UP, 2001), 3–29; see also Homi K. Bhabha, "The Other Question: The Stereotype and Colonial Discourse," *Screen* 24.6 (1983): 18–36. Julia Kristeva writes that " 'unconscious' contents remain . . . *excluded* but in strange fashion," clearly enough "for a defensive *position* to be established" yet "not radically enough to allow for a secure differentiation between subject and object"; Kristeva, *Powers of Horror: An Essay on Abjection*, trans. Leon S. Roudiez (1980; New York: Columbia UP, 1982), 7.

17. Doležal, *In Full Color*, chaps. 1–15; Mitchell Sunderland, "In Rachel Doležal's Skin," *Broadly* (7 December 2015), https://broadly.vice.com/en_us/article/rachel-dolezal-profile-interview; Ijeoma Oluo, "The Heart of Whiteness," *The Stranger* (19 April 2017), http://www.thestranger.com/features/2017/04/19/25082450/the-heart-of-whiteness-ijeoma-oluo-interviews-rachel-dolezal-the-white-woman-who-identifies-as-black; Slavoj Žižek, "Eastern Europe's Republics of Gilead," *New Left Review* 183 (1990): 57.

18. Doležal, *In Full Color*, chaps. 10, 13, 15; Judith Wilson, "Beauty Rites: Towards an Anatomy of Culture in African-American Women's Art," *The International Review of African American Art* 11.3 (1994): 11–17, 47–55; Kobena Mercer, "Black Hair / Style Politics," in Mercer, *Welcome to the Jungle: New Positions in Black Cultural Studies* (New York: Routledge, 1994), 97–128.

19. Walter Benn Michaels, "Autobiography of an Ex-White Man: Why Race Is Not a Social Construction," *Transition* 73 (1997): 122–43.

20. Doležal, *In Full Color*, 246, 232–33, 244; Allyson Hobbs, *A Chosen Exile: A History of Racial Passing in American Life* (Cambridge, MA: Harvard UP, 2014).

21. Norman Podhoretz, "The Know-Nothing Bohemians," *Partisan Review* 25 (Spring 1958): 311.

22. Interestingly, Vanilla Ice's biographer argues for his subject's racial indeterminacy: "Ice's family life was hardly the 'white bread' existence of *The Brady Bunch*. With regard to the rest of his family tree he claims to be 'part Apache. I am also part Cuban, but other than that I'm really not sure'"; Mark Bego, *Ice, Ice, Ice: The Extraordinary Vanilla Ice Story* (New York: Dell, 1991), 22. But see Armond White on the same performer: "What Vanilla Ice has to say (nothing) leaves his representation of whiteness as his only point"; White, "The White Albums: Is Black Music Under Siege?," *City Sun* 8.49 (1990): 19. For a chapter that beautifully covers this waterfront, see David R. Roediger, "Elvis, Wiggers, and Crossing Over to Nonwhiteness," in Roediger, *Colored White: Transcending the Racial Past* (Berkeley: U of California P, 2002), 212–40; see also Bart Bull, *Does This Road Go to Little Rock? Blackface Minstrelsy Then and Now, Now and Then* (n.p., n.d.).

23. Norman Mailer, "The White Negro," in *Advertisements for Myself* (New York: Putnam's, 1959), 314. Two excellent and necessary ripostes: James Baldwin, "The Black Boy Looks at the White Boy" (1961), in Baldwin, *The Price of the Ticket: Collected Nonfiction, 1948–1985* (New York: St. Martin's, 1985), 289–304; Kobena Mercer, "Skin Head Sex Thing," in Mercer, *Welcome to the Jungle*, 189–219.

24. For a now legendary account of Elvis's racial contradictions, see Greil Marcus, *Mystery Train: Images of America in Rock 'n' Roll Music* (1975; New York: Dutton, 1982), 141–209; see also George Lipsitz, *Class and Culture in Cold-War America* (New York: Praeger, 1981), 195–225. An acute reading of 1950s intellectual white-Negroism can be found in Andrew Ross, *No Respect: Intellectuals and Popular Culture* (New York: Routledge, 1989), 65–101.

25. Nelson George, *The Death of Rhythm & Blues* (New York: Dutton, 1988), 62–64.

26. The comeback special is available on video and record under the title *Elvis TV Special* (RCA). On Elvis's afterlife, see Greil Marcus, *Dead Elvis: A Chronicle of a Cultural Obsession* (New York: Doubleday, 1991); *I Am Elvis: A Guide to Elvis Impersonators* (New York: Pocket Books, 1991); Gilbert Rodman, *Elvis After Elvis: The Posthumous Career of a Living Legend* (New York: Routledge, 1996); and this book's Chapter 7.

27. Dyer, "White," *Screen* 29.4 (1988): 63; Wald, *Crossing the Line*, 152–81. When Griffin died in 1980, it was not, as is still widely rumored, as a belated result of his skin treatments (Sharpe, "Man Who Changed His Skin," 55)—a rumor whose persistence (roughly half of those I spoke to about this chapter repeated it) attests either to a continuing desire to punish Griffin for his transgressions and guard the color line or to a continuing fascination with white-liberal martyrdom. Either way, the tradition of all the dead generations weighs like a nightmare on the brain of the living.

28. Dreisinger, *Near Black*, 71–81.

29. Grace Halsell, *Soul Sister* (Greenwich, CT: Fawcett, 1969), 161, 212, 147, 215.

30. Dreisinger, *Near Black,* 41–92; Gaines, *Black for a Day.*

31. Richard Slotkin, *The Fatal Environment: The Myth of the Frontier in the Age of In-dustrialism* (Middletown, CT: Wesleyan UP, 1985). Cf. Amy Kaplan, *The Anarchy of Empire in the Making of U.S. Culture* (Cambridge, MA: Harvard UP, 2002), 92–120. For a pre–*Watermelon Man* take on Griffin that clarifies and ironizes this fact, see Dick Gregory, *What's Happening?* (New York: Dutton, 1965), 94–97. Thanks to Doris Witt for bringing this to my attention.

6. Tar Baby and the Great White Wonder

1. Sheila Weller, *Girls Like Us: Carole King, Joni Mitchell, Carly Simon—and the Journey of a Generation* (New York: Atria, 2008), 424–25; Mitchell tells the story herself in Malka Marom, *Joni Mitchell: In Her Own Words* (Toronto: ECW, 2014). The origins of this getup are told in, among other sources, Karen O'Brien, *Shadows and Light: Joni Mitchell, the Definitive Biography* (London: Virgin, 2002); another set of Mitchell tellings occurs in Carl Swanson, "Joni Mitchell, Unyielding," *New York Magazine* (9–22 February 2015): 88–94.

2. Henry Diltz, "Black Like . . . Joni Mitchell," *Spin* (October 2010): 88.

3. Daphne A. Brooks, "Tainted Love," *Nation* (29 September 2008): 36; see also Brooks, " 'This Voice Which Is Not One': Amy Winehouse Sings the Ballad of Sonic Blue(s)face Culture," *Women and Performance* 20.1 (2010): 37–60.

4. Joni Mitchell's Official Website: http://jonimitchell.com/library/video.cfm?id=412.

5. Greg Tate, "Black and Blond," *Vibe* (December 1998); Kevin Fellezs, *Birds of Fire: Jazz, Rock, Funk, and the Creation of Fusion* (Durham, NC: Duke UP, 2011), 148–82; Miles Park Grier, "The Only Black Man at the Party: Joni Mitchell Enters the Rock Canon," *Genders* Online 56 (2012), http://www.colorado.edu/gendersarchive1998-2013/2012/11/01/only-black-man-party-joni-mitchell-enters-rock-canon. See also the very fine volume by Sean Nelson, *Court and Spark* (New York: Continuum 33 1/3, 2007). Lloyd Whitesell's *The Music of Joni Mitchell* (New York: Oxford UP, 2008) is a blessing and a gift to any student of Mitchell's art. David Yaffe's forthcoming *Reckless Daughter: A Portrait of Joni Mitchell* (New York: Farrar, Straus and Giroux, 2017) promises to be eye- and ear-opening.

6. Robert Christgau, *Rock Albums of the 70s: A Critical Guide* (Boston: Da Capo, 1981), 263.

7. Charlie Gillett, *The Sound of the City: The Rise of Rock and Roll,* rev. and exp. ed. (1970; New York: Pantheon, 1983), 324–25.

8. Eric Avila, *Popular Culture in the Age of White Flight: Fear and Fantasy in Suburban Los Angeles* (Berkeley: U of California P, 2006); McWilliams quoted at 213.

9. Barney Hoskyns, *Waiting for the Sun: Strange Days, Weird Scenes, and the Sound of Los Angeles* (New York: St. Martin's, 1996), 21.

10. Newman quoted in Hoskyns, *Waiting for the Sun*, 107; Thomas Pynchon, "A Journey into the Mind of Watts," *New York Times Magazine* (12 June 1966), 4–5.

11. Barney Hoskyns, *Hotel California* (Hoboken, NJ: John Wiley, 2006) (Joe Smith on Joni Mitchell, 233); Michael Walker, *Laurel Canyon: The Inside Story of Rock-and-Roll's Legendary Neighborhood* (New York: Farrar, Straus and Giroux, 2007).

12. Shepard's take can be found in *The Rolling Thunder Logbook* (1977; New York: Da Capo, 2004), 117; more generally, see Judy Kutulas, "'That's the Way I've Always Heard It Should Be': Baby Boomers, 1970s Singer-Songwriters, and Romantic Relationships," *Journal of American History* 97.3 (2010): 682–702.

13. Michael Denning, "Bob Dylan and Rolling Thunder," in *The Cambridge Companion to Bob Dylan,* ed. Kevin J. H. Dettmar (Cambridge: Cambridge UP, 2009), 28–41.

14. Rubin Carter documentary; the quote appears as well, in Mitchell's own telling, in Mark Bego, *Joni Mitchell* (Lanham, MD: Taylor, 2005), 145.

15. Weller, *Girls Like Us*, 430.

16. Michael Szalay and Sean McCann, eds., "Countercultural Capital: Essays on the Sixties from Some Who Weren't There," *Yale Journal of Criticism* 18.2 (2005); and my response in the same issue, "Chants Demagogic": 471–72; McCann, *A Pinnacle of Feeling: American Literature and Presidential Government* (Princeton, NJ: Princeton UP, 2008).

17. Gayle Rubin, "The Traffic in Women: Notes on the 'Political Economy' of Sex," in *Toward an Anthropology of Women,* ed. Rayna R. Reiter (New York: Monthly Review P, 1975): 157–210; G. W. F. Hegel, *Phenomenology of Spirit,* trans. A. V. Miller (1807; Oxford: Oxford UP, 1977), 111–19. Tina Turner's version of "Edith" on Herbie Hancock's *River: The Joni Letters* strikes me as perhaps the definitive one, sung by one who was forced to know, and then left, the life.

18. David Yaffe, *Fascinating Rhythm: Reading Jazz in American Writing* (Princeton, NJ: Princeton UP, 2005), 150–98.

19. Justin Gifford, *Pimping Fictions: African American Crime Literature and the Untold Story of Black Pulp Publishing* (Philadelphia: Temple UP, 2013); see also Beth Coleman, "Pimp Notes on Autonomy," in Greg Tate, ed., *Everything but the Burden: What White People Are Taking from Black Culture* (New York: Broadway, 2003), 68–80.

20. Charles Mingus, *Beneath the Underdog: His World as Composed by Mingus,* ed. Nel King (New York: Vintage, 1971).

21. Joni Mitchell, *Mingus* (Asylum, 1979); Gene Santoro, *Myself When I Am Real: The Life and Music of Charles Mingus* (New York: Oxford UP, 2000), 374–76, 381–84; Bego, *Joni Mitchell,* 167–79; Katherine Monk, *Joni: The Creative Odyssey of Joni Mitchell* (Vancouver, BC: Greystone, 2012), 27–34.

22. I am indebted for these formulations to Alex Corey's illuminating, extended written responses to an earlier version of this work, personal communication, 29 July 2011; Grier, "Only Black Man at the Party"; Judith Halberstam, *Female Masculinity* (Durham, NC: Duke UP, 1998), 231–66. Subject for further study: Joni Mitchell exploring ideas contemporaneous with and closely adjacent to Luce Irigaray, *This Sex Which Is Not One* (1977; Ithaca, NY: Cornell UP, 1985).

23. Michael Szalay, *Hip Figures: A Literary History of the Democratic Party* (Stanford, CA: Stanford UP, 2012).

24. Mike Davis, *Prisoners of the American Dream: Politics and Economy in the History of the U.S. Working Class* (London: Verso, 1986), 157–80.

7. All the King's Men

1. Eco himself isn't nearly so doomy. See Umberto Eco, *Travels in Hyperreality* (New York: Harcourt Brace Jovanovich, 1982). A similar (though too cynical) view may be found in Arthur Kroker, Marilouise Kroker, and David Cook, *Panic Encyclopedia* (New York: St. Martin's, 1989).

2. William McCranor Henderson, *Stark Raving Elvis* (New York: Simon and Schuster, 1984).

3. Public Enemy, "Fight the Power," *Fear of a Black Planet* (Def Jam / CBS, 1990).

4. Living Colour, "Elvis Is Dead," *Time's Up* (Epic, 1990). For splendid coverage of Elvis's afterlife, see Greil Marcus, *Dead Elvis: A Chronicle of a Cultural Obsession* (New York: Doubleday, 1991); Gilbert B. Rodman, *Elvis After Elvis: The Posthumous Career of a Living Legend* (New York: Routledge, 1996); and Erika Doss, *Elvis Culture: Fans, Faith, and Image* (Lawrence: U Press of Kansas, 1999).

5. Marjorie Garber, *Vested Interests: Cross-Dressing and Cultural Anxiety* (New York: Routledge, 1991), 363–74. Impersonator Ron George told me that he (among others) was offered a part in *Honeymoon in Vegas* but turned it down because he was wary of being "bunched in" with "a bunch of other idiots out there"—his opinion of the general run of Elvis impersonators, like that of the corporate media, tending toward disgust and disavowal. For El Vez, see American Graphic Systems, Inc., *I Am Elvis: A Guide to Elvis Impersonators* (New York: Pocket Books, 1991), 48–51; henceforth cited in the text as *Guide*. Or check out one of his many albums, my favorite being *G.I. Ay, Ay! Blues* (Big Pop, 1996).

6. Besides interviewing impersonators and fans and watching the performances at the 1994 Elvis Presley International Impersonators Association convention, I conducted telephone interviews with impersonators and related people (managers, agents, organizers, etc.) from May 1992 to September 1993; all information and quotations are drawn from my personal interviews and observations unless otherwise noted.

7. The EPIIA was formed in 1989 by Ron and Sandy Bessette and was a "non profit organization dedicated to the preservation and continuing art form, style, and music of Elvis Presley thru Elvis performers and fans; to maintain professionalism, ethics, and standards for those performers who continue Elvis's creative and continuing art form" (quotations from EPIIA membership brochure). In addition to publishing a bimonthly newsletter, the Bessettes in the 1990s organized impersonator "mini-showcases," multi-impersonator shows, and the annual EPIIA convention, a massive affair first held in Chicago and then in Las Vegas. Ron Bessette told me that as of May 1993, the EPIIA sported approximately 200 performer-members (though there are vastly more impersonators in the United States and abroad) and 400 fan-members (one of whom was myself).

8. I refer here to Phil Cohen, "Subcultural Conflict and Working-Class Community," in *Culture, Media, Language: Working Papers in Cultural Studies, 1972–79,* ed. Stuart Hall et al. (London: Hutchinson, 1980), 78–87; Paul Willis, *Learning to Labour: How Working-Class Kids Get Working-Class Jobs* (1977; New York: Columbia UP, 1981); Willis, "Notes on Method," in *Culture, Media, Language,* 88–95; Janice Radway, *Reading the Romance: Women, Patriarchy, and Popular Literature* (Chapel Hill: U of North Carolina P, 1984); Donna Gaines, *Teenage Wasteland: Suburbia's Dead End Kids* (New York: Pantheon, 1991). See also Radway, "Reception Study: Ethnography and the Problems of Dispersed Audiences and Nomadic Subjects," *Cultural Studies* 2.3 (1988): 361; Stuart Hall, "Encoding/Decoding," in *Culture, Media, Language,* 128–38; David Morley, *The Nationwide Audience* (London, 1980); Tania Modleski, *Feminism Without Women: Culture and Criticism in a "Postfeminist" Age* (New York: Routledge, 1991), 35–58; and the pathbreaking precursor to my undertaking, Lynn Spigel, "Communicating with the Dead: Elvis as Medium," *Camera Obscura* 23 (1990): 177–204.

9. Willis, *Learning to Labour,* 125–26.

10. Rick Marino went on to write a book: *Be Elvis! A Guide to Impersonating the King* (Naperville, IL: Sourcebooks, 2000). See also Patty Carroll, *Living the Life: The World of Elvis Tribute Artists* (Burlington, VT: Verve, 2005).

11. Barbara Ehrenreich, *The Hearts of Men: American Dreams and the Flight from Commitment* (Garden City, NY: Anchor, 1983), 99–116.

12. See, for example, Andrew Tolson, *The Limits of Masculinity* (London: Tavistock, 1977), 63–64; Paul Willis, "Shop Floor Culture, Masculinity and the Wage Form," in *Working-Class Culture: Studies in History and Theory,* ed. John Clarke, Chas Critcher, and Richard Johnson (London: Hutchinson, 1979), 185–98; Nancy Chodorow, "Mothering, Male Dominance, and Capitalism," in *Capitalist Patriarchy and the Case for Socialist Feminism,* ed. Zillah R. Eisenstein (New York: Monthly Review P, 1979), 96–97; David Montgomery, *Workers' Control in America: Studies in the History of Work, Technology, and Labor Struggles* (Cambridge: Cambridge UP, 1979), 13–14; Sean Wilentz, *Chants Democratic: New York City and the Rise*

of the American Working Class, 1788–1850 (New York: Oxford UP, 1984), passim; Christine Stansell, *City of Women: Sex and Class in New York, 1789–1860* (New York: Knopf, 1986), 77–78, 81, 95–96, 137–41; Michael Denning, *Mechanic Accents: Dime Novels and Working-Class Culture in America* (London: Verso, 1987), chap. 9.

13. See Stanley Aronowitz, *False Promises: The Shaping of American Working-Class Consciousness* (New York: McGraw-Hill, 1973); Harry Braverman, *Labor and Monopoly Capital: The Degradation of Work in the Twentieth Century* (New York: Monthly Review P, 1974); Mike Davis, *Prisoners of the American Dream: Politics and Economy in the History of the U.S. Working Class* (London: Verso, 1986).

14. For an interesting treatment of the cinematic fate of white masculinity in this period of industrial decline, see Andrew Ross, "Cowboys, Cadillacs and Cosmonauts: Families, Film Genres, and Technocultures," in *Engendering Men: The Question of Male Feminist Criticism,* ed. Joseph A. Boone and Michael Cadden (New York: Routledge, 1990), 87–101.

15. Ehrenreich, *Hearts of Men,* 173–75; see also the special issue on post-Fordism of the *Socialist Review* 21.1 (1991).

16. Historians who have taken up the formation of American working-class whiteness include Alexander Saxton, *The Rise and Fall of the White Republic: Class Politics and Mass Culture in Nineteenth-Century America* (London: Verso, 1991); David R. Roediger, *The Wages of Whiteness: Race and the Making of the American Working Class* (London: Verso, 1991); Roediger, *Colored White: Transcending the Racial Past* (Berkeley: U of California P, 2002); Roediger, *Working Toward Whiteness: How America's Immigrants Became White* (New York: Basic, 2005); Matthew Frye Jacobson, *Whiteness of a Different Color: European Immigrants and the Alchemy of Race* (Cambridge, MA: Harvard UP, 1999); Jefferson Cowie, *Stayin' Alive: The 1970s and the Last Days of the Working Class* (New York: New Press, 2012); and Nancy Isenberg, *White Trash: The 400-Year Untold Story of Class in America* (New York: Viking, 2016). Nice ripostes to the alleged backwardness of working-class men may be found in Ehrenreich, *Hearts of Men,* 134–36; and Richard Sennett and Jonathan Cobb, *The Hidden Injuries of Class* (New York: Knopf, 1972), 217–18.

17. I am indebted here to the pioneering work on performance cultures in Stuart Hall and Tony Jefferson, eds., *Resistance Through Rituals: Youth Subcultures in Post-war Britain* (London: Hutchinson, 1976); and Dick Hebdige, *Subculture: The Meaning of Style* (New York: Methuen, 1979). See Lillian B. Rubin, *Worlds of Pain: Life in the Working-Class Family* (New York: Basic Books, 1976), 161, for a sense of the autonomy and fulfillment such activities might provide for men who are radically constricted on the job.

18. "Identity, because it is never in a moment of critical repose, because it resists the forces of suspension or negation, and because it neither begins nor ends at a point of total immobility, draws its very life-blood from the restless operations of identification, one of the most powerful but least understood mechanisms of cultural self-fashioning." Diana Fuss, "Fashion and the Homospectatorial Look," *Critical*

Inquiry 18.4 (1992): 716; more generally, see Marcus Boon, *In Praise of Copying* (Cambridge, MA: Harvard UP, 2010).

19. Laura Mulvey, *Visual and Other Pleasures* (Bloomington: U of Indiana P, 1989), 18.

20. Fuss, "Fashion and the Homospectatorial Look," 737.

21. See Steve Neale, "Masculinity as Spectacle: Reflections on Men and Mainstream Cinema," *Screen* 24.6 (1983): 7–8; Moustapha Safouan, "Is the Oedipus Complex Universal?," *m/f* 5 / 6 (1981): 85–87. I have also profited from Modleski, *Feminism Without Women,* chap. 4.

22. Christian Metz, *The Imaginary Signifier: Psychoanalysis and the Cinema,* trans. Celia Britton, Annwyl Williams, Ben Brewster, and Alfred Guzzetti (1977; Bloomington: Indiana UP, 1982), 71.

23. *Guide,* 123; *48 Hours,* August 1992.

24. Michael Abramowitz, "All Shook Up in Suburbia," *Washington Post* (10 June 1991), C1, 9.

25. For a similar argument regarding male spectators looking at men in film, see D. N. Rodowick, "The Difficulty of Difference," *Wide Angle* 5.1 (1981): 8.

26. Henderson's *Stark Raving Elvis* depicts a loaded scene in which impersonator Byron Bluford is fellated by a woman named Elvis who wears white satin-and-rhinestone jumpsuits and her hair slicked back—scarcely even a disguise for the same-sex erotics I detect generally in Elvis impersonation. "Byron's eyes closed and his face became a mask of domination. He grasped her head and held it in place. 'Stay there, Elvis,' he muttered. It was half speech, half grunt. 'Right there, baby'" (179). One might incidentally note here Byron's urge to invert the balance of power between Elvis and impersonator as well as the possible sham quality of that inversion ("mask of domination"). This captures the impersonators' quandary precisely.

27. In some ways the most explicit, and most misleading, of the charges of Elvis's impersonation of black cultural figures is Alice Walker's story "Nineteen Fifty-five" in *You Can't Keep a Good Woman Down* (New York: Harcourt Brace Jovanovich, 1981), 3–20.

28. Robert Cantwell, *Bluegrass Breakdown: The Making of the Old Southern Sound* (Urbana: U of Illinois P, 1984), 254–56; Greil Marcus, *Mystery Train: Images of America in Rock 'n' Roll Music* (1975; New York: Dutton, 1982), 196.

29. Once again, Homi K. Bhabha's terms in "Of Mimicry and Man: The Ambivalence of Colonial Discourse," *October* 28 (1984): 132.

30. John F. Szwed, "Race and the Embodiment of Culture," *Ethnicity* 2 (1975): 28.

31. For Alice Walker's own interesting spin on her earlier charge of Elvis's cultural expropriation of black material, see her *The Temple of My Familiar* (New York: Dell,

1989), 187–89, in which one character deems Elvis part Native American (thanks to Caroline Rody for bringing this to my attention).

32. Andrew Ross, "Ballots, Bullets or Batmen: Can Cultural Studies Do the Right Thing?," *Screen* (1990): 30–31.

33. Philip Cohen, "Tarzan and the Jungle Bunnies: Race, Class, and Sex in Popular Culture," *New Formations* 5 (1988): 27; see also Stuart Hall, "New Ethnicities," in *Black Film/British Cinema,* ed. Kobena Mercer (London: ICA, 1988), 29.

34. See Michael Rogin's excellent review of Roediger, "Black Masks, White Skin: Consciousness of Class and American National Culture," *Radical History Review* 54 (1992): 141–52; Roediger's subsequent work, for instance *Colored White* and *Working Toward Whiteness,* has produced increasingly supple accounts of white working-class racial ambivalence. Sennett and Cobb's *Hidden Injuries of Class,* 68–69, 136–37, has some acute remarks dispelling the myth of the racist, nationalist "hard hat"; Andrew Ross, *No Respect: Intellectuals and Popular Culture* (New York: Routledge, 1989), 229–32, has interesting things to say on the possibilities of exploiting moments of working-class ambivalence for emancipatory ends.

35. See Eve Sedgwick, *Epistemology of the Closet* (Berkeley: U of California P, 1990), 211, for a powerful analysis of the way same-sex desire may be transmuted into safer forms of male envy and identification; see also Robyn Wiegman, *American Anatomies: Theorizing Race and Gender* (Durham, NC: Duke UP, 1995), 115–46.

36. V. S. Naipaul, *A Turn in the South* (New York: Knopf, 1989), 225. More importantly, see Spigel, "Communicating with the Dead," 177–94.

37. T. S. Eliot, "Marie Lloyd" (1923), in *Selected Prose of T. S. Eliot,* ed. Frank Kermode (New York: Harcourt Brace Jovanovich, 1975), 172–74.

38. Impersonator Marc Roberts, a former Cleveland Ford worker originally from Selma, Alabama, confirmed this connection for me.

39. On "affective alliances," see Lawrence Grossberg, *We Gotta Get Out of This Place: Popular Conservatism and Postmodern Culture* (New York: Routledge, 1992), 79–87.

40. Georg Simmel, "Adornment" (1905), in *The Sociology of Georg Simmel,* ed. Kurt H. Wolff (Glencoe, IL: Free Press, 1950), 340.

41. Impersonator Ray Guillemette, who specializes in the young Elvis, amusingly remarked to me, "No matter how much you move, you'll always find somebody . . . you get off the stage, drenching wet, and they'll say, 'You gotta *move* more!' "

42. The April 1991 EPIIA newsletter carried an exasperated critique of the Oprah Winfrey Show for making Elvis fans and impersonators "look like fanatics and crazy people."

43. E. P. Thompson, *The Making of the English Working Class* (New York: Vintage, 1963), 9–11; Ehrenreich, *Hearts of Men,* 135.

44. Hebdige, *Subculture,* 113–27.

45. Abramowitz, "All Shook Up in Suburbia," C1.

46. Cf. Rubin, *Worlds of Pain,* 179.

47. The EPIIA vocally supported charity work by performer-members and fan-members alike; see, for example, the April 1991 EPIIA newsletter.

48. Marc Roberts spoke approvingly to me of Elvis's "down home" persona and his readiness to let fly with impressive acts of economic redistribution.

49. Mike Davis, "Armageddon at the Emerald City," *The Nation* (11 July 1994): 46–50.

50. "Bill and the King," *The New Yorker* 68 (1993): 32–33; Greil Marcus, *Double Trouble: Bill Clinton and Elvis Presley in a Land of No Alternatives* (New York: Henry Holt, 2000).

51. It may be worth noting that I tried one Saturday night to reach performers by phone for this project: none were home.

52. Walter Benjamin, "The Storyteller," in *Illuminations,* ed. Hannah Arendt (New York: Schocken, 1971), 102.

53. Ernst Bloch, *The Principle of Hope,* vol. 1, trans. Neville Plaice, Stephen Plaice, and Paul Knight (Cambridge, MA: MIT P, 1986), 367–68.

54. I draw this emphasis from Fuss, "Fashion and the Homospectatorial Look," 718; see also, for detailed remarks on the kind of masochistic moments I sense in Elvis impersonation, Kaja Silverman, *Male Subjectivity at the Margins* (New York: Routledge, 1992), 299–338.

8. Just Like Jack Frost's Blues

1. Ralph Ellison, *Shadow and Act* (New York: Random House, 1964), 55.

2. Bob Dylan, "My Back Pages," *Another Side of Bob Dylan* (Columbia, 1964). In 2016 the Nobel Prize winner was older than even *that,* turning to Frank Sinatra covers and the Great American Songbook generally on *Shadows in the Night* (Columbia, 2015) and *Fallen Angels* (Columbia, 2016).

3. Bob Dylan, *Tell Tale Signs, Bootleg Series Vol. 8* (Columbia, 2008). Greil Marcus put it to me this way: "I don't know that [Dylan's] read your book but wouldn't be surprised; he's a true scholar of old American music and all that goes with it." Marcus, email communication, 17 July 2001. See also Marcus, *Invisible Republic: Bob Dylan's Basement Tapes* (New York: Henry Holt, 1997) (reissued in paperback as *The Old, Weird America*); Marcus, *Like a Rolling Stone: Bob Dylan at the Crossroads* (New York: PublicAffairs, 2005); Marcus, *Bob Dylan by Greil Marcus: Writings 1968–2010* (New York: PublicAffairs, 2010).

4. Edna Gundersen, "Dylan Brings It All Back Home," *USA Today* (10 September 2001): 2D. See also Barry Shank, "'That Wild Mercury Sound': Bob Dylan and the Illusion of American Culture," *boundary 2* 29. 1 (2002): 97–123.

5. The best treatment of Delta blues in its context of Delta political economy is Clyde Woods, *Development Arrested: The Blues and Plantation Power in the Mississippi Delta* (London: Verso, 1998); for Woods on Patton, see 110–12, 118–19. See also Alan Lomax, *The Land Where the Blues Began* (New York: Pantheon, 1993) and Adam Gussow, *Seems Like Murder Here: Southern Violence and the Blues Tradition* (Chicago: U of Chicago P, 2002).

6. For the former, see Jon Pareles, "Plagiarism in Dylan, or a Cultural Collage?," *New York Times* (12 July 2003); for the latter, see http://www.whosampled.com/sample/394335/Bob-Dylan-Sugar-Baby-Gene-Austin-The-Lonesome-Road/. Scholar Scott Warmuth is the key expert in these matters.

7. "My early intention was to present this record with a cover photo of myself wearing blackface. Aside from providing controversy for hatemongers or offending the delicate sensibilities of the politically correct, my sincere intention was that it would provide a genuine focus on the real 'roots' of many of the tunes included; blackface minstrelsy. It's my contention that a blackface tradition is alive and well hidden behind a modern mask. I believe that 'blacking up' should be done correctly; as an exploration for the source of that hollow ring we mistakenly believe was immaculately conceived in Las Vegas, and in a context of true respect for the cultures we ape." Michelle Shocked, liner notes, *Arkansas Traveler* (PolyGram, 1992).

8. Run C&W, *Into the Twangy-First Century* (MCA, 1993); Robert Cantwell, *Bluegrass Breakdown: The Making of the Old Southern Sound* (Urbana: U of Illinois P, 1984).

9. Liner notes, Bob Dylan, *World Gone Wrong* (Columbia, 1993). It would be hard to overstate the influence of Benj DeMott on my thinking about Dylan, both his conversation and his writing in *First of the Month*.

10. The line comes from the song "Highlands," but it applies generally to the album on which it appears.

11. Gundersen, "Dylan Brings It All Back Home," 2D.

12. Interview with Ralph Ellison by Shelley Fisher Fishkin, quoted in Fishkin, *Was Huck Black? Mark Twain and African American Voices* (New York: Oxford UP, 1993), 90.

13. School-board conservative Christians voted in 1999 to change Kansas's science education policy, making evolution nonmandatory in statewide testing and thus opening the way for its creationist competitor; Kansas has see-sawed on the issue of Darwin versus God ever since, and the debates—and school-board elections—still rage.

14. Marshall Berman, "Love and Theft: From Jack Robin to Bob Dylan," *Dissent* (Summer 2002): 73.

15. See Richard Ellmann, *Yeats, the Man and the Masks* (New York: Dutton, 1973).

16. Michael Rogin, *Blackface, White Noise: Jewish Immigrants in the Hollywood Melting Pot* (Berkeley: U of California P, 1996).

17. See, for example, Marcus, *Invisible Republic*, 124.

18. Michael Gray, *The Bob Dylan Encyclopedia* (New York: Continuum, 2006), 239–40.

19. Howard Sacks and Judith Rose Sacks, *Way Up North in Dixie: A Black Family's Claim to the Confederate Anthem* (Washington, DC: Smithsonian, 1993).

20. Ibid., 157; Hans Nathan, *Dan Emmett and the Rise of Early Negro Minstrelsy* (Norman: U of Oklahoma P, 1962), 244–45.

21. "Sometimes it's not enough to know the meaning of things; sometimes we have to know what things don't mean as well," Jack Fate says in voiceover at the end of *Masked and Anonymous*.

22. This sentence condenses several debts: Albert Murray, *Stomping the Blues* (New York: McGraw-Hill, 1976); Farah Jasmine Griffin, *"Who Set You Flowin'?": The African-American Migration Narrative* (New York: Oxford UP, 1995), 56–57; Jani Scandura, *Down in the Dumps: Place, Modernity, American Depression* (Durham, NC: Duke UP, 2008); Erich Nunn, *Sounding the Color Line: Music and Race in the Southern Imagination* (Athens: U of Georgia P, 2015), chap. 3; Jennifer Lynn Stoever, *The Sonic Color Line: Race and the Cultural Politics of Listening* (New York: NYU P, 2016).

23. Sigmund Freud, *The Ego and the Id,* trans. Joan Riviere, ed. James Strachey (1923; New York: Norton, 1960), 18–20; Judith Butler, *The Psychic Life of Power: Theories in Subjection* (Stanford, CA: Stanford UP, 1997), 133. For this line of thinking I am indebted above all to Jonathan Flatley, *Affective Mapping: Melancholia and the Politics of Modernism* (Cambridge, MA: Harvard UP, 2008).

24. Stanley Plumly, "Sonnet," in *Out-of-the-Body Travel* (New York: Ecco, 1977), 31.

25. Walter Benjamin, *The Origin of German Tragic Drama,* trans. John Osborne (1928; London: NLB, 1977), 92; Butler, *Psychic Life of Power,* 174.

Coda

1. Fred Moten, "The Subprime and the Beautiful," *African Identities* 11.2 (2013): 237–45; see also "Race, Empire, and the Crisis of the Subprime," ed. Paula Chakravartty and Denise Ferreira da Silva, *American Quarterly* 64.3 (2012).

2. Matt Taibbi, "The Line That May Have Won Hillary Clinton the Nomination," *Rolling Stone* (28 April 2016).

3. Clarence Lusane, *The Black History of the White House* (San Francisco: City Lights, 2011); Michael P. Jeffries, *Painting the White House Black: Barack Obama and the Meaning of Race in America* (Stanford, CA: Stanford UP, 2013).

4. Jacqueline Rose, *States of Fantasy* (Oxford: Clarendon, 1996), 5.

INDEX